HOLOCAUST LANDSCAPES

HOLOCAUST LANDSCAPES

TIM COLE

B L O O M S B U R Y

LONDON · OXFORD · NEW YORK · NEW DELHI · SYDNEY

Bloomsbury Continuum
An imprint of Bloomsbury Publishing Plc

50 Bedford Square
London
WC1B 3DP
UK

1385 Broadway
New York
NY 10018
USA

www.bloomsbury.com

First published 2016

British Library Cataloguing-in-Publication Data
A catalogue record for this book is available from the British Library.

Library of Congress Cataloguing-in-Publication data has been applied for.

ISBN: HB: 9781472906885
ePDF: 9781472906908
ePub: 9781472906892

2 4 6 8 10 9 7 5 3 1

Typeset by Integra Software Services Pvt. Ltd.
Printed and bound in Great Britain by CPI Group (UK) Ltd, Croydon CR0 4YY

MIX
Paper from
responsible sources
FSC® C020471

To find out more about our authors and books visit www.bloomsbury.com.
Here you will find extracts, author interviews, details of forthcoming events and the
option to sign up for our newsletters.

For Jonathan, Jeremy and Matthew

CONTENTS

Holocaust Landscapes 1

Prologue: Returning Home/Leaving Home 9

Ghetto 21

Forest 45

Camp 69

Train 99

Attic and Cellar, Mountain and Sea 127

River 151

Road 173

Camp 195

Epilogue: Returning Home/Leaving Home 215

Moving Holocaust Landscapes 225

Acknowledgements 228
Notes 232
Index 257

Holocaust Landscapes

Joseph Elman recalled his father Benjamin drawing a rough sketch map to convey to his sons the hopelessness of their plight crammed into the ghetto set up in Proushinna after the Nazi occupation of eastern Poland in 1941. Safety, in his father's eyes, lay in a place. But the place he had in mind was one of the few countries during the Second World War that remained neutral, and such places were all achingly distant. 'Boys, look, here is Poland,' Joseph recalled his father telling them:

> and then he drew, you know, you got Czechoslovakia, he knew exactly all . . . Europe. He says, 'You haven't got a single country, neutral country. You got Sweden and Switzerland . . . even if you'll get out the ghetto,' he says, 'you got such a long way to go and you're going to be caught.'

Reflecting back on this conversation, Joseph wondered:

> I don't know to say if he was right or not right, who knows? I mean that geographically he was . . . right, because . . . if you have a border, you could . . . get out. But he didn't realize, you know . . . we did know there is some woods, partisans, we don't have to go. Now, if we wouldn't have the woods near, you know, it'd be a problem . . . from Warsaw . . . from Łódź, where they going to go?[1]

For both Joseph and his father, where they were mattered enormously in all sorts of ways. At its most basic level, they were in the wrong place at the wrong time, living in the borderland area of eastern Poland memorably dubbed the 'bloodlands' by historian Timothy Snyder.[2] Originally divided between Nazi Germany and Soviet Russia in 1939 under the terms of the Molotov–Ribbentrop non-aggression pact, eastern Poland was later occupied in the summer of 1941 as the launch of Operation Barbarossa saw the rapid eastward expansion of Nazi Germany deep into the heart of Soviet territory. Jews were caught up in this euphoric moment of German military success. Some were placed in rapidly constructed urban ghettos and work camps. Others were killed in waves of shooting, oftentimes in the forest on the edge of town. It was here in eastern Poland and the Soviet Union in the second half of 1941 that the so-called 'solution of the Jewish question' turned murderous.

But this was an event that never stayed still. Genocide was on the move, starting in the east but then heading westwards over the course of the war, and as it moved it changed shape. What began as genocide in the neighbourhood turned into killings and labour exchange on a continental scale before shifting to the more intimate, personal shootings of Jews – on the banks of the Danube in Budapest or the roadsides of Germany. Eventually, the tragic story culminated in men, women and children being transported to overcrowded camps such as Bergen-Belsen that are perhaps best seen as post-genocidal space. Instead of viewing the Holocaust as a single, monolithic event, rather different genocides were enacted in different places, at different times across the course of the war. Moving through these landscapes, I have been struck by how focusing on place highlights the shifting chronology of the genocide. Rather than geographies of the Holocaust being ahistorical, my sense is that probing ideas of place and space, as I do in this book, foregrounds histories as much as geographies of the Holocaust.[3]

But the Holocaust was not simply something that happened at particular times and in particular places. It was also a place-making event that created new places – ghettos and camps – within the European landscape, or reworked more familiar places – such as rivers or roads – into genocidal landscapes.

It was in one of these novel places – the ghetto built in Proushinna – that Joseph's father, Benjamin, delivered his geography lesson to his sons. Their family was, in a sense, fortunate to remain living in their family home, although this home was now repositioned within the city in a ghetto that physically separated Jews from non-Jews. Over the course of 1942, the ghetto population swelled as Jews who had survived the waves of killings in the local area were brought into Proushinna. Ultimately the ghetto was liquidated, its population transported to the most infamous of places associated with the Holocaust: the complex of camps at Auschwitz.

Neither Joseph nor his father ended up in Auschwitz. Joseph's father, along with other members of the Jewish Council who assumed leadership roles in the ghetto, committed suicide prior to its liquidation. Joseph, and a group that had made contact with the partisans in the neighbouring woods, escaped from the ghetto and survived the war living in the forest. There they dug bunkers into the soil, which was another act of Holocaust place-making.[4] Holocaust landscapes were not simply sites of incarceration and killing, but also of escape and hiding. While the Holocaust involved the construction of thousands of sites of incarceration by Nazi Germany and her collaborators, it also involved the construction of thousands of hiding places where Jews and non-Jews sought to carve out spaces beyond German control. Although the Holocaust involved the forced transfer of millions within and across national borders, it also meant that hundreds of thousands decided to flee within, and outside of, occupied territory.

For Joseph's father safety was a place, a neutral country, too distant to imagine ever reaching. However, for Joseph, safety lay much closer to home in the woods that surrounded Proushinna. There was a generational divide among Jews in how sites of safety were imagined. Although both father and son were in agreement that safety lay in a place, they differed in what that place was and where it was to be found. For Joseph's father, safety lay in the traditional political geography of national sovereignty and therefore could only be found in distant neutral countries. For Joseph, safety could be imagined in the unusual world of the forests that were increasingly coming under the control of Soviet partisans. However, even Joseph struggled to imagine sites of safety in the urban spaces of Poland's major cities, although it is clear that many others could.[5]

While Joseph's father saw Europe as divided between the unsafe places of German occupied territory and the safe places of neutral territory, on the ground things were much more complex. Many individuals and families did not adopt the kind of binary that Joseph's father worked with, but operated with mental maps that identified more or less safe places at a range of scales from the continental to the local. Even within the most iconic sites of Nazi control – the ghetto, camp or column of evacuees on a death march – individuals and groups adopted spatial strategies of survival as they tried to go here, rather than there, in a desperate attempt to stay alive. Across the shifting course of the genocide, survival remained profoundly spatial.

Driven by an interest in the range of spatial strategies of survival that individuals, families and groups developed, I have drawn heavily on the stories that survivors have told in diaries, memoirs and oral histories. In doing so, I am conscious that many voices are missing. Whereas we have Joseph Elman's voice, we only hear his father's voice echoed through his son's retelling. Stories of survival dominate over stories of murder. Like every other scholar of the Holocaust who uses oral history sources, I am aware that we hear almost nothing from those millions who were killed, meaning that in some senses we never really get to the very heart of the matter.[6]

This was brought home to me recently as I guided a group around some of the sites of the former ghettos and camps in Poland just as I was finishing off the last chapters of the book. I took the group to see fragments of the former ghetto wall in Warsaw and Kraków, as well as the barracks at Auschwitz and Majdanek. But I also took them to see the memorial sites at two of the Operation Reinhard camps – Treblinka and Belzec. These were sites built solely for murder and operated with a terrible efficiency during 1942 as Polish Jews were killed en masse. Belzec, the first of the Operation Reinhard camps, was a place where Jews from the surrounding regions were gassed shortly after arrival, with only a handful temporarily spared to work in the *Sonderkommando* that was forced to undertake the dirty work associated with the killings, before themselves being murdered. As far as we know, only two former prisoners survived Belzec, and one of these was killed in the immediate post-war years. Belzec is somewhere that we know relatively little about, certainly compared to Auschwitz, which was never solely an extermination camp and so is a place with thousands – rather than a handful – of survivors. Because I have gone to places in this book where the survivors' voices are richest, it means that I have not visited some of the deadliest sites – camps like Belzec, Sobibór and Treblinka – where the surviving human and material traces are so sparse.

While there are, inevitably, places that I miss out, the book is a journey through a number of key Holocaust landscapes that cover the years 1938 through to 1945, following the eastward and then westward thrust of the killings. I start with the ghetto (focusing on Warsaw where the largest ghetto in Europe was established), before moving to consider the role of the forest, camp (honing in on Auschwitz), train, attic and cellar, mountain and sea, river (where I examine rescue and murder on the banks of the Danube in Budapest), road, and finally returning once more to the camp (where I look at Bergen-Belsen at liberation). In the prologue and epilogue I turn my attention briefly to the years immediately before and after the war and to shifting ideas about home.

As I explore in the epilogue, the immediate post-war years saw attempts – some more, some less, successful – to unpick the years of dispersal of Jews across the European continent as the Holocaust became a trans-continental event. These attempts at reversing the impact of the Holocaust were specifically about reuniting families separated in the camp system. Here, men and women had been separated on arrival and this separation persisted and was hardened throughout the ensuing years, only breaking down in the chaos of the final months of the war. Although this separation was most marked in the case of the camp system, more broadly Holocaust landscapes were gendered landscapes. As well as being fluid places that were constantly evolving, these changing landscapes were also experienced differently by those inhabiting these sites. Men and women, rich and poor, young and old – as Joseph Elman's story of generational divides suggests – both occupied different places and often experienced the same landscapes in different ways.

These key ideas – the diverse range of victim experiences, spatial strategies of survival and the shifting landscapes of the Holocaust – are interwoven in this book that explores some of the landscapes where the Holocaust was implemented, experienced and evaded. In bringing these threads together, I hope to advance the nascent work that has begun on thinking spatially or geographically about the Holocaust.[7] Space, place, distance and proximity all mattered enormously during the Holocaust, as Joseph and his father were all too well aware. Being here rather than there was seen as literally the difference between life and death. It was not simply that the Holocaust was enacted in specific places, or through space, but it was also experienced by individuals for whom the idea of 'place' became paramount and the horrors they faced were evaded through the adoption of spatial strategies. Not only does the Holocaust have geographies as well as histories, it has micro-geographies as well as macro-geographies, and I try to capture something of that in this book that moves between the scales of the continent and cattle car. This sense of the Holocaust as a multi-scalar event tends to get lost in historical writing that often adopts a fixed scale of analysis and then works with a shifting chronology, rather than seeking to write about this event more dynamically as something moving through time and space.

Journeying through a number of Holocaust landscapes provides an opportunity to take a fresh look at a familiar event by focusing on the places where genocide was perpetrated or avoided. As Omer Bartov discovered when writing about the experiences of Galician Jews, bringing 'the protagonists of the event together into one place' enables us to move beyond 'bifurcated narratives of perpetrators and victims'.[8] Locating the Holocaust in specific places raises questions about the limits and possibilities of both German power and victim agency. It also brings into sharp focus the 'choice-less choices' that faced Jews like Joseph and his father as they sought to survive, oftentimes through spatial strategies, while their world was being reshaped around them.[9]

Prologue
Returning Home/
Leaving Home

On 10 November 1938, Gerda Blachman was woken early in the morning by the police. She and her fellow students at Munich's Jewish household school (a school for teaching girls domestic skills) were ordered to leave, taking nothing with them but the clothes on their back. Like the other girls, Gerda's first thought was to head straight home. In the immediate aftermath of the violent attack on Jewish property that became known as *Kristallnacht* – literally the night of broken glass, because of the glass-strewn pavements in towns and cities across Germany – home was the obvious place to go. In part, there were few other places Gerda could go in November 1938. More importantly, home was somewhere she hoped to find the rest of her family and she was desperate to find out what had happened to them.[1] Remembering the long train journey from Munich to Breslau, Gerda recalled her fear of what she might find – or not find – when she got back to her parents' apartment.

Making her way from the railway station through the centre of Breslau, Gerda saw the smashed windows of Jewish-owned stores and the smouldering remains of the synagogue. The view from the tram made it clear to Gerda that the events she had witnessed in Munich had been repeated in her home town.

As she made this journey, the full extent of the damage to Jewish property in Breslau was being proudly reported to his superiors by SS *Oberführer* Fritz Katzmann, who totted up the destruction wrought by one night of violence. One synagogue had been burnt and two others demolished, two Jewish meeting halls and one building of the Society of Friends had been destroyed, and over five hundred Jewish shops and ten Jewish inns had been damaged.[2] The devastation wreaked in Breslau was multiplied across the country as a whole, where 267 synagogues were destroyed and more than 7,500 Jewish-owned businesses were vandalized on the night of 9–10 November.

When Gerda finally made it home, she discovered – rather ominously – that no one was there. She decided that it was best to wait around for news of her missing parents. After a while, her mother arrived to tell her that her father had decided that he would be better off staying at the house of Gerda's grandmother than he would be staying at home. Discovering that Jewish men were being arrested at their home addresses as well as on the streets, her father had assumed that the authorities would not bother visiting a place where no Jewish men of working age lived. His hunch was proved right. Gerda's father was not arrested on the night of 9–10 November.[3] However, hundreds of others were. Ernest Heppner recalled watching as Jewish men were taken from their homes in his neighbourhood in Breslau. His brother was among those arrested and taken to Buchenwald, leaving his wife and baby alone in their wrecked apartment.[4] In total, close to 2,500 Jewish men were arrested in Breslau alone.[5] Across the country as a whole, the number of Jewish men arrested on 10 November was around 30,000. They were quickly dispatched to three of the concentration camps that had been established by the Nazi government for political opponents, with around 11,000 sent to Dachau, just under 10,000 to Buchenwald and 9,000 to Sachsenhausen.[6]

Although concentration camps had been established from the early days of the Nazi regime – Dachau in 1933, Sachsenhausen in 1936 and Buchenwald in 1937 – this was the first time that large numbers of Jewish men had been imprisoned en masse in the concentration camp system. Around 1,500 so-called 'antisocial' Jewish men had been arrested by the Gestapo earlier in 1938 and sent to concentration camps. However, the scale of arrests in November of that year was exceptional. A similar picture emerges with the destruction of Jewish property. Earlier on in the year, in the summer of 1938, a small number of synagogues – in Munich, Dortmund and Nuremberg – had been destroyed.[7] But the destruction in November was on a completely different scale both numerically and geographically. This was not a handful of minor incidents but a nationwide attack on Jewish property and persons, as Gerda Blachman discovered when she found almost identical scenes unfolding in Munich and Breslau.

The scope and scale of *Kristallnacht* signalled that this was a pogrom characterized by planned spontaneity, clearly stage-managed from the top. The immediate excuse for the violence was the attempted assassination on 7 November 1938 of the German diplomat Ernst vom Rath by a Polish-born Jew, Herschel Grynszpan, at the German embassy in Paris. Grynszpan's parents were among the nearly 18,000 Polish Jews who had been deported from Germany in late October 1938. When the Polish government closed the border, around 8,000 of these Jews were left to fend for themselves in the no-man's-land between Germany and Poland. The day after Grynszpan's attack, the German press threatened reprisals against Jews. On the afternoon of 9 November news came through that Ernst vom Rath had died of his injuries. That night synagogues, Jewish businesses, institutional buildings and homes were attacked with the active involvement and encouragement of the Nazi Party and German state. The police and firemen stood by and watched, having been instructed only to protect adjacent buildings from going up in flames. Writing approvingly in his diary on 10 November of the events going on around him, the Minister of Propaganda Joseph Goebbels – who appears to have been central to stage-managing the pogrom – recorded being driven back to his hotel in Munich amid shattering glass and burning synagogues.[8]

Simultaneous with this destruction, the Gestapo ordered the mass arrests of Jewish men.

Kristallnacht was a very public and visible pogrom. The flames from burning synagogues lit up the night sky and the smell of smoke persisted into the morning. The smashing of store windows could be heard and the results of this vandalism seen on the glass-strewn city streets the next day. Even those not directly affected could not fail to see, smell and hear what had happened. As well as being very public targets, synagogues and Jewish-owned stores were also highly symbolic targets. They represented an attack on German Jews as both a religious and an economic community. The presence of Jews on the high streets and main squares of German towns and cities was punished through attack and erased through destruction.

But these high-profile Jewish synagogues and stores in the city centre were not the only targets on the night of 9–10 November. Further out into the suburbs, Jewish homes were also vandalized as intruders broke into the intimate space of the bedroom and slashed mattresses, pillows and comforters, leaving feathers scattered on the floor.[9] For Lore Gang-Saalheimer the overriding memory of *Kristallnacht* was the contents of her parents' sideboard being systematically smashed, spelling the sudden end of the family's best china.[10] This was a widely shared Jewish experience. One survivor recaled the terrible moment when 'they came to our house' and 'threw all our furniture and dishes and everything out the window'.[11] Smashed crockery on the floor of the apartment and broken furniture in the courtyard outside mirrored the imagery of broken glass on the pavements of the city's main streets, but it also brought the reality of destruction much closer to home. It was this combination of 'broken glass in public and strewn feathers in private,' writes Marion Kaplan, that 'spelled the end of Jewish security in Germany'.[12] While strewn feathers, smashed china and broken furniture could – like the broken glass on the city streets – be swept up, psychologically the damage wrought and sense of violation they represented took far longer to repair.

All assumptions that home was a place of safe retreat were quite literally overturned overnight.

Just where safety lay, if not at home, was a critical question being urgently asked by German Jewish families on and after the night of 9–10 November. On that night Gerda's father realized early on that his home was no guarantee of safety and so he decided to lie low in another apartment in the same city. The next morning, on 10 November, Ernest Heppner recalled a vigorous discussion with his family over whether they should leave Breslau – a place where they were known – for the anonymity of a large city like Berlin. Retelling this discussion to his interviewer, Ernest explained that on the morning following the violence, he and his family were still unaware that what had happened in Breslau was not simply 'an isolated incident' but was occurring 'all over the country'.[13] Once the picture of a nationwide pogrom emerged, then both local solutions – hiding in someone else's apartment in Breslau – and national ones – leaving Breslau for Berlin – became redundant. Potential sites of safety became ever more distant as knowledge of what had happened across Germany as a whole emerged in the hours and days following *Kristallnacht*.

This sense of the pieces of a jigsaw quickly falling into place in the hours after *Kristallnacht* can be seen in a diary entry written on 10 November 1938 by a Jewish woman living in Hamburg, Luise Solmitz. Like Gerda Blachman's family in Breslau, Luise was not directly impacted by the events that took place. Her first hunch that something was wrong came on the night of 9 November when her husband conveyed the rumours he had heard in the grocery store. The next morning Luise and her husband saw something of the destruction themselves while out shopping in the city where they found 'areas blocked off, all the big Jewish stores closed, all the windows were broken in Robinsohn's place and Hirschfeld's. An incessant rattling and clinking from the splintered windowpanes on which glaziers were working. I've never heard such a clattering in all my life.'

A big jump in Luise's understanding of what had happened and its significance came later that evening when she and her husband heard the announcement 'on the radio around 6:00 p.m.: demonstrations and actions against Jews must end immediately. The Führer will order regulations regarding the murder of Herr vom Rath – Goebbels has issued this message.' From hearing rumours, through seeing the destruction on the streets of her own city, to finally hearing a national radio broadcast, Luise came to the realization over the course of twenty-four hours that destruction had not been confined to the streets of central Hamburg but was spread across Germany. It all added up, Luise confided in her diary, to 'a terrible, terrible day' that she saw as a premonition of worse to come. Concluding her diary entry for this 'terrible day', Luise wrote that what had just happened 'means that our fate is relentlessly approaching doom. I always thought, now we have reached the worst point. But now I see it was always just a prelude to the next thing. Now the end is near.'[14]

Once the national scale of violence was understood, the impact of *Kristallnacht* extended beyond those directly affected through attack or arrest.[15] It became clear that what had happened on the night of 9–10 November to the property or body of others – someone else's synagogue, store, apartment, husband, father or son – could now be imagined as something that could happen to you. All felt the ripple effect of this night. This single night of violence – including the deaths of around ninety Jews – and the mass arrests of Jewish men had an impact on German Jewish families not witnessed by half a decade of anti-Jewish legislation. '*Kristallnacht*,' Ernest Heppner recalled, 'was the turning point.'[16] While the first five years of Nazi rule saw a raft of anti-Jewish laws and measures, it was the dual attack on Jewish property and (male) bodies at a national scale in November 1938 that was a watershed moment for German Jews, especially in their perceptions of places of danger and places of safety. It was not just that home was no longer safe, but Germany was no longer safe. These events radically reframed German Jewish understandings of vulnerability and ultimately their relationship with the nation itself.

In the five years before the events of November 1938, German Jews had been excluded from a number of spheres. The earliest anti-Jewish legislation – the Law for the Restoration of the Regular Civil Service introduced on 7 April 1933 – removed Jews, or 'non-Aryans' as they were called, from government. Over the following years, Jews were increasingly removed from the economic sphere. This had a serious impact on Jewish families. Those who were children at the time often remember the moment in the mid to late 1930s when their father lost his job as a result of 'Aryanization' and conditions became so much harder for the whole family. Another frequent reference point – seen for example in Gerda's and Ernest's stories – was the removal of Jewish children from state schools in 1936. One of the reasons Gerda was at the Jewish household school in Munich in November 1938 was because German Jewish families had to turn to providing their own separate schooling for their children. The removal of Jews from the German economy and institutions was extended in November 1935 to their separation out from the German population at large through the so-called Nuremberg Laws, which outlawed marriage and sexual relations between Jews and Germans. Here was an attempt to turn back the clock on decades of mixed marriages and assimilation and create clear water between Jews and Germans.

While German Jews did emigrate during these years of 'Aryanization', it was in the days, weeks and months following *Kristallnacht* that attempts to emigrate were pursued with a new sense of urgency. Something had changed. What *Kristallnacht* spelt out dramatically was that safety could only be found outside the borders of Germany. And therefore like so many others, Gerda's family started making plans to leave Germany. 'We knew then and there that the time had come to leave,' Gerda later recalled of the winter of 1938–9.[17] Whether to stay or go had been a long-running conversation between Gerda and her parents. As in many German Jewish families, there tended to be a generational and gendered division.[18] Her father, with a good job, was on the side of staying. Gerda was keener to leave. However, in the weeks after

Kristallnacht it became clear to all of them that they had to leave Germany. They were not the only German Jewish family coming to the same conclusion. Over half of the Jews living in Breslau had left the country by the time war broke out in September 1939.[19] Many of those – like Gerda's family – left during the ten months between November 1938 and September 1939. This picture was repeated across the country. In the winter of 1938–9 an estimated 120,000 Jews left Germany, meaning that roughly the same number of Jews left the country in a matter of months after *Kristallnacht* as had left in the five years following the Nazi rise to power.

However, emigration from Germany in the winter of 1938–9 was far from a simple process. Legally it required permission to leave Germany as well as to enter a new country. As Gertrud Grossmann explained to her son in a letter in January 1939, 'Getting out . . . is at least as difficult as getting into another country.'[20] While Gerda Blachman and her parents were adamant that they needed to leave Germany, it seemed to Gerda that they had left it 'pretty late'.[21] Relatively few options were available. A new, and strange, geography of emigration was created that quite literally spanned the globe. Something of that new geography can be seen in the diverse range of destinations considered by Gerda's family and those closest to them in the weeks following *Kristallnacht*. Gerda and her parents were trying to get hold of papers to go to Cuba through a cousin who lived there. Close family friends were planning on making their way to Shanghai. The boy who would later become Gerda's husband had decided not to bother with getting hold of exit and entry papers but instead to attempt to cross illegally into Belgium. Whether to go to places like Cuba or Shanghai, and whether to leave with or without papers, were the new questions being urgently asked by German Jews during the winter of 1938–9. The result was a scattering east and west, near and far, to wherever they had contacts, could get papers, or could physically get to without papers.

The attraction of Shanghai to Gerda's family friends and some 8,000 other German Jews was that the International Settlement there was a multinational space that did not have the normal demands of entry visas that characterized the post-First World War world made up of sovereign nation states. In short, Shanghai was a place you could get into, if you could get hold of an exit visa out of Germany and afford – and obtain – a ticket to make the long journey east. Ernest Heppner was one of those who successfully made this journey, leaving Breslau with his mother bound for Shanghai. Going to China seemed, Ernest later recalled, like making their way to 'the other end of the world . . . or perhaps the moon'. However, his mother managed to use her contacts and her portable wealth to get a cabin for two on the *Potsdam*, which left Hamburg via Egypt, Singapore and Japan, before steaming into Shanghai in March 1939.[22]

Even with tickets and the requisite papers, emigration was not assured. Gerda Blachman and her parents were among the 937 passengers – mostly Jews – aboard the *St Louis* that left Hamburg in May 1939. Heading west involved a journey in which they danced, played ping-pong and had 'a good time'. However, having been turned back by officials first in Havana and then later Miami, their journey back east was rather different. 'There was a terrible mood,' Gerda explained, with, 'no more parties . . . no more fun'. Her family left the ship when it docked at Antwerp and they moved to Brussels. Although they had failed to make it to Cuba, at this moment in time what was important was less where they were than where they were not, namely Germany. However, what Gerda and her parents did not know in the early summer of 1939 was that although Brussels was not Breslau, within a year it would be occupied by Germany as part of the westward push that took place in 1940.

While a limited number of options were still available in 1938–9, there was huge demand for passages on ships. Ernest's mother used her networks and wealth to secure places on the *Potsdam*. Others had neither. The competition for visas and tickets was fierce. Gerda Schild remembered the 'rivalry' to get one's hands on the limited number of visas and ship tickets. Her mother, living with relatives in Munich, was unsuccessful in getting hold of the necessary paperwork, but other relatives were more fortunate. However, this was very much a clandestine operation. The first Gerda's mother knew of their success was when they left 'kind of secretly' and 'all of a sudden'. Given the rivalry for scarce opportunities, Gerda explained that 'people who were lucky like that kept that very secret, very much to themselves. They didn't say.' For those like Gerda and her mother left behind, 'there was a great jealousy . . . against those who could leave'.[23]

Leaving had both its financial and emotional costs. German Jews were 'fleeced, totally and completely' as they secured the necessary paperwork to leave the country. Adopting the model developed by Adolf Eichmann in Vienna after the *Anschluss* in March 1938 that saw Austria incorporated into the Reich, a Central Authority for Jewish Emigration was established by the Gestapo in Berlin in early 1939. This became 'an assembly line' where Jews 'entered . . . still a German citizen', but then systematically had their various possessions removed by one official after another. A typical Jew would leave 'reduced to the status of a stateless beggar with the only thing he possessed clutched in his hand: an exit visa.'[24] After making their way through this process, Jews left the country with very little.

It was one thing to leave possessions behind, but another thing entirely to leave family members – or be left by them. One of Gerda Blachman's overwhelming memories of this time was the 'terrible, terrible moment' when she with her mother and father said goodbye to her grandparents.[25] Leaving grandparents behind was a relatively common story.[26] However, for some, emigration meant the separation of nuclear families. When Ernest Heppner headed for Shanghai with his mother, he left behind his father, disabled sister and brother – who 'was trying to go to England'. Retelling their final farewell, he remembers getting a 'severe nosebleed that couldn't be stopped when I said goodbye to my sister'.[27] Equally 'traumatic' was the moment when Gerda Schild's father left as part of a group of skilled Jewish men heading to England in the summer of 1939. He left Gerda, her mother and sister behind, with the oft-repeated hope of finding a way to bring them over a little later. Her father's departure without the rest of his family was almost incomprehensible to Gerda. 'Families were sacred,' she explained, 'you didn't separate . . . you didn't leave your family. You didn't separate. You didn't leave your family alone.'[28] That Gerda's father did the unthinkable by leaving without the rest of his family in 1939 points to the exceptional situation and appalling dilemmas that German Jews faced in the aftermath of *Kristallnacht*.

In many ways Gerda Schild's story parallels that of Gerda Blachman. Like Blachman, in November 1938 Gerda Schild was living away from her parents at a Jewish school – in her case in Berlin. Also like Blachman, Gerda Schild headed home after *Kristallnacht*, passing the burning synagogues and smashed shop windows in Berlin as she headed by train to Ansbach. However, unlike Blachman, the men in Gerda Schild's family – her father, uncles, cousins – were arrested and sent to Dachau, leaving her mother to pack up their home that they had been ordered to leave. When her father returned – with his head shaven – 'we began to wake up,' Gerda Schild recalled. The impact of imprisonment was palpable to those at home once the men started to return after a few weeks. Although they might refuse to talk about their time in the camp, it was clear from the very visible signs like lost weight and teeth that this place had been brutal.[29] This direct experience of the violence of the camp system was critical in meaning that Gerda's father pushed through with plans to leave. As one of those who had been arrested he had to. Writing of how the 'November Pogrom decisively tipped the balance toward emigration,' Marion Kaplan notes that 'for those in camps, the only way out was proof of readiness to emigrate, and for those not in camps, the violence influenced their decisions'.[30] Yet, at this point, Gerda explained, 'we still only thought that the men were in danger', and so her father left alone, as part of a group of young skilled workers who were taken to Britain. 'We thought that my father could find domestic positions for us and bring us over after him,' Gerda Schild explained, 'but the war ended that.'[31]

At the end of 1939 the shutters came down and the borders were closed. Emigration was no longer an option. Gerda Schild, her sister and mother never made it to England to join her father. Around three-fifths of the Jews living in Germany when Hitler came to power in 1933 had managed to leave the country by the end of 1939. Small numbers continued to escape, illegally, across wartime borders or go into hiding. However, for most left behind – those like the women in Gerda's family – emigration was replaced by deportation to the 'east', as Germany occupied first Poland and then the Soviet Union during a period of highly successful wartime conquest. While Ernest Heppner's brother did manage to make it to England, he was unsure what happened to his father and sister. Once their letters from Germany stopped coming, all he knew was that they had been 'sent east and that was the last I heard of them'.[32] In November 1941, Gerda Schild's mother was deported from Munich to Riga in Latvia and to a newly created Holocaust landscape: the ghetto.[33]

Ghetto

In the autumn of 1940, Janina Bauman and her family found themselves asking a 'new question'. Faced with the order that all Jews were to move into the newly created ghetto area of Warsaw, Janina's family wondered whether it would 'be better to stay in the ghetto, or hide on the "Aryan" side?' Ghettoization divided this city, along with hundreds of others across Poland and later on elsewhere in eastern and central Europe, into separate Jewish and non-Jewish living space. In Warsaw, the first stages of dividing the city along ethnic lines had begun in the aftermath of the German occupation a year earlier, although the priority initially appeared to be to create a Jewish 'quarantine area' off-limits to German troops.[1] Later, roughly defined German, Polish and Jewish quarters began to be formed in the Polish capital by regulating where people lived when they changed apartments.[2] By October 1940 this move towards ethnic segregation was hardened and made concrete as a single area of the city was designated for all Jews to move into, which was then closed off by fences and walls. Dividing the city up like this into Jewish and non-Jewish space forced families like Janina's to ask which side of the wall might be safer.

In order to even seriously consider the possibility of surviving on the so-called 'Aryan side' of the wall, it was widely assumed that certain things needed to be in place. A set of non-Jewish social networks and the money to pay for their services was something that the Bauman family did have. However, what they felt they did not have were the necessary looks to pass as non-Jewish, and so, Janina recalled, 'we were resigned to living behind the walls'.[3] The significance of physical appearance was heightened for Jewish men, whose circumcision meant that their Jewishness was marked on their bodies. Facing a sense that their face or body did not fit, or a lack of contacts and money, many felt that moving into the ghetto was their only option. But as they asked this 'new question,' Jews not only had to decide whether they had what they thought it would take to survive outside the ghetto, but also to decide what this new place was, and in 1940 that was not entirely clear.

Concentrating Jews into ghettos emerged as a policy in the aftermath of the German invasion of Poland in September 1939. As they expanded eastwards, Germany carved Poland up into three zones. The area in the west – the *Warthgeau* – was incorporated into the Reich. The area in the east became part of the Soviet Union, as a result of the secret non-aggression pact that saw Poland invaded from the east as well as the west. The large area in the middle became the *Generalgouvernement*, or an occupied zone under the rule of Hans Frank. It was here, in this occupied land between the expanded Reich and the Soviet Union, that the Germans encountered large numbers of Jews, including the so-called *Ostjuden* so central to their antisemitic imagination.[4] The three million Jews across the country dwarfed the numbers in Germany, Austria and Czechoslovakia. While Jews in Germany in 1933 made up roughly one person in every one hundred, in Poland that figure was closer to one in ten. There were more Jews in Warsaw alone than in the whole of pre-war Germany.

During the early years of occupation, makeshift urban ghettos were set up across occupied Poland to house the Jewish population in a concentrated place in each town, city or region. The first ghetto was created in Piotrków in November 1939. Ghettos took a little longer to get established in the Polish capital, Warsaw. After a series of abandoned ghetto plans, the Warsaw ghetto was finally sealed a year after its equivalent had been set up in Piotrków. Down in the south of the country, in Kraków where Hans Frank established his headquarters, a ghetto was not established until the spring of 1941. Across the *Generalgouvernement* it seems that ghettos were set up as temporary measures driven by local agendas.[5] More permanent measures were being discussed in Berlin. In 1940 a series of territorial solutions were considered that would involve the expulsion of Jewish populations, either to the far edges of German-controlled space – in the so-called *Nisko* plan to create a reservation east of Lublin in Poland – or outside of Europe altogether – in the so-called Madagascar plan that envisioned relocation literally to the other end of the world. While ghettos brought Jews, oftentimes, to the centre of Polish cities, the utopian plans being aired in Berlin imagined pushing Jews to the very ends of the earth.

In the end, these plans to expel Jews to live and die in some godforsaken spot never came to anything because in 1941 far more radical plans emerged, which imagined extermination rather than expulsion. But when ghettos were constructed from the autumn of 1939 onwards, they were not places designed primarily to kill Jews – in the way that, for example, the purpose-built death camps established in 1942 were. Warsaw in 1940 was not Treblinka in 1942. It was both a different time and a different place. And in that different time and space – the autumn of 1940 in Warsaw – the Bauman family decided that they were better off in the ghetto than trying to pass to the other side of the wall where they feared they would be caught.

Initially it was unclear whether the family would even have to move. They lived on a street 'right on the border between the two worlds' and so one subject to claims and counterclaims as the final location of the ghetto wall was decided upon.[6] There was plenty of horse-trading going on over the inclusion or exclusion of specific streets and buildings in the autumn of 1940.[7] At first glance, creating a ghetto was a relatively quick and simple process. It did not involve designing and building something from scratch, but simply drawing lines on a city map and then building walls around that demarcated space – something paid for by the Jewish community as so often happened during this 'self-financing genocide'.[8]

However, in reality, things were far more complex. Ghetto walls were built in towns and cities with complex histories and geographies of Jewish and non-Jewish residential and business patterns. While Jews lived in larger or smaller proportions in different parts of a city like Warsaw, nowhere did they make up the entire population of a single street, let alone an entire district of the city as the total separation of ghettoization demanded. Choosing a site for the Warsaw ghetto was a long, drawn-out process that took close to a year. Initial plans appear to have been to shift Jews out of the historic centre of the city entirely and create a ghetto in one of Warsaw's suburbs, due to fears of the economic impact of walling in part of the city centre that would impede transport routes and the free movement of people and goods.[9] But these plans were abandoned in favour of locating the ghetto where large numbers of Jews already lived – and therefore by implication, relatively few non-Jews lived – in the traditional Jewish quarter close to the city centre.[10]

The street where the Baumans lived ended up being excluded from the ghetto during the final changes that were made to the precise location of the boundary, and so they did have to move. In the autumn of 1940 they moved in with relatives who had arranged to swap their apartment outside the walls with one inside the ghetto. Janina remembered packing some belongings onto a horse and cart and walking behind it to their new home. Explaining that they made their way to the ghetto on foot, she noted that 'it was only a ten minute walk, after all'.[11] That the ghetto was only a short walk away was not unusual. Ghettos were not created in *terra nulla*, but oftentimes in those parts of the city where Jews traditionally lived and that were generally close to home if not home itself.[12] Of course this was not the case for everyone. For Jews living in smaller communities, ghettoization might mean moving to the nearest larger town.[13] For German Jews like Gerda Schild's mother, deported to the 'east' in 1941, the ghettos of Poland or the Baltic states where they were sent were quite literally foreign places. But Janina Bauman's ten-minute walk across Warsaw – rather than a train journey to the other side of the continent – was one replicated across Poland and further afield in central and eastern Europe when Jews first moved into ghettos.

While Janina and her family had to move into confined quarters, it did not mean moving to an entirely unknown place. This comes across strongly in Janina's description of the apartment they moved into. It was clearly a domestic space, with Janina's eye drawn to the vivid colour scheme. But it was a very different kind of home to those that Janina, with her privileged upbringing, was used to and was far more overcrowded. 'The flat was small but nice,' Janina recalled. 'Never before had I lived in a multi-story annex meant for the less prosperous inhabitants of a smart apartment building; never had I had to climb five steep flights of stairs to find myself at home.' In this new home, Janina and her mother and sister lived in one room – painted bright yellow – that doubled as their dining room, with two others in the other room with its 'sky blue' walls and one more in the 'pea-green' corridor. All six shared the kitchen and a toilet, and the absence of a bathroom meant they washed in their own rooms. For Janina, 'all this was so unusual, so different from all the other homes I had ever known,' but 'we settled down somehow and began a more or less normal existence, living from one day to the next'.[14]

Relocation to the familiar domestic space of a brightly painted apartment was of course not the case for everyone. In some places, ghettos were established in institutional buildings such as synagogues, or in industrial premises such as a brick works. Moreover, while people did tend to search out a chance to swap flats and move in with friends and family, this was not always possible. However, moving into the ghetto was not the rupture that characterized later deportation to one of the camps. As Debórah Dwork and Robert Jan van Pelt perceptively suggest, 'the inhabitants of east European ghettos were connected to the history of the place in which they were now compelled to live. These streets, synagogues, and markets had grown over centuries to meet the Jewish community's needs; they now suggested that life could go on.'[15]

It is all too easy, with the benefit of hindsight, to assume an overly monolithic view of the Holocaust, seeing it as a single event that unfolded in a series of inevitably linked steps. But this fails to grapple with the contingency that marked every stage. The phrase, 'the Holocaust' is, as Martin Jay notes, 'a *post facto* conceptual entity not in use at the time, which no one individual ever witnessed'.[16] For the perpetrators, there was innovation and radicalization, with policies developing in a piecemeal fashion across both time and space. For the victims, what we know as the Holocaust was experienced as a series of discrete events and 'individual experiences' in a variety of different places. 'They may have been momentous experiences for some,' Joan Ringelheim suggested, 'but . . . that momentousness often occurs after we've identified what the event is. There was no such language for those experiences when people were going through them.'[17]

Reading Janina Bauman's memoir, it is clear that the moment when she and her family moved into the Warsaw ghetto was significant enough to be recorded, and both the nature of the apartment that she moved into and specifically the overcrowding in her new home were striking. However, it was perhaps not as 'momentous' an event – initially at least – as we might imagine. This can also be seen in the oral history interview with another Janina – Janina David. Born in Kalisz, Janina David's family were forced to leave after the German occupation, which led to her grandfather being arrested and the family business confiscated. As she retold her wartime story, it was the move from Kalisz to Warsaw, which was a place where they knew no one, that assumed greater significance than the moment when the ghetto was closed. In her oral history narrative there is a blurring of the precise chronology of the closing of the ghetto, a narrative that moves from arriving in Warsaw from Kalisz as refugees in desperate need of a home, to that new home becoming, and being, part of the ghetto. The creation of the ghetto happens very much offstage in a story where being forced to leave their home town and move to the capital assumed for the family a much more central role as Janina described the initial post-war years.[18]

However, as Janina David noted in her memoir, once the ghetto was closed in November 1940, 'the trap was sprung'.[19] As weeks in the ghetto turned to months, and then months turned to years, the terrible living conditions became the central concern in these survivors' narratives. In 1941 and 1942 it was now clear what life in the ghetto meant in a way that could not be imagined in those early weeks when Janina Bauman and her family were facing the 'new question' of where they should go. Most obviously perhaps, individuals had become increasingly aware that ghettoization meant being trapped in a terribly overcrowded space. Ghettoization everywhere involved concentration, within an event that Elie Wiesel recalled as a progressive experience of a 'shrinking' universe.[20]

Although the ghetto where Janina Bauman and her family lived was the largest in wartime Europe, it was inadequate given the size of Warsaw's Jewish population. This numbered around 360,000 in 1939, but an inflow of Jews from elsewhere in Poland meant that the ghetto housed as many as 460,000.[21] Crammed into this shrunken city within a city, a terrible lack of housing meant that each room held, on average, seven people.[22] For a young woman like Janina Bauman, the lack of personal space was particularly pressing when she got a new boyfriend. For two young lovers, living in the ghetto meant that they had 'nowhere to go' and 'no way to be alone'. Neither the crowded street nor their crowded apartment offered privacy. It seemed to Janina that in July 1942 the 'streets moan and yell with a thousand voices, they reek of rotten fish and dying bodies', and while their apartment provided some respite 'from sounds and smells', their attempts to find a place to be alone in the corridor were thwarted by the constant stream of visitors to the toilet.[23]

As Janina's recollections from the early summer of 1942 make clear, this overcrowded space was also a place of dying and death. One early writer, playing with the Nazi notion of *Lebensraum* – or imperial expansion creating new living space for ethnic Germans within an expanded Reich – dubbed ghettos *Todesraum*, or dying spaces.[24] Although ghettos were established for a variety of local reasons – in the case of Warsaw, on the pretext of limiting the spread of epidemics – they quickly became deadly places.[25] In these concentrated and segregated places a combination of overcrowding and an inadequate diet proved devastating. Confining very large numbers of people into an overcrowded part of the city meant that diseases such as typhus spread rapidly. In the spring of 1941 a typhus epidemic broke out in the ghetto that worsened during the summer and early autumn of 1941. In October 1941 the number of deaths from typhus in the Warsaw ghetto peaked at 3,438 during that month, although the actual number was most likely higher still.[26]

But Warsaw's Jews were not simply dying of disease. They were also dying of starvation in large numbers. By sealing off the ghetto, supply lines could be tightly controlled. A punitive ration was imposed on ghetto inhabitants that was completely insufficient. Official daily rations for the majority of inhabitants shifted between roughly 200 and 300 calories per day, which was only around 10 per cent of what an adult needed.[27] This meant that Jews in the ghetto received a lot less food – and not only lived in a lot less space – than others in the city. No wonder then that Janina David's dominant memory of her years in the Warsaw ghetto was of being constantly hungry. On her birthday in 1940 she received a copy of Charles Dickens' *Little Dorrit*, a story that resonated with her own experience of imprisonment. Years later, when she re-read this book, she was surprised to find that she kept wanting to eat. It seemed to her that the act of re-reading this book took her back to another time and place that was dominated by an overwhelming experience of constant hunger.[28]

Rising mortality was not simply a statistic, but something visible to all as death from starvation and disease took place out in the open on the streets of the ghetto. Questioned on what the Warsaw ghetto was like, Icek Baum struggled to summarize this other world, but honed in on a set of images of the dead. As he sought to paint a picture for his interviewer, Icek described seeing 'people lying outside starving . . . the people are dead, all dead. You don't have nothing there, nothing there. No food, cold. People . . . outside begging you for pieces of bread . . . I can't explain to you. I can't explain.'[29] When his brother Erwin was asked a similar question, his immediate response was a checklist of ghetto suffering – 'well, hunger, starvation, sickness' – before recalling, as his interviewer pushed him to provide more details, his memories of 'virtually' walking 'over corpses' because 'there were corpses lying around everyday, everywhere' on the ghetto streets.[30]

The presence of the dying and dead on the streets of the ghetto are recurring images in survivors' memoirs, oral history accounts and ghetto diaries. One ghetto diarist was Mary Berg – Miriam Wattenberg – who kept a diary while living in the Warsaw ghetto and then later rewrote it, first when her family was transferred to Pawiak prison in the city in July 1942. She then rewrote it again when developing a manuscript for publication in conjunction with a Yiddish journalist in New York after the family – privileged because of her mother's American citizenship – arrived in the United States in March 1944.[31] In a long entry dated 5 February 1941, Mary described leaving the warmth of her apartment to venture out briefly onto the winter streets that fascinated and repulsed her in equal measure, so that she could 'gaze at the faces of the passers-by, blue with cold' and 'try to learn by heart the look of the homeless women wrapped in rags and of the children with chapped and frozen cheeks'. Away from her 'warm room where I can smell the appetizing odors of good food cooking', Mary spotted a man whom she dubbed one of the 'dreamers of bread' that were found on the streets of the ghetto. With enough money for quarter of a pound of bread but no more, 'all he can do now,' she wrote, 'is lie down in the snow and wait for death'. He was a ghetto everyman in a place where it seemed that 'each morning another body of an old man with a blue face and clenched fists will be found lying in the snow'.[32]

Reading through Mary's diary it is clear she realized that the situation within the ghetto was getting worse and that more and more were joining the ranks of the 'half-dead' and dead on the streets. In October 1941 she described taking a 'ghastly trip' on the streets of the ghetto on her birthday, where among the 'huddled human figures like discarded bundles of rags' she stumbled over a 'half-naked corpse, covered only with a few fluttering newspapers', which she 'did not notice' in the darkness.[33] A month later, Mary reflected that there were 'fewer beggars' on the nearby streets than the year before because 'they have simply died off', and she noted that 'frozen human corpses' were becoming 'an increasingly frequent sight' on the ghetto streets.[34] In February 1942 she wrote that 'more and more frozen bodies can be seen in the streets . . . This is a hair-raising sight, but the passers-by are used to it.'[35]

For one self-proclaimed ghetto 'wild boy', David Kochalski, the bodies of the dead lying on the ghetto streets presented an opportunity. 'It was horrible,' he told his interviewer, before explaining that he would wake at five in the morning 'hoping' to find 'a lot of dead people on the street'. 'I wasn't the only one,' he assured his interviewer, as he described rifling through the pockets of the corpses hoping to find a piece of bread or something of value that he could trade for food in order to survive this place that he described years later as 'hell on earth' and 'worse than hell', where 'children my age and worse was smaller children, were just laying in the street begging for food, dying and nobody even paid attention'.[36] Adjusting to the constant presence of the dead among the living was, Erwin Baum suggested, critical for survival. When his interviewer asked him what he thought when he saw corpses on the pavement, Erwin replied with only one word – 'callous'. Later on, he reflected on how the bodies of those starving to death on the ghetto streets became normalized and how he 'found it natural, I said, oh just another poor soul, another poor soul. Just make sure I'm not going to be in that position'.[37]

To make sure that they did not end up among the corpses on the ghetto streets, Erwin and Icek Baum became, as they put it, 'hustlers'. In order to be able to eat, they joined the massive smuggling economy that was crucial to survival. Erwin learnt 'how to jump out of the ghettos'. His brother knew how to get in. Both used well-known weak spots in the boundary where the so-called 'Aryan side' and ghetto coexisted – the courthouse and the tramline that ran between the so-called large and small ghettos – to get in and out of the ghetto. The municipal courts on Leszno Street were open from both sides of the city and so were a 'third space' between these two worlds where strict spatial segregation became blurred, while the corridors inside the courthouse were a crucial meeting point for Jews and non-Jews.[38] Like the courts, the tramline that initially continued running through the ghetto was another lifeline connecting the worlds each side of the wall.[39]

Icek decided to live outside the ghetto on the 'Aryan side' but use the tram to enter the ghetto in order to deliver smuggled meat. By bribing a Polish policeman and jumping off and on when the tram slowed down at a bend, he reckoned that he brought 'maybe 25 kilo, 30 kilo' of meat into the ghetto at a time. 'And when I sold the meat,' Icek recalled, 'I have some money so I could buy something, potatoes or something like that,' which he 'took . . . home, I give them, and I go out'.[40] Back at home, his brother Erwin made the reverse journey, leaving the ghetto to buy loaves on the 'Aryan side' before passing them back over the wall to his mother who resold the bread for a higher price within the ghetto. She passed the money earned back to him so he could buy more bread, and so the business continued, leaving them with a small profit 'by the end of the day'.[41]

As he retold the account of this family business, Erwin's interviewer appeared incredulous that Erwin managed to leave the ghetto with such apparent ease. In a lengthy exchange he asked Erwin in increasingly minute detail to describe how he managed to cross this boundary that he clearly assumed was nigh on impossible to breach. Patiently answering his long series of questions, Erwin explained how his mother 'used to put her hands like creating a step ladder' so he could climb over a stretch of fence made from wooden boards that 'wasn't very high' and blend in with those 'going to the Court House'.[42] Although Erwin's interviewer seemed surprised to learn of the permeability of the ghetto boundary, this was something that contemporaries were well aware of. While a German report in 1941 made much of the total separation of the ghetto by three-metre high walls with another metre of barbed wire on top backed up by police surveillance, the reality on the ground was a little different.[43]

Even the seemingly most impervious of boundaries can be clambered over or wriggled through and it is clear that the Warsaw ghetto – like other ghettos – was far from impenetrable.[44] Each journey in and out of the ghetto undermined the logic of segregation so central to ghettoization. The ghetto walls that portended not only overcrowding but also the very real threat of starvation seemed to Erwin Baum to be 'like a border' between two different nations, such were the contrasts within and beyond the walls.[45] But there were 'ferrymen' who – for a price – would take you across the 'river' to the other side, and there were smugglers like Erwin who would risk it to feed both themselves and by extension those in the ghetto who could afford to pay.

The scale of smuggling and the size of the black market within the ghetto was considerable. While there were attempts to supplement the meagre rations by turning patches of earth in the ghetto into vegetable plots under the auspices of the *Toporol* Society for the Support of Agriculture,[46] the vast majority of the food consumed in the ghetto had been smuggled in. In December 1941, the Chairman of the Jewish Council, Adam Czerniakow, estimated that more than 95 per cent of the food in the ghetto had been brought in illegally.[47] The Jewish Council recognized that smuggling was essential if the ghetto population was not to starve, but fears were expressed over the toleration of large-scale organized smuggling undertaken by gangs. Moreover, the presence of so many child smugglers, in particular, was troubling to Czerniakow and made plain the limits of what the Council was able to provide. While the Council sought to ameliorate the plight of the ghetto poor through a host of mechanisms and organizations set up at either the scale of the ghetto or the individual house committees established in each building, the size of the challenge was simply too great.[48] Initially, it seems that the

German authorities had a mixed response to smuggling that combined official intolerance with unofficial tolerance. However, as time went on, attitudes hardened. The tram running through the ghetto was re-routed in March 1941 and boundary changes were made that saw the wall being moved to the more visible middle of streets. Crossing the ghetto boundary was punished with a death sentence from November 1941 onwards, and increasing numbers of those caught smuggling were shot.[49]

Despite the risks, smuggling was an everyday occurrence in the ghetto. It had to be if those within the ghetto were not to starve to death. Indeed, it seemed to contemporaries that some stretches of the ghetto boundary had semi-permanent holes in them that were in constant use for smuggling in food.[50] In the late summer of 1941, Emmanuel Ringelblum described what he dubbed 'the immortal hole connecting the former post-office building on Leszno Street with the finance-ministry building', as a favourite with smugglers. Its longevity stemmed from the fact that while 'the hole is regularly walled up by the Germans,' wrote Emmanuel Ringelblum, 'before the day is over the hole, the immortal hole, is open again'. This hole that seemed to be constantly filled and then broken through again lasted for just over six months before the action had moved elsewhere.[51] During the early summer of 1942 it was another long-lived hole – or 'target' – that fascinated one of the ghetto's diarists. The 'gap in the wall' outside the window where Abraham Lewin sat writing was, he estimated, 'wide enough for a sack with 100 kg of potatoes or corn or other foodstuffs'. Here 'smuggling goes on without a break from dawn at half past five until nine in the evening'. Although this 'hole in the wall' – like Ringelblum's 'immortal hole' – had 'been blocked up countless times', 'each time the Polish and Jewish policemen on both sides of the wall are bought off and before the lime has a chance to dry the bricks are taken down and the smuggling continues'.[52]

Smugglers did not only knock 'immortal' holes in the eleven miles of ghetto wall. Indeed Adam Czerniakow reckoned that in September 1941 only 5 per cent of the food and other goods smuggled into the ghetto came 'through the walls', with most coming in through the ghetto gates.[53] The variety of places utilized to bring things into the ghetto was a matter of some interest to contemporaries. In the lengthy entry when he made his first reference to 'the immortal hole' in the ghetto wall, Emmanuel Ringelblum extended the variety of places where smugglers operated in the late summer of 1941 to include 'certain places where the Wall runs through a courtyard', the rooftops at Rymarkska Street, 'latticed windows' on Kozla Street, and 'via a gate on Nalewki Street, through which a German post wagon drives'.[54] In her diary, Mary Berg was just as interested in the multiple sites where smugglers entered the ghetto, noting down the use made of tunnel-like cellars in houses on the borders to go under the ghetto boundary,[55] the law courts on Leszno Street that was Erwin Baum's preferred location,[56] or via the services of the 'kindly guard' positioned at 'the ghetto boundary at the corner of Sienna and Zelazna Streets'.[57]

As both Mary Berg and Emmanuel Ringelblum suggested, smuggling did not only take place over, under or through the ghetto wall, but most significantly through the gateways into and out of the ghetto provided that guards could be bribed or those authorized to enter the ghetto to undertake official duties.[58] Indeed, it seemed to Emmanuel Ringelblum that attempts to patch up holes in the ghetto wall by Polish police were motivated primarily because unregulated access into the ghetto bypassed opportunities for bribery. He retold an incident when police captured a crowd of smugglers using a ladder to scale the wall and forced them to pay a large fine, which Ringelblum surmised was 'the sum that the police claim to have lost because the smugglers used the Wall to bring goods in, rather than taking them through the watch at the Ghetto gate, where the police get a cut'.[59]

While for those – German, Polish and Jewish – guarding the gates and those doing the smuggling, bringing goods into the ghetto was a source of enrichment, for ghetto inhabitants it was essential for survival. As Janina

David explained to her interviewer, 'the rationing was so severe that if you really wanted to survive on what you were allowed, you'd starve very quickly'.[60] Janina Bauman was adamant that 'it was the black market, thriving in the ghetto despite its borders and heavily guarded gates, that kept us alive'.[61] However, to participate in this thriving black-market economy required money.[62] Smuggled food could be brought for a price, but these prices were high and rising.[63] Food prices on the black market were routinely 20–50 per cent higher than on the other side of the wall, and sometimes up to twice those on the other side of the ghetto boundary.[64] In the ghetto, food was by far and away the single biggest cost for everyone living in this inflated market within a market. It is estimated that an average family working and living in the ghetto in the spring of 1942 spent three-quarters of their family income on food, and that half of the income that they needed to pay these inflated prices came from selling off any remaining possessions.[65] Without work and possessions to sell, one was in trouble. Somewhere in between the Baum brothers hustling to survive and the Bauman family selling off their possessions to buy food, were those who were neither smugglers nor had enough to buy smuggled goods. Excluded from the smuggling economy, they were effectively destined to starve to death. Alive, they were the beggars who crowded the ghetto streets. Dead, they were the corpses stretched out on the pavement.

The existence of the smuggling economy in the Warsaw ghetto served to heighten pre-existing class differences as well as create a new class of smuggling nouveau riche who enriched themselves through large-scale organized smuggling. As contemporaries were well aware, the ghetto was not a single, homogeneous space nor a single homogeneous community. Rather it was made up of a variegated patchwork of streets that housed richer and poorer Jews who lived very different lives. Certain streets gained a reputation for being the home of a ghetto elite. Sienna Street, where the Berg family first lived, was one of these. Described by Emmanuel Ringelblum as 'the street where the Jewish aristocracy lived', Sienna Street was, he wrote:

a broad street, with good air, little poverty, few beggars, kept clean – literally, an island in the Ghetto. In the evening you could see well-dressed women, wearing lipstick and rouge, strolling calmly down the street with their dogs, as though there was no war. There was none of the confinement, hullabaloo, or nervousness of the Ghetto here. An isle of repose. A survival of the expansiveness of pre-war life in the middle of the Ghetto.[66]

Just a few streets away, it seemed like another world entirely. Walking down Komitetowa Street was, Mary Berg wrote in her diary, to enter 'a living graveyard of children devoured by scurvy', where older people without 'the strength to rise from their cots' in the 'long cellar-caves into which no ray of the sun ever reaches', stretched out 'a bony hand' to beg for bread.[67]

During their more than a year and a half spent living in the Warsaw ghetto, the Berg family inhabited the most privileged streets in the ghetto. When the ghetto was first closed off, it included the apartment building at 41 Sienna Street where Mary had been living since January 1940. She remained here until early October 1940 when this peripheral street was excluded from the ghetto during one of the periodic alterations to this ghetto that changed shape and shrank over the three years that it was in existence. When they were forced to move, the Bergs initially found an apartment on Leszno Street, before ending up living at 10 Chlodna Street where the so-called little and big ghettos met. Here they joined members of the ghetto elite on a street where those 'who could afford to bribe the officials of the housing office, got the best apartments on this street with its many large modern houses'. Well aware of her privileged status, Mary noted that 'Chlodna Street is generally considered the aristocratic street of the ghetto, just as Sienna Street was at the beginning'.[68]

Those occupying these different parts of the ghetto lived radically different lives within this shared but divided place. For a privileged inhabitant like Mary Berg, the Warsaw ghetto was somewhere that she could rightly claim in April 1941 to be the site of a 'flourishing' 'artistic life' centred around a series of thriving theatres that she listed on Leszno and Nowolipie Streets.[69] The sheer number of places of entertainment that sprang up in the ghetto is striking. Drawing on advertisements in the ghetto newspaper, Barbara Engelking and Jacek Leociak list literally hundreds of concerts and plays and other cultural activities that took place in this city within a city.[70] Against this backdrop of life seemingly going on as normal, contemporaries were painfully aware that the ghetto was also a place where life and death coexisted.

At the time, and subsequently, those who were aware of their relatively privileged status reflected on the ethics raised by the proximity of the living and dying within this troubling place.[71] As she wrote of the presence of 'so much misery and starvation' just outside her door, Mary Berg was well aware of her own selfish desire 'to fill my stomach'.[72] In one poignant passage in her memoir, Janina Bauman recalled eating with her mother and sister at one of the restaurants on Leszno Street where black-suited waiters served fine food to diners at tables with white tablecloths, while a wild, naked beggar could be seen on the street through the restaurant window – physically proximate but experientially a world away.[73] Writing of meeting 'living skeletons from the ranks of the street beggars' in June 1942, Adam Czerniakow, who confessed that he had been reduced to tears by these 'eight-year-old citizens' who 'talked with me like grown-ups', ended his diary entry for that day with the words, 'Damned be those of us who have enough to eat and drink and forget about these children.'[74] The stark contrasts between those who had the means to participate in the smuggling economy and those who did not, had to be navigated by those who still had money every time they left their apartment and came face to face not just with beggars on the streets but also with corpses.

While the contrast between those with money to buy food and those without was most marked, there was also a contrast between those like Mary and Janina who lived relatively privileged lives in the ghetto, and those like the Baum brothers who felt they had no option but to join the ranks of the smugglers. This comes through strikingly in the interview with Erwin Baum, who when asked whether there was any schooling in the ghetto, simply said no. Pushed on this, he conceded, 'there might have been, but who had patience for that. It was just a daily way how to survive, how to get . . . something to eat'. As he explained, 'I didn't want to go to school, I didn't want to participate in anything, only hustle. My best activities was jumping over the gate, run to the Polish market, buy a few loaves of bread, throw over. That gave me pride that I could do it.'[75] As his brother Icek explained, schools were certainly not for children like them, although 'sometimes you have the teachers, the Jewish teachers were teaching in the school before the war. They're teaching their own children. They can do that for nothing. Nobody want to pay.'[76] However, there were those who were willing and able to pay for schooling. Despite German restrictions on Jewish schooling, a host of ad hoc schools sprang up within the ghetto, in part as a potential source of income for former teachers. Without any 'major daily tasks', Janina Bauman spent her days translating 'Horace from Latin' or toiling 'over the theorems of Pythagoras', and she later managed to join students studying 'an almost standard unofficial university course in medicine' that 'immersed' her 'in the world of genetics'.[77]

While the contrasts in experience within the ghetto were stark, the contrasts between life inside and outside the ghetto were even more marked. This comes across well in a couple of passages from Mary Berg's diary written during the first spring she spent in the ghetto. She was still living at the time on Sienna Street at the very southern edge of the ghetto, and the glimpses of the world just the other side of the wall that ran through the courtyard served to highlight the differences between the ghetto and the remainder of the city. On 20 May 1941, Mary bemoaned:

On the other side of the barbed wire, spring holds full sway. From my window I can see young girls with bouquets of lilac walking on the Aryan part of the street. I can even smell the tender fragrance of the opened buds.

But there is no sign of spring in the ghetto. Here the rays of the sun are swallowed up by the heavy grey pavement. On a few window sills, long, scrawny onion stalks, more yellow than green, are sprouting. Where are my lovely spring days of former years, the gay walks in the park, the narcissus, lilac, and magnolia that used to fill my room?

A few pages on, after writing of her longing for green space, Mary reported the opening of the *Bajka* (literally Fairy Tale) garden cafe in the ruins of a bombed-out house in the little ghetto in Warsaw, which offered her the chance to don a bathing suit, pay the entrance fee, and 'bask in the sun here for an entire day'.[78] Mary was one of those privileged enough not only to have plenty of food to eat, but also to be able to pay to make use of the ghetto gardens that sprang up. However, as she noted, these were not the kind of gardens that existed outside of the ghetto, but were sited on waste ground. The image of Mary sunbathing in a garden cafe in the ruins of a bombed-out house captures something of the stark differences within the ghetto landscape and its population, as well as the dramatic contrast between life inside and outside the ghetto walls.

As Mary wrote this diary entry that longed for escape in May 1941, there was more happening than simply a sense that spring was holding full sway outside, rather than inside, the Warsaw ghetto. In the spring of 1941 a typhus epidemic broke out in the ghetto, which posed a threat to all of those imprisoned in this space. While participating in the smuggling economy could meet the challenge of a severely limited food supply, the onset of a typhus epidemic was more problematic. Smuggled medicine could be, and was, bought for a price. Reading through Mary Berg's diary and Janina Bauman's memoir, it seems that these two relatively privileged individuals adopted spatial strategies to deal with the threat posed by typhus. They both avoided the crowded streets of the ghetto, or perhaps more specifically, certain streets in the ghetto.

Overcrowded streets full of beggars were seen as a breeding ground for typhus. Therefore, out on the streets, Janina Bauman explained, 'physical contact with strangers was what we tried most to avoid'. Although she was well aware of the irony of seeing poor Jews on the ghetto streets in terms akin to 'Nazi propaganda' claiming 'that Jews were the carriers of lice and germs', Janina persisted in seeing those 'homeless, tattered, undernourished people we brushed against in the streets' as 'covered with lice' and suffering 'from infectious diseases'.[79] She was hardly alone in these assumptions. Mary Berg shared such fears of contamination, writing in her diary that 'it is enough to walk in the street and rub against someone in the crowd to become infested'.[80]

One solution was to avoid the streets altogether, but it seems that rather than seeing all streets as equally dangerous, Mary Berg mentally mapped out the ghetto as consisting of those places where typhus was 'particularly acute' and those places 'where the situation is somewhat better'. She identified a shifting micro-geography to the spread of typhus during the summer of 1941. On 29 July it seemed to her that Gesia, Nalewki, Nowolipiki and Nowolopie Streets were diseased places, with the 'little ghetto' where she lived a safer place, 'because it is inhabited by relatively well-to-do people who can afford private medical care'.[81] A couple of days later, it was Grzybowska Street – a place much closer to home and one that Mary had to go near when visiting friends in the southern end of the main ghetto – that was described as 'a terrible breeding ground for typhus'.[82] A month and a half later, Karmelicka Street in the large ghetto was somewhere that was best avoided given that 'the epidemic is particularly severe', prompting one of her friends to flee her home to the relative safety of Mary's apartment on Sienna Street in the little ghetto.[83]

As individuals navigated their way around this city within a city, it seems that they avoided certain streets or areas. When Mary's family was forced to move from Sienna Street in October 1941, her journey by rickshaw to look for a new apartment took her to 'the remotest corners of the ghetto'.

She travelled from the far southern edge of the ghetto to Stawki Street at the far northern edge, which was somewhere that Mary had never been to before and was described by her as if it were a wasteland made up of 'nothing but ruins and piles of ashes'.[84] This journey took Mary well beyond the geographical limits of her everyday use of ghetto space. Her daily experience of the Warsaw ghetto were the roads that ran from Sienna Street in the far south of the little ghetto to Leszno Street at the southern end of the large ghetto. This limited day-to-day use of a fraction of the ghetto area was also true of Janina Bauman. Describing making her way to the cemetery in the far north-western corner of the ghetto, she walked 'through the worst, most appalling part of the ghetto', which was 'a part I hardly knew'.[85]

In many ways there were few reasons for someone like Mary Berg or Janina Bauman to go to these poorer districts in the northern part of the large ghetto. They were not the site of the shops, cafes and theatres they frequented, nor the streets where friends or family members lived. But it also seems that these were the kinds of places to be avoided because of fears of contracting typhus in overcrowded streets occupied by the ghetto poor. As well as being divided from the world outside by the physical walls that made up the ghetto boundary, it would seem that its inhabitants mentally erected a series of (shifting) invisible walls within the ghetto. These demarcated those places they felt it was safe for them to go and those places – and people – that they kept well away from. However, despite trying to avoid typhus-ridden places and people, Janina Bauman discovered that even home was not safe. As she explained, 'the first enemy to violate our home and ruin the illusory peace of our daily life did not wear a Nazi uniform', but was the dreaded disease typhus caught by one of the men who shared their apartment and who volunteered in the ghetto hospital.[86]

Ironically, the threat of typhus largely kept the Germans out of the ghetto, although not entirely. There was a steady trickle of ghetto tourists, who came into the ghetto in search of the *Ostjuden* of their antisemitic imagination, and – as David Kochalski put it – took photographs to 'show how Jewish people are dirty, how they live in poverty, how they just are a heap of people who wouldn't be so bad to kill'.[87] There were also German guards, who as well as shooting those suspected of smuggling, seemingly took potshots at random for bloody 'entertainment'.[88] One gendarme became synonymous with such shootings and earned the nickname 'Frankenstein' for 'his notorious cruelty'.[89]

Such was the threat of being caught up in the violence that by the spring and early summer of 1942, Mary felt that it was 'now very dangerous to take long walks' through the ghetto and people were 'afraid to walk in the streets'.[90] This was a period when larger numbers of smugglers were shot. The dangers facing smugglers at this time were a particular cause of concern to Abraham Lewin. His interest in reporting the gap in the wall – the 'target' – that he could see from his window, was precisely because this was a site of murder. In his diary he recorded for posterity, often with painstaking detail, the individual atrocities taking place on the ghetto streets and along its walls, seeing smugglers as particularly vulnerable. This meant, Abraham Lewin informed his future readers, that 'each piece of bread that we buy on the open market is soaked with Jewish blood'. As the deaths of smugglers continued to mount up day by day, he wrote that the 'smugglers have reached the stature of heroes in my eyes, and the day will come when the whole people will surely sing of them in celebration of their great heroism'.[91]

While there were deaths due to German bullets, the vast majority of ghetto inhabitants who died, during the roughly two years between the setting up of the Warsaw ghetto in the autumn of 1940 and the beginnings of the mass deportations in the summer of 1942, did so because of starvation and disease in this overcrowded and walled-in space. With an average of around 2,500 dying each month, the question of whether Jews were to be sustained as a viable workforce in the ghetto, which was the assumption of the Jewish Councils, or left to starve, was much debated by local German officials.[92] However, these debates were ultimately supplanted by orders coming from Berlin in late 1941 and early 1942.[93] The radicalization of Nazi policy and practice in the second half of 1941 led to ghetto populations being liquidated en masse from 1942 onwards. German estimates put the number of Jews deported over forty-six days between July and September from the *Umschlagplatz* on the northern edge of the Warsaw ghetto to the extermination camp Treblinka at over 250,000, although the total may be closer to 300,000.[94] By the time that these mass deportations were taking place, the question of whether there was somewhere safer than the ghetto was being asked with greater urgency, and the answer appeared clear. Janina Bauman and her family decided that it was safer to risk it on the 'Aryan side' and left the ghetto for the last time in January 1943 during the second wave of deportations.[95] Janina David left around the same time.[96] Others stayed and fought it out during the final wave of deportations in April 1943 when they remade the ghetto by occupying hundreds of bunkers that formed not only hiding places but also sites of armed resistance against German troops.[97] In the aftermath of the Warsaw ghetto uprising, Jewish labour was brought in to demolish remaining buildings and recycle anything of value.[98] After the war, the Muranów district was built not only on the site of the ghetto, but out of the very fabric of the former ghetto with the innovative use of 'crushed-brick concrete' incorporating the broken bricks that were all that remained.[99]

But the shift in policy and practice from a situation in 1940 and 1941 when Jews were left to starve to death in overcrowded ghettos, to the implementation of mass deportation to the death camp of Treblinka in 1942, was not a shift in policy and practice centred on Warsaw or the *Generalgouvernement*. It came as Germany pushed further eastwards and invaded the Soviet Union in the summer of 1941. For Jews living in former Soviet territories that came under German control, seeking to survive necessitated doing more than participating in the smuggling economy or avoiding those parts of the ghetto where typhus was seen to be rife. It was not simply starvation or disease that Jews sought to evade during and after the second half of 1941, but genocide. And that demanded a new set of spatial strategies.

Forest

Earl Greif grew up on a small farm in Chlopczice, an agricultural community in eastern Galicia. His family farm lay in the eastern part of Poland that ended up in Soviet hands in 1939. In June 1941, German troops invaded Soviet territory. Initial rapid victories meant that much of Ukraine, Belorussia and the Baltic States were occupied within less than a month. The German advance continued apace, reaching Leningrad in September. As a result, large numbers of Jews – including the Greif family – came under German control. The occupation of the western and central part of Poland in 1939 had brought approximately three million Jews under control of the Nazis. Two years later, several million more Jews living in former Soviet territory now came under German control after the rapid success of Operation Barbarossa.[1]

In the aftermath of the German occupation, every member of the Greif family decided it was best to move. The oldest daughter – Reizel – had already left the family farm during the Soviet occupation to become a bookkeeper for a store and restaurant in Chaykovice, a small town just a few miles east of the family farm.[2] When the Germans invaded, Reizel did not head home to be with her parents, but went to live with an aunt near Lvov fearing what her membership of the Communist Youth might now mean. Ultimately, she joined the estimated one and a half million Jews who fled eastwards into the Soviet Union, just before the advancing German army.[3] She spent the war working as a lab technician for a field hospital, only returning westwards with the Soviet advance at the tail end of the war.

While Reizel joined the lines of refugees heading east, her parents (Izak and Miriam) and brothers (Earl and Leibel) and baby sister (Dvorah) stayed in German-controlled Galicia. However, they did decide to leave their small village for the promise of greater anonymity in the nearby city of Rudki. It was not the occupying German forces that they sought to flee as they moved to the city, but rather the threat of violence meted out by their neighbours as two years of Soviet control followed by German occupation presented new opportunities for antisemitic nationalists. Once in Rudki, they discovered that things were no better there. So, in the autumn of 1941 the family moved again. They left the urban space entirely and headed to the forests where they 'moved from one spot to another in the woods, sleeping in hollows on the ground where we laid out our blankets'.[4] As winter approached, the family split up and hid with three farming families they knew. In the spring of 1942 they returned once more to the forest where they were again constantly on the move through the summer and early autumn. Facing another winter and finding food harder to get hold of, they decided that life might be better in the ghetto-cum-work camp that had been set up for Jews in Rudki.

They quickly discovered that entering the ghetto had been a big mistake. They did survive the winter here in terrible conditions, but in April 1943 troops surrounded the ghetto and cleared the buildings. While Earl, his brother Leibel and father Izak hid in a brick oven, his mother Miriam and little sister Dvorah were taken into nearby woods. Here, along with the remaining Jews from the ghetto, they were shot into a large ditch and their bodies were covered over with soil. Like so many other Jews escaping the final liquidation of ghettos in eastern Poland, Earl, Leibel and Izak once more made their way to the forests, where they slept on leaves under a makeshift tent fashioned from tree branches. With the onset of another winter, this shrunken family of three separated. In his memoir, Earl explained that his father had decided to send his two sons away from the forest to find work on local farms under newly assumed non-Jewish identities, and so he and his brother left their father and the woods. Both Earl and Leibel survived the war, and were liberated by Soviet troops in the summer of 1944, but their father's fate remained unknown.[5]

Like thousands of other Jews living in the Polish-Soviet borderlands, most members of the Greif family did not experience deportation – or escape – on a continental scale, Reizel aside. Instead they underwent a far more localized and intimate experience of killing and evasion much closer to home in the ordinary spaces of densely wooded eastern Galicia. During the four years following the German occupation of this part of south-eastern Poland that was briefly occupied by the Soviets, Izak, Miriam, Earl, Leibel and Dvorah only moved a short distance from their family farm. Miriam and Dvorah were both shot just outside the main market town up the road from where the family had lived. Earl and Leibel hid in forests and on farms in the rural hinterland. The place of Izak's death remains unknown, but it was most likely also close to home.

It was in this region, in the summer and autumn of 1941, that German policy towards the Jews first turned murderous. Rather than being part of a 'preconceived plan', it seems that in the weeks and months after the German invasion of Soviet territory, 'an evolving policy with ever widening effect' developed through a series of orders issued to commanders on the ground.[6] Accompanying ground troops on their march east were *Einsatzgruppen* – mobile killing units – that initially targeted those suspected of being potential enemies of the new order. However, commando leaders were ordered to broaden out the categories of Jews being shot to include first of all able-bodied men, and then increasingly also women and children.[7] By late August entire Jewish communities were being targeted and killed on the outskirts of the towns where they lived.[8]

As the four main *Einsatzgruppen* swept eastwards – from *Einsatzgruppe* A in the north through the Baltic States, through *Einsatzgruppe* B in Belorussia and

C in the Ukraine, to *Einsatzgruppe* D in the southern part of Ukraine – larger numbers of Jews were killed. *Einsatzgruppe* C passed through Rudki – where the Greif family moved in the aftermath of the German occupation – early in the summer of 1941.[9] Because Rudki was early on in their path, it was not the site of mass killings of Jews at this point in the war. These first took place a little further into Soviet territory in those villages, towns and cities reached a couple of months after the invasion at the time when policy radicalized from targeting political opponents in the early summer to genocide in the late summer and early autumn. The intersections of time and space mattered. However, while Rudki was in some senses passed over in the initial rapid movement of *Einsatzgruppe* C, this did not mean that the Greif family had been spared. The first wave of killings that resulted in perhaps as many as half a million Jews being shot in the late summer and autumn of 1941 was only the first of several waves.[10]

After the first wave of killings, Jews tended to be placed into ghettos or work camps. As the late Raul Hilberg noted, 'the function of these ghettos, unlike those established in the *Generalgouvernement* during the preceding year and a half, was to be neither open-ended nor ambiguous. The goal was in sight from the start.'[11] In *Reichskommissarat Ostland* – the former Baltic states and Belorussia – a second wave of killings started in the autumn 1941.[12] In *Reichskommissarat Ukraine* – eastern Ukraine – a second wave of killings commenced during the late spring and early summer of 1942. This developed from a policy of killing Jews deemed unfit for labour into one of wholesale murder, meaning that by the end of the year 'there were almost no Jews left'.[13] A little further west, in Rudki that was now part of the *Generalgouvernement*, Jews were still living in the ghetto-cum-work camp at the end of 1942, and it was not until 1943 that Miriam and Dvorah Greif were killed in a wave of mass shootings that targeted the ghettos and work camps set up in this area. In broad terms, Jews in former Soviet territory were killed in three waves of shootings – either initially during the early occupation period in the second half of 1941, in a second and very bloody wave of killings that took place in the main during 1942, or in a final mopping-up exercise as ghettos and work camps were liquidated in 1943. In total, at least one and a half million Jews were murdered.

Whether in 1941, 1942 or 1943, these waves of killings tended to take place very close to home on the edge of town. Use was often made of existing indentations such as pits and ravines, or areas of sandy soil that was easy to dig.[14] Shooting into pits or hastily dug mass graves meant that the act of killing and corpse disposal was combined in one streamlined act. In many cases the killing sites were in forest glades where, as Andrew Charlesworth notes, the 'trees acted as camouflage from prying eyes both during the killings and after the graves had been covered'.[15] Although 'forests were convenient places of secrecy', the killings that took place here were something of an open secret.[16] The sound of gunshots echoed through the visual screen presented by the trees. Non-Jewish neighbours living in Rudki may well not have seen the killings, but they certainly heard them. And in the days that followed, it would seem that some ventured to see the mass graves in the woods.[17] Many of these graves were later dug up as part of a systematic attempt from the summer of 1942 onwards to hide the traces of these mass killings. The Germans implemented Operation 1005 with the express aim of exhuming and burning the bodies of those who had been shot.[18]

More recently those traces have been uncovered, in particular during the systematic forensic archaeology undertaken by a French catholic priest, Patrick Desbois, who has led a team uncovering the hundreds of sites of mass shootings hidden by decades of neglect and silence. They have found not only human remains, but also spent cartridges – thousands and thousands of them. Tallying up these cartridges has become for Desbois a way of counting the number of Jews killed during this more hidden phase of the Holocaust in the eastern borders of Europe between 1941 and 1943. Although initially 'convinced that all the mass graves were hidden in the forests', Desbois discovered that this was not always the case and that in some places Jews had been killed in far more visible spots, including 'in the middle of the village'.[19] These murders took place in the most ordinary of places, generally just a short walk from where the victims lived.

Because killings took place so close to home, those who survived and returned lived literally next door to the massacre sites. Polina Pekerman, a survivor from a town in Ukraine where killings had taken place in fourteen pits in the park, explained how 'when I lived in Chudnov, there was not a single day that I wouldn't be there. My feet would take me there. I know where the third grave was; and there my mum is.'[20] These sites were part and parcel of the lived geography of post-war daily life. Not only was the geography of genocide profoundly local in the former Soviet territories, the geography of memory was also similarly local.

Given the proximity of killing sites to villages and towns, it would seem that no one living in the area during the war could have any doubts about what German occupation meant, including those Jews spared the initial waves of killings. Writing of the situation in eastern Ukraine, Timothy Snyder notes that 'because these actions took place in public and over months', those who survived the first waves of killings 'had few doubts about their fate'.[21] Nechama Tec suggests that a similar situation played out in western Byelorussia where, because 'most mass shootings happened close to home', those 'Jews who had eluded the killings had a hard time denying the grim reality'.[22] However, referring back to his own experience of hearing the shootings in the forest, Josef Perl – a Czech Jew who ended up in Poland – was careful to point out the difference between hearing and seeing the massacres. As he explained, 'you can hear now and again "tat-tat-tat, tat-tat-tat", machine gun going, but . . . when you don't see it, it doesn't bother you, forgot shooting, and it's far away . . . it doesn't somehow connect you with anything, but as you come nearer and nearer and nearer you . . . come to see faces a little, so you know what's being killed, you can see who's being killed'.[23]

Snyder notes that while 'the very openness of the "Final Solution" . . . encouraged some Jews to flee for their lives' in this part of Europe, 'leaving the ghetto' was 'the easiest part'.[24] Deciding where to go was another matter entirely. Although large numbers of Jews who fled the waves of killings did end up hiding in the forest, for many this was a place of last resort because there was simply nowhere else to go. Even for someone like Abram Bobrow who came from a family intricately involved with the surrounding forests through their lumber business in eastern Poland, the woods were freighted with childhood stories of the forests surrounding his home as a 'frightening' and 'magical . . . forbidding netherworld', filled with 'wolves . . . and quicksand'.[25] For Samuel Gruber, who came from a small town on the Polish-Ukrainian border, forests were alien and alienating places. 'The beginning was so hard, it's unbelievable,' Samuel explained to his interviewer half a century later, as he described entering the forest for the first time with some others. 'I was really scared. I didn't know where I am.' In particular, it was the strange sounds that they heard in the woods at night that alarmed Samuel, who recalled the noise of the 'wind' and 'animals' and a broken tree that sounded like 'a wounded animal', which left him and the group with him 'really scared' as they navigated a strange landscape not knowing 'where you are'.[26] For a predominantly urban Jewish population, drawing on a wider repertoire of traditional assumptions, forests – especially at night – were an unknown and feared space.

No wonder then that Charlene Perlmutter Schiff, like many urban Jews, never intended to hide out in the forests. The plan had always been that Charlene along with her mother and sister would escape from the ghetto in Horochow in eastern Poland in the late spring of 1942 and go into hiding with farmers they knew 'on the edge of town'. Because no one was willing to take a family of three, her sister headed off to one farmer, and then a few days later she and her mother escaped from the ghetto in order to go to hide at another farm. However, in the chaos of escape, Charlene found herself separated from her mother. She continued on alone to their prearranged hiding place, only to be told once she got there that she was not welcome. For the next couple of days, Charlene hid out in the nearby fields. It was here she came to the conclusion that she 'would have to go to the forests' where she hoped that she might find her mother.[27] Her route into the forests via the tall wheat fields was a typical story of a short period spent in this space in between farm and forest. It was a semi-domesticated transition zone, which she occupied for a few days before plunging into the woods with more than a certain degree of reluctance.

Another woman who survived the war hiding in the forests was Sonia Orbuch, although her experience was very different from Charlene's one of hiding on her own. Having escaped from the Luboml ghetto in the Polish-Ukrainian borderlands just prior to its liquidation in October 1942, Sonia and her parents spent the next two years hiding in the woods. Initially, they met up with her uncle Hershel, who became both guide and teacher for this small family group. Living in a series of forests well known to their uncle, and close to his former home, contacts with a local farmer – Tichon – were vital in providing both food and information. Over the next six months or so, Sonia survived in a series of shelters built from 'branches, twigs, leaves, moss and bark'. The family moved 'about every two weeks on average' within the forests close to Tichon's home. In March 1943 they moved further away to escape the threat posed by antisemitic Ukrainian nationalist groups. For a short while Sonia and her parents switched a series of hand-built shelters for the hayloft of a widow who lived in 'a decrepit one-room wooden dwelling in a remote corner of the forest', which was a hiding place sourced by Tichon. When this site became unsafe, they moved further into the forest to seek acceptance by a group of pro-Soviet partisans. 'I was sure we'd be rejected,' Sonia later wrote, 'but as soon as Uncle Hershel began relating his experience as a scout in the Polish Army and his vast knowledge of the region, the *Politruk* showed interest. He told us to follow him through the trees to the camp. We would no longer have to face the forbidding forest on our own.'

From being a transient family group of four, Sonia, her parents and uncle now entered the highly organized space of a large partisan camp, especially when they left the partisans' summer camp for the winter camp in the Lubieshov forest, where they 'no longer slept in tents but rather in sturdy wooden *ziemlankas* [bunkers], camouflaged, insulated and heated'. For Sonia, living in this 'forest republic' felt like joining 'another world, an independent city-state . . . right in the midst of Nazi-occupied Ukraine'. Here, in the pro-Soviet partisan-controlled forest in 1943–4, Sonia discovered a 'third space' between Nazi-occupied and Soviet-occupied territory, where she and her family experienced their first – and more significant – 'liberation'.[28] It might not have been one of the neutral nations that Joseph Elman's father dreamt of reaching. However, as another woman recalled, one who – like Sonia – experienced both modes of hiding in the forest, entering the partisan camp did feel like discovering a place where 'people . . . can breathe free . . . you don't have to worry about the Nazis'.[29] More prosaically, but no less importantly for Sonia and her family, the superior living conditions within the winter camp meant that 'lice, which had caused us such distress when we were on our own the past winter, were no longer a major problem'.[30]

Making her way deeper into the forest in 1943, Sonia moved from one type of forest and forest living to another. She went from the forest edge into its heart, or as another survivor put it, from the 'little woods' to the 'big woods'.[31] Her different phases of forest hiding made clear that as Jews headed to the woods to escape the killings, they did not share either a single common space or experience. Rather, these experiences ranged from hiding alone or in a small family group and moving frequently at the edge of the forest – as Charlene Schiff and Earl Greif did, and Sonia initially – to living in more established and structured partisan camps deep in the woods, like the camp where Sonia spent the last year of the war.

Sonia's story of experiencing an early sense of 'liberation' in partisan-controlled forest in the last year of the war resulted from the shift in the balance of power after the German defeat at the Battle of Stalingrad in February 1943. This defeat spelt, in the east at least, the slow beginning of the end. The shifting fortunes of the war were felt on the ground by those hiding in the forests. Reflecting back on 1941, Nahum Kohn – who was originally from western Poland but spent the war hiding in the forests in Ukraine – remembered this as a time when 'the Germans were very strong . . . they were confident. They were the masters – the world was theirs. There were no Russian partisans – nobody had heard of any such thing.'[32] A couple of years later, things had changed. While 'at the beginning of the war, the Germans hunted us all hours of the day and night', one survivor recalled that 'by May of 1943 they had stopped hunting at night, and it became relatively safe for us to move around under the cover of darkness'. Another recalled that 'as winter was slowly ebbing away in 1943, there were many more partisans in the Bagdanovka forests. Some small areas were now controlled by the resistance, and the Germans could not enter then, even in force.'[33] Indeed, by June 1944, with the rapid westward advance of the Red Army it seemed to some that 'the partisans and the Germans had switched roles: now the partisans were hunting down Germans . . . The Germans, at this point, were like hunted, frightened animals, trying to escape, hiding in the bush, hungry and exhausted.'[34]

However, while it was true that forests gradually became safer hiding places as German power in the east waned across the war, Jews living outside the ghettos and camps were nevertheless hunted down in the so-called 'rabbit hunts' that followed the final wave of killings in this part of Europe in the summer and autumn of 1943.[35] Although relatively small in number, 'Jews in the forests and marshes were a special problem' to the German authorities, Raul Hilberg suggested, 'because they were no longer under control.' As a result, 'they were more important than their numbers (in the thousands) would indicate', and German forces sought to track them down and kill them.[36] These 'rabbit hunts', along with the dangers of being killed or reported by neighbours and the sheer difficulties of surviving for months or years in the forests, meant that less than 10 per cent of the tens of thousands of Jews who headed to the forests survived.[37]

In order to survive, those in hiding needed to find food and shelter and avoid detection. In the spring, summer and autumn, Jews ate what they could find in the forest, gathering plants, wild berries, mushrooms, nuts, eggs from birds' nests, as well as insects and worms. Drinking water was found in streams, on moss, or pools on the forest floor.[38] However, there was a need to supplement foraged food, 'and for that,' recalled one survivor, 'we had to leave the woods'.[39] It was this, above everything, that meant small family groups or individuals tended – like Sonia and her family during their first year in hiding – to stay close to the edge of the forest so they could easily get to neighbouring farms or maintain contact with pre-war acquaintances to ensure a supply of food. As Charlene Schiff explained, 'I had to find forests that were near villages where I could sneak into a garden, or a yard, or a potato cellar, or something where I could get something to keep me from dying from hunger.'[40]

While Charlene survived by stealing potatoes from the potato stores that were a feature in every farm in the region, others received food from contacts in the world outside the forest. A network of contacts was of inestimable value to those in hiding. Abram Bobrow recalled that 'it was not easy to keep changing places', as 'we couldn't go too far away from the peasants who were friendly to us. New, safe contacts were hard to come by'.[41] When Abram 'was forced to leave this familiar area and go to places where I did not know anybody', he discovered just how hard it was to live in the forest as one of the 'newcomers' rather than someone with an established set of contacts and the advantage of intimate, local knowledge.[42] One newcomer, Samuel Gruber, who ended up living in a forest some distance from home, explained that he was reliant on those with local knowledge who 'knew the terrain', knew 'where to go' and 'knew every piece, every house, every farmer . . . they knew everything around there'.[43]

While living on the edge of a forest close to home presented opportunities to maintain contacts with a known world, it did leave Jews vulnerable to being captured not only by German troops but also caught or blackmailed by forest wardens and opportunistic neighbours.[44] One young woman was well aware of the dangers of staying close to home in the small-town world where everyone knew everyone else and it seemed like her 'mother . . . was known throughout the area'.[45] It was therefore of paramount importance to choose a good hiding place to avoid being caught. Menachem Katz had escaped from the Brzezany ghetto in eastern Poland in June 1943. Avoiding neighbours searching for firewood was prominent in his mind as he and his friends sought out a site for their first bunker in the autumn of that year. His choice of an area of 'young forest' was intentional because no one went there to collect firewood.[46] Moreover, he was careful to choose 'a thicketed area at the side of the road, where no signs of carts and other traffic could be detected. The wheel marks were covered with thin grass, which indicated that the road had not been in use for quite some time.'[47]

Within the least-frequented parts of forests, Menachem and his friends chose a thicketed area for their hiding place. Living close to the forest edges, it was not primarily the trees that provided camouflage, but rather the 'undergrowth' or 'underbush'.[48] Recalling his escape from the ghetto in Brzezany, Menachem dismissed his idea of hiding in the closest forest with a post-facto rhetorical question directed at himself: 'What would I do in a pine forest near a town, a forest with no undergrowth to hide in?'[49] Later, he rejected another 'large pine forest' on the grounds that it also 'had little undergrowth at its edges and would not make a good hiding place'. Instead he chose a 'mixed and dense' forest 'with bushes and earth folds, where you cannot see a person even from a few yards away'.[50] The camouflage offered by the natural topography was fully utilized, with the final decision to construct a bunker in 'a small mound in a not very densely thicketed area, so that we don't have to ruin the natural look, and mark the digging area'.[51]

As they built bunkers and shelters, Jews made use of what they found around them on the forest floor. Tree trunks and branches provided structural beams, while smaller twigs, leaves, pine needles, pine cones and grass were used for roofing.[52] Utilizing natural materials for roofing meant that shelters, 'camouflaged with branches and grass . . . could not be seen from the air' by German pilots.[53] The careful choice of site and design could lessen the likelihood of a hiding place being discovered. Alongside this, those hiding were cautious about when – and if – to light fires. The plumes and smell of smoke that breached the forest canopy were a clear giveaway as to the location of even the most hidden shelter.[54] The choice of firewood was important. 'Green branches' were avoided because they 'would cause too much smoke that someone could notice from a distance'.[55] One survivor from Ukraine recalled being instructed by more experienced forest fugitives to use birch wood, 'since wet birch tree would not smoke'.[56] Some avoided lighting fires at all, or did so 'if we felt our environment was safe enough'.[57] Others only lit fires at twilight or at night to avoid smoke being seen by farmers during the day.[58] This reflected a broader reorientation of life to a quasi-noctural existence, whereby one only left the forest at night to search for food on neighbouring farms.

Surviving in the woods for several years meant not only adjusting to the rhythms of night and day, but also of the seasons. During winter, thick snow meant that few entered the forest, and bunkers were both insulated and camouflaged with a blanket of snow, thereby making this, in some ways, the safest season to live in the forest. However, these benefits were more than outweighed by the problem of coping with harsh conditions, sourcing food, and the likelihood of hiding places being given away by a line of footprints.[59] One way around this was to leave and return to the bunker during a blizzard so that fresh snow covered the tracks, to walk backwards, or to use branches to brush away tracks. Other options included leaving the shelter infrequently and stockpiling and rationing food.[60] In effect, this meant going into hibernation for the winter.

One Ukrainian survivor's recollection of seasonal migration – 'in summer we lived in the forest, in winter in villages' – was shared by others.[61] Charlene Schiff sought out warmth in farm buildings in the winter, hiding in potato cellars. Here she adopted a seasonal pattern of movement in and out of the forest that characterized the wartime experience of Earl Greif and his family and many others in hiding on the forest edge. The forest was oftentimes one place among many of hiding, rather than the sole place of more permanent hiding. Chaim Melcer – who had fled to the forest after escaping from a train taking him and his family to Sobibor – lived a transient life between barns and 'holes in the ground, empty tree trunks, and secluded brush'. 'After a night of foraging for food,' he recalled, 'we retreated to our shelter in the hay loft or holes in the ground underneath bushes to disguise ourselves. During the day, if we felt our environment was safe enough, we made a fire and cooked what we had found.'[62]

Living a transient existence within a fairly well-defined area close to key contacts and a reliable food supply meant that each move was accompanied by a careful attempt at erasing, as Abram Bobrow explained, 'all evidence of our stay, burying anything not a necessity and smoothing over the ground with dirt and weeds, and then spreading newly fallen leaves over that', to ensure that signs of their existence were kept to a minimum.[63] In the case of larger, more semi-permanent camps, this careful erasing of traces that Abram described was far more difficult. Julia – who was later to become Abram's wife – explained that 'it was hard to remove all evidence of a camp of 200 people'.[64] However, for those, like Julia or Sonia Orbuch, who experienced forest life first as part of a small group and then within the semi-permanent world of a partisan group, the contrast in living conditions was striking.

Nahum Kohn was originally the leader of a small and highly mobile group of Jewish men in hiding. 'We never remained long in one place – one day, or two at the very most,' he recalled. 'Today we were here, tomorrow we were far away, and on the third day we were even further than that.' Moving through the forest 'according to our instincts . . . sleeping comfort was not too important, since we rarely slept in the same place twice. We would dig individual holes half a metre deep, line them with moss, post a rotating guard and sleep.'[65] As Nahum moved from leading this small group of men, through to being a member of Felyuk's Ukrainian partisan group of fifty people, then to joining the massive Soviet *Medvedev atrád* made up of 1,500 partisans, he experienced the radical difference of leaving behind a world of sleeping in holes dug into the ground to entering what seemed to him to be 'a whole city' in the woods.' As he explained:

> my own group had numbered 18 men; Felyuk had 50 men, and I thought that his group was the most modern and organized possible. But here I saw hundreds if not thousands of men! I saw cars, trucks, cavalry, a hospital; I saw antitank guns, artillery pieces, horses, cows . . . it was a whole new world for me. I couldn't imagine that these were partisans. They looked like a regular army. As I was being led in, I saw that they were slaughtering cows for their kitchens. I was quite bewildered.[66]

Nahum's amazement at what was happening in the heart of the forest was shared by others. Dov Cohen – who had fled the ghetto in Novogrodek in Belorussia to go into hiding in the woods – found 'the whole scene simply unbelievable' when he was taken to the Bielski camp 'bustling with activity'.[67] It seemed that a 'little town' had been built in the woods, complete with 'streets', 'a bakery, a salami-maker, show workshops, tailoring and engineering workshops and, later, a tannery'.[68] It is no surprise that this settled existence from autumn 1943 onwards meant this camp seemed almost like a 'shtetl', and was dubbed 'Bielsk' or even 'Jerusalem'.[69]

What struck those who had moved from the forest edge to its heart was not only the infrastructure of these cities in the heart of the woods, but something as simple as the pleasure of sitting around a camp fire at night.

Deep in the forest, fires could only be seen by airplanes flying over the forest and not by farmers or patrols looking into the forest from the outside. It is striking how in many memoirs and oral histories, accounts of evenings spent around the camp fire were markers of safety and normality for those entering the partisan camps. Abram Bobrow, reunited with his brother in his partisan group, remembered:

> that night, David gathered the entire company around an evening bonfire. They were deep enough in the Mizelyschchatz, to not worry about Germans or peasants. For the first time in a year, I thought, the smell of a wood-burning fire is good, and the warmth is like paradise. For the first time in a year, I could take pleasure in such a simple sight as the sparks flying upward against the backdrop of the tall trees.[70]

For Josef Perl, memories of sitting round a camp fire in the evening – singing and playing accordions – represented a return to a life approaching normality.[71]

However, despite the greater comforts of life within large partisan groups, 'the problems of feeding and protecting the group were enormous', given the sheer number of mouths to feed.[72] The large quantities of food that were needed could only be sourced from outside the forest by raiding parties that sometimes had to travel vast distances. Dov Cohen recalled how his partisan group in the Naliboki forest was fed by 'groups of 10 to 15 young armed men [who] would go out, leaving the safety of the forest and travelling up to 100 kilometres to bring back food for the group'.[73] As he explained:

> in order to provide for a camp of 1,200, our supply units had to travel long distances and operate very close to the cities. It took days and sometimes weeks before the units returned with supplies, meat, flour and other basic provisions. The roads were bad, and there were ambushes and traps. Many men died on these missions, but they were vital to the camp, and we did them out of a sense of responsibility.[74]

Feeding large partisan camps such as the one that Nahum was part of became more challenging as 'the woods were flooded with partisans' during what survivors remember as 'the invasion of the forests' in the final years of the war.[75] Jews were neither the first nor the only temporary residents of these borderland forests during the Second World War. In Belorussia, as Nechama Tec points out, the first wave of forest fugitives were Soviet soldiers evading capture by German troops in the summer of 1941. They were followed in 1942 by young Belorussian men escaping call-ups to labour service in Germany. Jews only started heading from the ghettos to the forests in significant numbers from the summer of 1942 onwards.[76] Following the German defeat at Stalingrad, increased emphasis was put on developing the existing Soviet partisan movement, and men were parachuted into Belorussian forests, bringing their expertise with them.[77] The result was that many of the larger forests became home to multiple and quite divergent groups, with 'the territory . . . divided into sections and each part . . . ruled by a different partisan group'.[78]

It was perhaps inevitable that there would be conflicts between different partisan groups competing for scarce resources. One leading member of the group to which Abram Bobrow's brother belonged – the *Kaganovich Atrad* – made the mistake of stealing clothes from a farmer who 'was a contact for another partisan brigade made up of Soviet soldiers': a mistake that resulted in his summary execution.[79] Another dispute arose between the Bielski group and the Soviet group headed by Victor Panchenko, who were competing for the same limited food in the area outside the forest.[80] The solution was a division of the area outside the forest, with the Bielskis being given the area around the towns of Lida and Novogrodek and Panchenko taking the area around Zdzieneiol.[81] The end result – and a pattern you see elsewhere – was the effective division of the hinterland outside the forests into separate supply zones to avoid conflict between groups or over-burdening a particular set of villages or farms – especially those close to the woods. As Joseph Elman recalled, 'there was so many brigades already in the woods [at] that time, that each brigade had their own territory'. His group was assigned 'a territory where we had to operate, far away from our camp', where the brigades went 'to the rich farmers' to obtain food.[82]

Joseph's experience of going to rich farmers increasingly further and further away from the forests is one that was mirrored elsewhere. The group that Abram Bobrow belonged to stopped taking food from local farmers, who were becoming overwhelmed by the demands being placed upon them, and instead began seizing food from towns and larger landowners further away from the forest.[83] The increasing challenge of food supply meant not simply a shift in where food was sourced, but also how it was sourced. Negotiations with local peasants turned to large-scale theft.[84] As a result, being armed was essential. 'You could get food then only with a "convincer," a gun,' Nahum Kohn remembered. As he explained, in the forests in the last years of the war, 'a revolver was gold, diamonds, *everything* – without it you were regarded as a cockroach. With it you became a respected person.'[85]

Weapons were a valuable and valued asset in the partisan-controlled forests. It was hard, as Sonia Orbuch acknowledged, to gain entry into these groups without marketable skills or commodities. In her case, it was her uncle Hershel who was the entry ticket for the family group. He brought a skill very much in demand, namely, his vast knowledge of the region. Also needed were doctors, barbers and musicians.[86] For others, it was not skills but weapons that secured access.[87] This was Leib Reizer's experience when he, along with a group of others hiding in the Grodno ghetto during the first deportations, attempted to contact partisans in the Nacza forest. Arriving in the forest after a long journey undertaken at night, their presence in this regulated space was tolerated by the partisans because they brought weapons and ammunition with them. As Leib noted with purposeful play on the wording of another ideologically controlled space, it was ultimately the partisan leader Bucko who 'could declare us "citizens of the forest" and offer us "*lebensraum*".'[88] Bucko assigned Jewish partisans to settle Leib and his group 'in a safe location' and then act as their 'teachers in the forest kingdom' where Bucko was clearly king.[89] Charlene Schiff's one, half-hearted, attempt to join a partisan group that she came across in the forest ended up with her being sent away because, unlike Leib and Sonia's uncle Hershel, she had neither weapons nor skills to offer.

Entering into partisan-controlled space generally necessitated planning, connections with the underground, and skills and weapons. In some cases, those seeking admission who were deemed a threat given their knowledge of the location of the partisan base, were executed outside the camp.[90] Partisan-controlled woods during the later years of the war were highly regulated spaces under semi-military discipline.[91] This militarization of the forest – what one dubbed as the time 'when the rule of the jungle finished' – was seen by many as essential for survival.[92] When Samuel Gruber became part of a larger and more settled group that he described as a 'real army' and 'military establishment', he contrasted the successful organizing of supply groups that ensured a steady flow of food with the precarious existence of a less disciplined group living in a nearby swamp. As he told his interviewer, he had warned them: 'Listen people. You want to live. You have to behave. You have to do something else. You cannot just go to the farmers, rob them. Wait for us. Organize something. There should be some organization because otherwise . . . you will perish and we will perish altogether.'[93]

However, this militarization of the forests could, and did, present a threat. The partisan-controlled forests in the last years of the war were – in the vast majority of cases – male-controlled space where Jewish women were doubly vulnerable: firstly as Jews and secondly as women.[94] This was something that Sonia Orbuch was well aware of when she moved from the more isolated existence of hiding with three family members into the male-dominated space of the partisan camp. Although it was a personal 'liberation' for her, she was aware that it presented dangers for women more generally. As was the case in other partisan groups, the commander's wife recommended that Sonia choose a man from the camp to be her protector.[95] In her memoir, Sonia suggests that her father and uncle played this role for her, and her mother, meaning that they were seen as sexually 'off limits'. As she later recalled, 'I was lucky in this respect, but many other young women . . . had a different fate. There was much sexual harassment and even rape, and for that reason single females did tend to pick a defender, often a brawny labourer, the sort of person with whom they likely would have had no contact before the war' – a prospect that left her 'horrified'.[96] However, from reading through Sonia's memoir, it seems that the presence of her father and uncle were not seen as sufficient. Instead, the role of male protector was taken by another man in the camp, Piotr Menaker, who Sonia was quick to make clear 'never touched me'.[97] In order to survive within this male-controlled space, women needed to be under the control – or protection – of a man.[98]

There tended to be clearly defined gendered roles for men and women within partisan camps. Sonia's uncle Hershel went on partisan raids given his knowledge of the locality and his background as a scout in the Polish Army – the very skills that led to their acceptance into the partisan camp – and her father left the camp to forage for food and raid farms. On the one occasion when Sonia left the camp to go on a mission, it was in her role as assistant medic, rather than armed combatant.[99] This mirrored the picture elsewhere, where Jewish – and non-Jewish – women tended to be assigned traditional gender roles – in particular cooking and cleaning – within the 'forest kingdom', rather than being armed and partaking in raids. There were noteworthy exceptions.[100] One was when Leib Reizer and his group made their way into the Nacza forest and first encountered the wife of the partisan leader Bucko. Rejecting the 'fur coat and schnapps' that Reizer's group brought with them, she was only interested in weapons, not such fripperies. 'This simple White Russian peasant woman,' wrote Leib in revealing gendered terms, 'who assessed the guns' great value in so manly a fashion, grew considerably in stature in my mind.'[101]

While particularly marked in the partisan camps, traditional gender divisions were also replicated in the search for domestic normality to which Menachem Katz and his small family group aspired. Forced to move from their initial bunker after the roof collapsed in a cycle of freezing and thaws, they started work on a second, superior bunker in the late spring of 1944. In his post-war descriptions of life in this place, Menachem rendered it as the successful carving-out of a domestic space in the woods. Outside the bunker in the morning sunlight, the boys chopped wood and removed waste, while the women aired the bedding and prepared breakfast. 'Everyone was busy,' he recalled, 'as if they were ordinary householders running their normal life in their own premises in the forest.' Inside, small touches domesticated this cave carved out of the earth. Pebbles provided flooring between log-hewn bunks, 'cloth bags and braided onions and garlic hung on the wall as decoration, and a saw, an ax, sticks and several cooking utensils completed the display of equipment stolen from farmers of the nearby villages'.[102] In relocating to the forest, Menachem sought to recreate at least some of the norms and comforts of home in this alternative, carved-out space. Through domestication or quasi-urbanization in the partisan camps, the alien space of the forest was transformed into a 'home'.[103]

This re-creation of home extended to the scale of the forest and not just individual bunkers or camps. There was an attempt to reunite scattered rural communities and reconstitute the pre-war geography of the region on the forest floor. In the first forest where Leib Reizer's group was settled, he ended up heading a 'forest family' of eighty. However, there was another group of seventy Jews from another town – Lida – living less than half a mile away, and sixty Jews originally from another place – Radun – a couple of miles away, who made it clear that they did not want Leib's group 'hanging around as guests'.[104] After his final forced move into a new forest, Leib was reunited with Jews from his home town of Grodno, leading to a time that he recalled 'felt like living in a small *shtetl*'.[105]

Finding others from a shared pre-war world brought a sense of familiarity to the alien space of the forest. During his final period of hiding in the forest in the spring and summer of 1944, Menachem Katz met two men from his home town. Returning to tell of this discovery, Menachem recalled an initial nervousness among the rest of the group about anyone – even Jews from their own town – knowing the whereabouts of their bunker, and there were days of 'frequent arguments for and against the meeting'.[106] This scenario was played out in the hiding place of the two men Menachem had encountered, as both 'groups, in their respective Kuropatniki forest hiding places, went through two days of tension, arguments and guessing'. However, when the two groups finally did meet, 'hugging, kissing and crying' gave way to hours of talking together over a meal. 'This day was different from all the others during the past year,' Menachem recalled, 'simply because it brought together two groups of Jews who wanted one thing – to be free and live like human beings.'[107]

Menachem's account of a fond reunion between two small groups of Jews from Brzezany in the Kuropatniki forest points to a time and place where the events of what we know as the Holocaust – whether extermination or evasion – were played out very much at the local scale. This was not a story of mass movement across the European continent, whether through forced deportation or flight. In the forests of eastern Poland and the former Soviet Union, both hiding and killing took place close to home. There were plenty of Jews like Polina Pekerman's mother or Earl Greif's mother and baby sister who were killed close to home in a park or the woods just outside the town where they had lived all their lives. And there were other Jews like Menachem Katz and Charlene Schiff who escaped these killings by hiding in the woods near their former homes.

But this experience of genocide in the neighbourhood was transformed in 1942 and 1943 into a continent-wide programme of killing that brought Jews often over vast distances to a handful of purpose-built killing centres that were alien rather than familiar places. In his classic account of the Holocaust first published in 1961, the late Raul Hilberg distinguished between the early phase of killings from the summer of 1941 onwards, when 'small units of the SS and Police were dispatched to Soviet territory, where they killed Jewish inhabitants on the spot', and the later phase in 1942 and 1943 when 'the Jewish populations of central, western, and southeastern Europe were transported to camps equipped with gassing installations'. Hilberg drew attention to a marked shift from a geography of genocide where 'the killers . . . moved to the victims' to one in which 'the victims were brought to the killers'. This shift involved increased 'complexity', and necessitated a 'much larger apparatus that had to deal with a host of constraints and requirements' in order 'to accomplish the final solution on a European-wide scale'.[108] It meant not simply digging pits in sandy soil, but building death camps.

Camp

After the liquidation of the Starachowice ghetto in southern-central Poland, Renia Laks Gelb was taken with her father and two sisters to the nearby Majowka labour camp. During the ghetto liquidation, Renia's mother had become separated from the rest of the family and been sent to an unknown destination.[1] In 1944 this shrunken family of four – a father and his three daughters – were on the move again, when they were taken by train to Auschwitz-Birkenau. In 1944, Auschwitz lay at the epicentre of the shifting Europe-wide geography of killings. This had started in 1941 with *Einsatzgruppen* shootings in the occupied Soviet Union, and then moved westwards through the experimental death camp at Chelmno and the Operation Reinhard camps of Belzec, Sobibór and Treblinka in 1942 and 1943, and on to Auschwitz-Birkenau. Ultimately, the killings continued to move westwards onto the road network of Austria and Germany in 1945 and the overcrowded concentration camps in Germany that became a dumping ground for emaciated prisoners evacuated from camps in the east. If there were 'bloodlands' during the Second World War, then these were less a static, fixed space than a constantly evolving (first increasing and then shrinking) shifting murderous zone in the space between the Axis and Allied forces and the euphoria of Nazi victory and the desperation of Nazi defeat. In 1943 and 1944 that zone was very much centred on Auschwitz-Birkenau, where trains from across Europe converged on this site that was, for a year or so, the killing capital of the continent.

Before she arrived in Auschwitz, Renia's horizons of persecution revolved around a highly localized story of the forced labour of the Jews from the region around her home town. It was only in Auschwitz, this most international of all the camps at the heart of the European rail network, that Renia began to grasp for the first time that her community was not alone in being subjected to imprisonment and killings, but was one community among hundreds of others across Europe that were being similarly persecuted. Auschwitz was the place where what we know as the Holocaust was first comprehended by individuals like Renia as a project of killing and enslavement on a massive, continent-wide scale.

The continental scope had been sketched out a couple of years before Renia arrived at Auschwitz, at an infamous meeting held in the Wannsee villa in the suburbs of Berlin in January 1942. A gathering attended by leading officials, we only know about this secret meeting because someone chose not to destroy the minutes. Reading through these, the Europe-wide ambitions of the so-called 'final solution of the Jewish question' clearly emerge, with over thirty European countries and their Jewish populations listed.[2] Very few within the Nazi state were privy to this top-secret paperwork. Completely unaware of the scale and scope of these plans were, of course, their intended victims. For Jews like the Laks family, their experience of persecution was profoundly local and limited, a few rumours aside. But in Auschwitz, as Renia later put it, 'you get thrown into a situation of different nationalities, so you are beginning to understand the scope of this entire drama'.

For Renia, one of the hardest parts of discovering 'the scope of this entire drama' was coming to terms with the likely fate of her mother, separated from her family a few years before and sent to an unknown destination. Now that Renia was living cheek by jowl with Jews from across Poland and across Europe, it became 'very easy to piece things together' and work out what might have happened to her. First in Auschwitz, and then later on in Ravensbrück, Renia and her sisters came to the conclusion that their mother was most likely dead, 'because we'd seen too much and heard too much . . . having now been mixed in with all the people . . . from every conceivable part of Poland'.[3]

It was not only prisoners from all over Poland that the Laks sisters encountered at Auschwitz, but from throughout Europe. While they could not understand the words that other prisoners said, their presence spoke powerfully of the European-wide scope of the persecution. Reading through a surviving block book from Auschwitz-Birkenau, one glimpses a moment after the Hungarian deportations in the late spring and early summer of 1944 when Jewish and non-Jewish women from all across Europe were crammed into overcrowded barracks. Here, in Block 22b, hundreds of women from Belgium, France, Germany and Holland to the west, from Italy, Greece, Hungary, Slovakia and Yugoslavia to the south, and from Latvia, Lithuania, Poland and Russia to the east, were temporarily housed together in a crowded multilingual space.[4] This picture was repeated across the camp. In Auschwitz no one was at home. Deportation from ghetto to camp was not simply about being taken from one closely guarded and bounded space to another more closely guarded and bounded space. Rather it was about being taken from a place close to home to an alien and disorienting landscape.

Auschwitz was a constantly shifting linguistic landscape with additional languages being added to the mix as each new national group of prisoners were brought in. For Lilly Malnik, transported to Auschwitz-Birkenau from Belgium in 1944, it seemed that 'transports were coming in every day from all different countries. People with all kinds of different languages – Hungarians, Poles, Czechoslovakians, from Holland, from France, from Belgium, from Germany, Italy, Russians. They were from everywhere. It was a melting pot. And everybody spoke in different languages.'[5] Asked who was housed with her in Auschwitz, Nina Kaleska who came from Grodno on the Polish-Belarussian border responded:

I have no idea. They were speaking all different languages. I did not know German. I did not know Hungarian. Actually the Hungarians came later.

Mainly I think the people at that time were from Poland. Polish Jews. Uh possibly Czechoslovakian but I really am not totally sure so I can't tell you.[6]

Another survivor remembered Auschwitz as a place where it seemed that 'every language on the European continent could be heard . . . because people had come to Auschwitz from all the places Nazi Germany had conquered. I thought of the Roman Empire and the adage "All roads lead to Rome." Now it seemed that all roads led to Auschwitz.'[7] The train lines that converged at Auschwitz made it a strange meeting place where in 1944 a German Jewish teenage girl called Ruth could befriend another Jewish teenager called Nini from Salonika, and through this encounter understand for the first time 'that the Nazis were trying to eliminate even the Jews of as far south as Greece'.[8]

The specific camp – Auschwitz-Birkenau – where the Laks sisters arrived with their father in 1944 and discovered a multilingual prisoner population, was only one of a number of camps within a much larger complex. Auschwitz was, one survivor sought to explain to her interviewer, not just a camp but 'a big . . . complex' and like 'a whole city you know'.[9] Within the 40 square-kilometre SS zone of influence that made up the Auschwitz complex, the major elements of the Nazi camp system – concentration camp, POW camp, death camp and labour camp – could all be found in this one place.

The original camp – Auschwitz I – with its iconic ARBEIT MACHT FREI gateway where modern-day visitors begin their tour, was created in the spring and early summer of 1940 to house Poles deemed political opponents of the Reich. A compound of barracks was recycled to form the seventh concentration camp (after Dachau, Sachsenshausen, Buchenwald, Flossenbürg, Mauthausen and Ravensbrück) at a moment of expansion of the camp system, when Stutthof, Natzweiler and Gross-Rosen were also being planned and established. The construction of Auschwitz II – or Auschwitz-Birkenau – which is where the Laks family were taken in 1944, began in the autumn of 1941. Originally planned for Soviet POWs captured during the German invasion of the Soviet Union, this increasingly became a site of the mass killing of European Jews. Jewish transports began arriving there in March 1942, with systematic killings beginning a few months later. In June large gas-chamber and crematoria complexes were constructed, and additional killing facilities were ordered at the end of the summer. By July 1943 there were sufficient gas chambers and crematoria in place to mean that several thousand corpses could be gassed and burnt here each day.

This transformation of Birkenau into a death camp brought Auschwitz into the handful of sites purpose-built for mass killing. The technology for mass killing had been developed in Chelmno and then Belzec, Sobibór and Treblinka, where Polish Jews were deported and murdered en masse in 1942 and early 1943. Once the killings had ended at these four camps, they were razed to the ground and the area was planted over as a forest. By 1944, Auschwitz was the only death camp with mass killing facilities still intact and so was used, as Debórah Dwork and Robert Jan van Pelt put it, 'to mop up the remnants of the Jewish communities of Poland, Italy, France, the Netherlands, and the rest of occupied Europe'.[10]

Auschwitz-Birkenau was a relative latecomer to mass killings. As Dwork and van Pelt point out, none of the estimated 1.1 million Jews killed in 1941 died in Auschwitz. In 1942, the bloodiest year during the Holocaust, it is thought that 2.7 million Jews were killed. Less than 10 per cent of those killed in this seminal year – probably around 200,000 – were gassed in the newly established bunkers 1 and 2 in Auschwitz. In 1943 around half a million Jews were killed, roughly half of these in Auschwitz. At the end of that year more Jews had been killed in Treblinka and Belzec than at Auschwitz.[11] However, all that changed in 1944, when Auschwitz-Birkenau became the single most important site of mass killings. As Sybille Steinbacher points out, this was largely due to 'pragmatic reasons' related to the changing fortunes in the war.[12] When the largest single national community of Jews remaining in occupied Europe – Hungarian Jews – were deported in mid-1944, they were sent to Auschwitz-Birkenau because there was nowhere else left to send them.

Beyond functioning as a concentration camp for political prisoners and playing an increasingly important role as an extermination site for Jewish deportees in the second half of the war, the Auschwitz complex also housed forced labourers employed in the vast agricultural estates and industrial facilities such as the I. G. Farben works built in 1941 to produce *Buna* – a synthetic rubber. As well as working in agriculture and industry, thousands of prisoners were employed on multiple construction projects. Around 10,000 prisoners from Auschwitz were initially assigned to construct the I. G. Farben works, followed by an expansion of the slave-labour population to 30,000 to work in the newly built factory. In 1942 a new concentration camp – Auschwitz III – was built specifically for I. G. Farben, located much closer to the factory in Monowitz than the main camp of Auschwitz a few miles away. This model of the co-location of factories and labour camps was reproduced across German-occupied territory. Prisoners were sent to these camps from Auschwitz in 1943 and 1944, when the camp played a key role as the central node in a wide network of labour camps.

Although Auschwitz was made up of a multiplicity of camps and sub-camps with different functions, most prisoners only saw a fraction of this vast space. When survivors return, as many have done to show their children or grandchildren their former sites of incarceration, they are often astounded at seeing the full extent of a single camp like Auschwitz II, or when walking around the former camp Auschwitz I.[13] Writing of revisiting Auschwitz sixty-three years after she was sent there from wartime Hungary, Eva Olsson described how 'this time, I saw things I was not aware of when I was there before'. For the majority of prisoners, Birkenau, let alone the entire complex of camps in Auschwitz, was not a place of free movement. It was only when Eva joined a tour guide on her return visit that she was able to see Auschwitz I for the first time, and go to parts of Auschwitz-Birkenau that were out of bounds in 1944. Doing so, Eva realized that 'there was so much more going on at Auschwitz-Birkenau' than she saw as a prisoner. As she tried to explain the limited scope of her knowledge of this place in 1944, 'it's like when you are in a room in a huge building. You know what's going on in that room and that building, but if you don't get out of that room or building, you don't know what's happening in the next building or the next room'.[14]

Eva's revelatory experience on her return visit to Birkenau and the main camp points to the importance of boundaries that separated zones within the camp as well as different camps from each other and not just the camp from the world outside. The external-facing perimeter fence was perhaps the most obvious of the boundaries in this heavily segregated space. Michael Vogel – deported here from Slovakia in late 1942 – was struck by the way that Birkenau was encircled by a boundary both physical and human. As he explained his visual memories of the camp, he recalled seeing 'guard towers all around the complex, all around, constantly manned by SS'.[15] The physical boundary at Birkenau – made up of eighteen steel gates, twenty-seven guard towers and more than seventeen kilometres of fence[16] – was something that struck George Havas when he first arrived there.

Brought in on one of the Hungarian transports in 1944, George immediately saw the difference between where he had been sent from, the rapidly constructed ad hoc ghetto sited in the brick works on the outskirts of Munkács, and his new site of imprisonment. 'As soon as I stepped out I looked around,' George recalled, quickly coming to the conclusion that this 'place is ominous'. 'Whereas in Munkács, the brick factory . . . had a three-foot high wooden plank fence and wooden towers', George realized that there 'was no temporariness about this place', where:

the fence posts were solid concrete and all identical and you could look down along them and they ran . . . into infinity. And from this platform

I could see buildings . . . lines and lines there were, all of them were black and huge and as far as the eye could see, there was no end to them and then I could see there's more of these guard buildings.

As he was marched from the unloading ramp, George saw that the 'barbed-wire fence with the concrete poles' was 'electrified and on every pole there were insulators, electric insulators, which I knew what they were, I wasn't that simple and I knew that wire passing through an insulator had high voltage in it'.[17] That voltage was, as those who threw themselves against the wires discovered, strong enough to kill.

But, as prisoners quickly became aware, barbed-wire fencing not only formed an external boundary to the camp, but also a series of internal boundaries that divided Birkenau into sectors with different functions and prisoner populations.[18] Michael Vogel came to realize that the camp was actually made up of 'rows of camps' with 'a ditch' and 'wires in between the camps'.[19] As recalled by Thomas Buergenthal – who arrived in Auschwitz-Birkenau in 1944 after having been moved through a number of ghettos and camps in Czechoslovakia and Poland – Birkenau was made up of 'a number of camps . . . surrounded by barbed wire'.[20] These separate camps, or zones, within Birkenau meant that this was a prison where 'prisoners were not incarcerated in individual cells, but confined within geometric fields'.[21] Eva Olssen's experience of confinement operated at the scale of the barracks and the sector where that barracks was located alongside rows of others. Living 'in just one barrack', Eva recalled that 'going to the kitchen to get the soup was as far as I went. You didn't go from one section of Auschwitz-Birkenau to another section unless you were taken for a reason', meaning that she 'had no way of knowing what was going on in the next section of the camp'.[22] Although prisoners were counted during the frequent roll calls as members of a single barracks,[23] there was some limited freedom of movement within zones after work details had returned in the evening. This was a 'very important part of the day'. Felicia Berland Hyatt, who was originally from Chelm in eastern Poland, remembers the evening offering an opportunity to 'go from one Block to another' within their zone, 'visiting relatives or friends, or buying and selling merchandise', or doing what survivors generally called 'organising', which was 'the most important word in the Auschwitz language'.[24]

Confining prisoners to individual zones or sections within the wider camp was not simply a way of controlling the prisoner population through boundary making. It was also a way of separating out different prisoner populations from each other, which was something that prisoners sought to overturn. The internal fences in the camp reflected, replicated and made concrete the initial twofold separation of prisoners when they first arrived in the camp. Memories of the 'two selections, one to choose those able to work and the other to separate the females from the males', loom large in survivors' oral history interviews and memoirs, given that it was for many the place where families were permanently wrenched apart.[25] Elie Wiesel's powerful rendering of the moment of separation as just eight words that sent him and his father to the left and his mother to the right, captures the speed of these initial separations as a fast-moving blur in this disorienting space: 'Men to the left! Women to the right!'[26] For Leo Scheneiderman, deported to Auschwitz with his family from the Łódź ghetto, permanent separation from one's family was accomplished with the simple repetition of the two words 'left' and 'right'. 'We got out of the train,' Leo remembered, 'and everything went so fast: left, right, right, left. Men separated from women, children torn from the arms of mothers, the elderly chased like cattle. The sick, the disabled, were handled like packs of garbage.'[27]

This dual separation of Jews into the living and dead, and those chosen for labour into men and women, assumed spatial form as these groups entered distinct zones within Birkenau. Men and women selected for labour were sent to separate men and women's camps within the camp. Those selected for murder were taken to the death zone where the gas chambers and crematoria stood. This zone replicated the spatial form of Operation Reinhard camps such as Treblinka whose sole function was designed to be rapid mass murder, with only a small cadre of prisoners permitted to live to ensure the functioning of production-line murder. One of those men in Treblinka, Samuel Rajzmen, was called by the Soviet prosecutor to give evidence at the post-war Nuremberg trials. In their exchange, it is clear that what shocked the prosecutor was the sheer speed with which killings at Treblinka could be achieved. It seemed almost unbelievable to him that within ten to fifteen minutes of their arrival at the camp, these prisoners could be dead.[28] The rapid mass killing developed in the Operation Reinhard camps was replicated and perfected within the death zone constructed in Birkenau. Here, the separate elements developed in the Operation Reinhard camps – undressing room, tube, gas chamber – were concentrated within a single building (that could be, and was, replicated) made up of distinct rooms that also contained massive crematoria to burn the bodies.

The death zone in Birkenau was separated out from, and screened off from, the remainder of the camp and was out of bounds for the majority of prisoners.[29] The exception were members of the so-called *Sonderkommando*, Jewish prisoners who were forced to carry the bodies out of the gas chambers and take them for burning. *Sonderkommando* members were routinely killed because they had seen too much by dint of going to places where no one should go and leave alive – into the gas chambers at Birkenau. After the *Sonderkommando* members had been killed, the gas chambers themselves were blown up as a final act by the retreating camp command in January 1945. This was a place to be erased, as were all those prisoners who entered there. But it was not only the camp authorities who sought to destroy this place. Members of the *Sonderkommando* managed to smuggle explosives into the death zone and succeeded in blowing up one of the crematoria in October 1944.

As this suggests, the boundaries between zones within the camp were not completely impermeable. Prisoners in one section could see and hear prisoners in another. William Lowenberg – who had been deported from the Netherlands where he and his family had earlier fled to escape the growing antisemitism in Germany in the mid-1930s – recalled hearing an incongruous mix of violin music and screams coming from the gypsy camp, and seeing women prisoners from 'a distance', even while 'you couldn't talk to anybody from any other camp, any other compounds'.[30] As well as being a single visual and auditory landscape, Auschwitz was also – more problematically – a single olfactory landscape. The death zone was glimpsed in the chimneys that rose up above the barracks and smelt throughout the camp. What unified the discrete and separate spaces in the camp for one survivor was the sight and smell of burning. 'You could stand, for example, outside your barracks in my camp,' Thomas Buergenthal recalled, 'and see the smoke billowing out from the, from the crematory. And not only the smoke, and even almost fire, but also the stench that would come out. So you couldn't be in any place in that environment and not know what was happening.'[31] Birkenau is remembered as a unified olfactory landscape, drenched in a 'gruesome, overpowering stench', where 'the chimneys were very high and the smell of flesh was very prominent'.[32] As Renia Laks explained, 'when we came, you could smell, you could see the fire out of the chimney. And of course, burning flesh has a very strong odour that is nothing like anything else that you know. So, that was unmistakable, the burning of human bodies, unmistakable.'[33] It did not take much imagination to comprehend what might have happened to others, and what might happen ultimately to you, although there could be resistance to believing either or both.[34]

While prisoners might begin to piece together what had probably happened to family members in the aftermath of the initial selections, it was impossible to be certain. In the case of family members of the opposite sex, the gendered separation of the camp into distinct men's and women's camps meant that finding out about what had happened to grandfathers, fathers, husbands, sons and brothers, or to grandmothers, mothers, wives, daughters and sisters, was near impossible. Magda Blau – deported from Slovakia – recalled husbands and wives screaming to each other to communicate between sectors, 'or sometimes the man, if he has a chance to get something extra, so he put it in a piece of paper . . . in a rock and he threw it over'.[35] However, overcoming gendered separation was difficult in this internally segregated space. The experience of separation from her father, as much as the physical removal from home, is what made Auschwitz feel alien to Renia Laks who later recalled:

> I do know that I felt . . . less fear in Majowka than in Auschwitz because Majowka was still Starachowice and Father was still on the premises and it was really home town, my home town, even though there was no semblance to life or home or anything, this was the place that was a familiar – not the camp, but the town was a familiar town. Auschwitz was a totally different situation, where everything was threatening from day one. The mixture of fatherless, the total terror of being surrounded by electrical barbed wire, by a system in place.[36]

Within this segregated, gendered space, freedom of movement between zones was highly prized precisely because it held up the chance to find out something about family members of the opposite sex. Certain roles offered opportunities to cross between zones. This was something that William Lowenberg's 'big brother' Hans Gelpter enjoyed, who 'could walk around the camp a little bit more than anybody else' by dint of his job within the camp as a mechanic.[37] Two male prisoners who were doing some repairs in the women's camp seized upon the chance to access a normally forbidden zone to ask Felicia Berland Hyatt 'where I came from, when, and what was happening on the outside'.[38] Work details inside or outside the camp might bring a chance to exchange a few words with prisoners of the opposite sex.[39] One survivor recalled always being on the look-out for work 'details where I could get out of this particular camp' to go to another sector to look for his parents and brother. He succeeded in getting onto work details cleaning toilets, but 'I went and I never found anybody. Never found anybody in the camp . . . I never found anybody.'[40]

Renia and her sisters had a similarly fruitless search for information about their father. Marching to work presented opportunities to walk close to other parts of the camp and search out information on family members who might be living in other sectors of the camp. Renia's sister Chris remembered times when they passed 'by an area where there were men', and how 'during the day when they saw others moving along the roads, they used to come close to the fences to look whether they will spot someone who is familiar'. Other times, she recalled:

> we could see groups that were passing by as we were marching to work, and in some cases – among them there were women – we usually tried to communicate in passing to find out where the people were from, so that if they mentioned a familiar name, you called somebody's name from that town that you knew, and if they were among them, they answered and this is how we found my aunt who was from Radom. They were coming from the opposite direction and they asked, 'Where are you from?' And we said, 'Starachowice'. And, she started to call our names, and she says, 'Remember, I'm here, too, and I'm still alive.'

Despite the fact that 'people told us that there was a way of contacting men, because there were always male inmates that were coming as electricians, as plumbers, to the camp', the sisters never managed to find out 'anything about Father'. It was as though they were living in entirely separate – yet parallel – worlds. During what was close to a year in Auschwitz, Chris explained, 'from Father, we didn't hear at all'.[41]

As well as seeking to breach the internal boundaries within the camp to find out something about their father, the Laks sisters also sought to breach the external boundaries of the camp to hear news of what was happening outside the camp. The arrival of each new transport presented opportunities for exchanging information between the worlds outside and inside the camp fence. With 'so many new transports coming' in, Chris explained, 'we could inquire of where the people are from and whether they know anybody that we were looking for' as they queued up together to use the latrine block that served the 'twenty barracks' in their section. When she was a new arrival herself, Felicia Berland Hyatt remembered being bombarded at Auschwitz with questions from inmates who 'told the names of our home towns, and . . . asked, "Did you know this one?" "Did you see that one?"'[42]

But this exchange of knowledge between old and new prisoners was very much two-way. While new arrivals promised more up-to-date news of the progress of the war or the fate of relatives incarcerated elsewhere, those newly arriving prisoners themselves were dependent on existing prisoners for learning the skills needed to negotiate the camp world. Writing about her early days in Auschwitz, Felicia repeated again and again all the new information she and her friends 'learned'. They learnt where in the camp not to go, which bunk to avoid, what could be bought with a ration of bread, and of the need to try to get hold of a second bowl so that one could be used for food and the other as a toilet – what she called a 'pishka' and a 'pushka'.[43] Newcomers needed to learn quickly the rules of the game in this place, which Kitty Hart thought boiled down to trying to make yourself 'invisible'.[44] However, as one survivor discovered, knowledge was not always that easy to come by, let alone act on. While she 'learned there were "commandos" that could leave and work outside the camp', these were 'coveted by every prisoner, because it was almost impossible to get any supplemental food on the premises'. Prying these kinds of 'secrets' out of 'older prisoners . . . stingy with information' was difficult and getting access to one of these coveted work details seemed nigh on impossible in a place where 'everybody tried to hoard whatever secrets might improve his everyday existence'.[45]

One open secret that runs through many survivors' narratives is that the greatest improvement to camp life was in getting an inside, rather than an outside, job. As Magda Blau succinctly explained, 'everybody wanted an inside job naturally'.[46] Survival boiled down to spatial strategies. Explaining why she managed to survive, one woman put it down to getting a job as a seamstress, which meant she had an 'inside job with better conditions' rather than 'working outside' where 'the sun burned through you, the rain drenched you, the wind dried you out, and in the winter you froze'.[47] Getting an inside job was in part about being sheltered from the elements. Bela Blau – who was later to become Magda's husband – was relieved to swap digging a channel, which meant 'working up until here in mud', for an easy inside job as a scribe, which only meant doing a few hours' work each day. For poorly fed and poorly clothed prisoners, an inside job was seen as the difference between the chance of life and the certainty of death. But securing an inside job also often offered more. For Bela, it meant getting hold of extra rations.[48] Thomas Buergenthal, who got a job working as an errand boy for one of the *kapo* – or prisoner functionaries – in the *Sauna* where new arrivals chosen for labour undressed and washed, got not only relatively easy work but also privileged access to knowledge of what was going on that provided him with 'a certain protection'.[49]

As they retold their story of wartime survival, the Laks sisters recognized that the critical 'turning point' was the moment in the autumn of 1944 when they got hold of an inside job sorting clothes. That way they no longer had to work outside and face the elements. Like Bela Blau, the Laks sisters had been working in one of the outside details in the marshes that Birkenau was built on, standing in water for hours cutting bulrushes. As Chris Laks, who lost her 'good shoes' in the mud, recalled, 'by the middle of October, it was a pathetic thing to look at us. We were hungry. We were beaten. We didn't have any clothes.' Securing 'a job inside, office work, office quote unquote',[50] felt to Renia nothing less than a 'heaven-sent' miracle.[51] It seemed to the sisters that they had not only left the harsh world of outside work details on the cusp of winter for a job inside, but they had entered into another 'camp that was pretty much separated from the rest of the camp', working in a 'unit, which was separate and apart from anything that was going on in Auschwitz', living 'a new life – a new life that we didn't even know existed in Birkenau'.[52] As Hania Laks recalled, 'I didn't believe it's Auschwitz', because of the improved living conditions and a world without the incessant roll calls.[53]

This job not only gave the three Laks sisters shelter from the elements during the winter of 1944–5, but it also offered the chance to steal clothes and shoes from the piles they were packing.[54] Starting this job with few clothes, the sisters left it 'wearing proper clothes'.[55] Not only were they able to get hold of clothes for themselves, but Chris recalled returning to their original barracks to share clothes with friends from their home town. This occasion served, she suggested, to reveal the nature of the transformation that getting hold of an inside job meant to her and her sisters. As she explained, 'we went back to the barracks, to the original barracks to the group from Starachowice, and when we came in nobody could recognize us, nobody. Because we looked so different. We had all these clothes and everything. So, you know what we did? We undressed and we shared our clothes.'[56] These few months were seen by the sisters as critical, in Renia's words, in giving them 'a little breathing space which restored the soul and the body before we would face the other horror'.[57] For Chris, 'in a way those two and a half months gave us self-esteem, brought us back to kind of a little bit of a normal life', which 'prepared us for the death march and then for all these next six months that were not so good'.[58]

With access to clothes and shoes, the Laks sisters were able to get hold of one of the most critical commodities in the camp that had a high exchange value in the internal market and could be traded for extra food rations or other favours. Another survivor with access to clothes and shoes was Michael Vogel, who worked in the *Kanada* commando sorting clothes that came in with the transports. 'I must be very blunt,' Michael explained, 'I survived because of *Kanada* commando. Good, bad or indifferent, I survived because I was assigned to work in *Kanada* commando.' He explained his survival not primarily because he was working inside rather than outside and so was sheltered from the elements. Rather it was what working inside meant, and in Michael's case – like the Laks sisters – it meant getting hold of commodities that he could trade in a world that 'was constant *organizierung*, organising, constantly going on. Between the *Kapos* you had to pay off, the *Blockälteste* [block elder] who you had to pay off . . . for better treatment, for taking care of our friends who got typhus'. Crucially, he could trade commodities in order to get hold of something as basic as 'more food'.[59]

Although Renia saw their privileged job as miraculous and Hania considered that they were 'lucky',[60] the sisters were also aware that this job came through connections with their block secretary, Felicia Hyatt.[61] She was, Chris explained, 'an acquaintance that you run into'. Felicia – who was Polish like the Laks sisters – 'knew some people . . . had some friends who came to live in our town before the war, and they lived in the neighbourhood'. Therefore, 'there was a little bit of contact right there that we had established'. It was a case, Chris recalled, of meeting someone with friends in common. 'You know some people that she knows or that she was fond of, who were from her home town,' Chris explained, 'and that was all.'[62] The importance of these kinds of pre-war connections in the camp in getting hold of privileges such as an inside job were widely recognized. Ruth Meyorowitz – a German Jew – and her mother ended up in the privileged space of *Kanada*, 'somehow, through knowing someone'.[63] This was a common experience. You either 'had to have connections' to get privileged jobs, or rely upon bribery.[64]

But those connections had to be with someone who had some power to help or something to offer. In the case of the Laks sisters, Felicia was in a position to help because of her place within the prisoner hierarchy as a block secretary. Explaining how she had managed to rise to this position, Felicia put it down to being 'good with languages', and so she had managed to learn

Czech and speak with some of the long-standing prisoners in charge of the barracks. That privileged positions tended to be held by veteran prisoners was typical across the camp system. One survivor recalled, towards the end of the war, arriving in a camp where he discovered that 'naturally the better jobs is taken already, being an old camp'.[65] As Felicia Hyatt explained, 'the longer you were there, the better the likelihood that you would get a better position'. Having picked up some Czech, Felicia was able 'to be helpful' and 'did what I was told', so earning the trust of the Czech prisoner elite. 'When there was something important to do,' Felicia recalled, 'they would come to me and I would try to help them', including arranging 'lists of prisoners in numerical order'.[66] Her opportunity came with the expansion of Birkenau and the opening up of Lager B, which necessitated a new raft of *Blockälteste*, assistants and secretaries.[67]

The story of Felicia's rise to a position of some power within the prisoner hierarchy, and the way that her help was critical in the Laks sisters getting a coveted inside job, points to the importance of language and place-based connections within the multilingual and international space of Auschwitz. While the block book from one of the barracks in Birkenau powerfully evokes Auschwitz as a multilingual space where the broad scope of the persecutions was experienced by the Laks sisters for the very first time, it does not show the kind of strategies that prisoners adopted to build coalitions and communities amid this babel.

A shared language was critical in forming alliances within barracks that were a collision of Jews and non-Jews from across the continent. For the German Ruth Meyerowitz and the Greek Nini, English provided a common language for two middle-class Jewish girls who had been taught foreign languages before the war. For most, it was their mother tongue that formed the basis for relationships. Lilly Malnik – caught in hiding in Belgium and deported to Birkenau in 1944 – explained that she befriended a young French Jewish girl called Christiane who she remained close to through her time at Auschwitz and the subsequent evacuation to Bergen-Belsen, because 'we both spoke French'.[68] A common language could be very useful, as Felicia discovered, for developing connections with the prisoner hierarchy. William Lowenberg felt that his knowledge of German helped him to gain the favour of his *Blockälteste* who 'never hit me' and 'every so often used to give me a piece of bread'.[69] As all prisoners were well aware, the barracks were social spaces. They were occupied, rather than empty, spaces, and those occupying and overseeing these buildings mattered enormously. While from the outside all the barracks might appear entirely uniform, inside they varied enormously depending on just who the prisoners and prisoner-functionaries were.

But, as the story of Felicia and the Laks sisters shows, communities were created in the barracks that were far more parochial than these broad linguistic connections. In a parallel to the ways that pre-war geographies were re-formed on the forest floor, pre-war extended family groups and local communities were – whenever possible – recreated and maintained in the crowded, multilingual spaces of the barracks. As Felicia Hyatt put it simply, 'those of us who came from Kraków took care of each other'.[70] In the midst of the dislocation that deportation to the mixing pot of Auschwitz entailed, prisoners sought to hang on to something of the known-ness of home by creating small networks of individuals from their locality wherever possible.

For those, like the Laks sisters, who had been brought into Auschwitz with friends and family, they sought to sustain these communities through the initiation process into the camp and then through the camp system. Staying together through the induction process meant that friends or family received consecutive numbering. This, as Renia explained, was critical. She recalled how she and her sisters:

were tattooed, and I really always stress the fact that we lined up together for tattooing so that we had consecutive numbers, which really contributed to our survival as a unit, the three of us. Because, you know, not having a name, you are always referred as a number, and when they call X number of people for detail or work somewhere, you happen to be in the same unit of numbers, so that was lucky.[71]

In a place where you became a number and were officially stripped of a name, it mattered enormously who had the numbers immediately before and after you tattooed onto their arms.

Because Renia had been brought into Auschwitz as one member of what she described as a 'unit' of women from Starachowice, she managed to stay together not only with her sisters, but also a handful of other young women from her home town. Her triple-decker bunk bed was a 'nine people's perch' where they 'talked all the time' to their 'heart's content' in a language they could all understand, of people and places that they shared in common. Renia carved out her 'own little world' of 'privacy' peopled by her sisters and other women from Starachowice whom she knew she 'could always depend on'.[72] In the alien and alienating landscape of Auschwitz, prisoners like Renia, her sisters and friends sought to hang on to some semblance of the familiarity of home through building and maintaining monolingual, profoundly local sub-groups within a block of bunks miles from their former homes.

However, not everyone arrived together with family members or on a transport from their home town. Much depended on when, and from where, you were deported. When prisoners arrived alone within a transport of strangers, ad hoc communities had to be created from scratch within the camp as best they could. Unlike the Laks sisters, who arrived in the camp system together, William Lowenberg was sent from Westerbork on his own, as a boy in his mid-teens in 1943. While he spent the train journey with a girlfriend he had got to know in the camp, they were separated on arrival in the gendered space of Auschwitz. Here, he found Hans Gelpter – 'a family friend' – who became his partner, assisted him in negotiating the camp system and helped him 'to survive'. As he explained, this man he chanced upon, 'knew me . . . and he knew my family, and I knew his family, only by name, but he knew more about my parents . . . he knew my uncles'. With this shared history, Hans became William's 'so-called big brother', who told him 'what to do and what not to do'. The two managed to stick together through a series of relocations across the slave-labour system, first to Dachau and then to Warsaw where they worked on demolishing the remains of the Warsaw ghetto.[73]

While William and Hans' relationship survived two transfers within the camp system, others were not so fortunate. One man still recalled with utter disbelief what he saw as his stupidity in losing his friends because he left them while he went to seek out another ration, meaning that he ended up during the evacuation from the camp 'with people I don't know'. In a lengthy exchange he explained to his interviewer half a century after the event how he, alone among his friendship group, went back to get hold of a second ration, and then realized:

> I made perhaps a terrible mistake, because all my friends had gone. So now I was with people I don't know and the most important thing is that you are always with some people. I . . . knew people, I was talking with people and I was separated from them. I said, 'you stupid fellow, you got yourself another ration but you lost all your friends.'[74]

As he was well aware, social networks were vitally important, but each transfer within the camp system threatened to break those networks and communities of home apart.

In the end, it was the evacuations from Auschwitz in January 1945 that ultimately broke apart the 'little world' of women from Starachowice that the Laks sisters belonged to. Although this group had survived the half-year that they spent in Auschwitz, it crumbled in the more chaotic space of Ravensbrück, which was a camp 'overrun with people' being evacuated from camps across Poland and Germany. Here Renia and her sisters ended up in an overcrowded tented camp, 'completely disconnected from the original group . . . because we were not evacuated with the Starachowice people, we came there with another group, and then we got mixed in with all kinds of nationalities and people'.[75]

Entering into a new camp was a time when it was easy to end up separated from family members or a fellow *landsman*. Leaving the rail cars, going through selections, being inducted into the camp, and ending up in barracks, were all chaotic processes, in which it was easy to lose hold of friends and family. After having their hair shaved and being kitted out with ill-fitting uniforms, people looked different. As one survivor recalled, entering into the barrack in Birkenau for the first time, 'we couldn't even recognize each other. No hair. The hair was shaven off. Dressed in striped uniforms – too small, too big, too large, too short. We all looked like clowns.'[76] His experience was one repeated across barracks in the men's and women's camps.[77] In this context it often took time to piece together extended family or locality-based groups. In the midst of the chaos of a transit barracks full of shaved women where 'nobody recognized anybody', Bella Pasternak, who had been deported from Transylvania in the early summer of 1944, quickly set about trying to find familiar faces. 'Because the trains come in constantly and there were people not from our ghetto alone and everything got mixed up,' Bella explained, 'so when I was talking I say, "Gee, somebody there said she is from the same place".' After four days she discovered that two of her sisters and two cousins were in the same barracks. 'And then we stuck together,' Bella recalled, 'the five of us. Whenever we went, they counted us. We were together.'[78] This group of five extended family members expanded further as it doubled in size with the addition of five more, including 'a daughter of my mother's cousin who was by herself' and 'a girl from our town' who had been separated from her two brothers in this gendered space. Ultimately, Bella's group of 'ten together' managed to 'stick together' through to liberation.[79]

Both Bella's 'ten together' and Reina's 'nine people's perch' were groups intimately shaped by the geography and geometry of the camp and its system.

This was something to which Bella herself alluded. 'Everybody had their own group,' she explained, 'you see, like when they were counting . . . we were ten. So they counted ten. So we tried to be together.'[80] Counting off prisoners in rows of five meant that, for Bella, units of five were units of potential togetherness that had a chance to persist through the camp system. As another survivor remembered the moment when her group was being moved out of Auschwitz to another camp, 'I hurry to our barracks, where people are already standing in rows of five. My four friends, Sarah, Judith, Hela, and Ruth, are waiting for me. They don't want anybody else in their row.'[81] Alongside units of five, the triple-decker bunk beds with three prisoners to a bed in Birkenau created a space to be occupied by Renia's group of nine. The very spaces of Birkenau – whether within the barracks, on the *appelplatz* (the roll-call square), or in the columns of prisoners being marched to work five-abreast – could be and were drawn upon to create small, familiar worlds.

These lived experiences of Auschwitz, where prisoners reworked the architecture and processes of the camp system, contrast with overly monolithic understandings of concentration camp space as absolute. For sociologist Wolfgang Sofsky the concentration camp was:

> a system of rigorous surveillance, a receptacle for violence. The inter-relation of human beings and space had been abrogated, discontinued. The possibility for prisoners to appropriate space for themselves has shrunk to virtually nil. Absolute power destroys space as a domain for acting and living. It packs people together, ordering them to and fro, hounding them back and forth. The individual is no longer the centrepoint of his or her world, but only an object in space.[82]

However, as the words of survivors reveal, there were attempts to reorder this space along more familiar lines, marking out the internal worlds of the barracks into (single-sex) extended family and home-town units. Even in this most 'totalitarian' of spaces, individual acts of place-making created a more variegated landscape than the seemingly uniform block system – and the alphabetized block book – would suggest.

In some ways perhaps our view of Auschwitz depends on where we position ourselves to look at this place. Observing from the guard tower over the main gateway into Birkenau offers up this site along the lines given by Sofsky – a panoptical gaze extending over a landscape of surveillance. Heading higher still and adopting the bird's-eye view of the aerial photographs taken by Allied planes in 1944 suggests a highly efficient modernist space constructed on the block system. What it fails to show is that Auschwitz was a place, as one survivor recalled, where 'when I arrived in 1943, there was still construction going on. It wasn't finished, not everything was finished.'[83] In this place that was a chaotic perpetual building site lay opportunity as well as threat. It is perhaps not surprising that the majority of prisoner escapes took place during the peaks of construction.[84] But looking from the guard tower or the bird's-eye view offered by a reconnaissance flyover fails to deal with these kinds of stories that can be found on the ground. At the level of the lived experience of survivors, this place – like all Holocaust landscapes – emerges as a variegated social space. But I want to shift our gaze and focus in closer still, literally to ground level, to explore the very soil of Birkenau, which offers up a different place than more monolithic tellings of totalitarian landscapes suggest.

On the ground, Birkenau was a very, very muddy place. This was something that struck two male prisoners who arrived from the original camp at Auschwitz I where 'everything is brick. Even the road, the streets are made of brick.' In contrast, Birkenau appeared to them to be 'nothing but mud'.[85] It is hard to find a survivor who fails to mention the cloying clay mud that it seemed everyone was always 'sinking in'.[86] It was Birkenau as a muddy field that Kitty Hart sought to stress to her son David, who accompanied her there in 1978 for a television documentary. Walking around the site, she told him, 'Now I know you are seeing grass, but I don't see grass. I see mud, just a sea of mud.'[87] This was a place where it seemed that, as one put it, 'we were always in mud up [to] our ankles'.[88] And this was the kind of mud that threatened to condemn you to a rapid, shoeless death.[89]

In order to navigate this mud, shoes assumed a heightened importance and became something of an obsession. Hana Bruml – who arrived in Birkenau from Theresienstadt in the autumn of 1944 – described her 'wooden shoes' as 'killers, absolute killers' in 'the mud of Auschwitz'. Trying to explain to her interviewer, who did not seem to understand quite how important having the right shoes was, Hana went on to tell of the deathly challenges of having 'no socks in the cold, the wooden shoes were rubbing your feet. Also, they were sticking in the mud. You couldn't pull them out. And when you had a sore on your feet, it would never heal. The shoes were killers.'[90] One woman recalled having to slip out of her line during selections, after 'the heel of one of my shoes fell off in the Birkenau mud, which made me look as if I was limping'.[91] Given the importance of having the right shoes to navigate the mud of Birkenau, it is no wonder that these were the first things to disappear off a corpse when a prisoner died in the barracks.[92] Although the German Jewish girl Carola Steinhardt managed to hang on to her own shoes when she arrived at Auschwitz from Berlin, after a few days she found that the soles were coming off. She tried to tie them together with a rag but struggled with inadequate footwear. Her luck changed once she managed to leave construction work for an inside job, first cutting the hair of the new arrivals and then cleaning their clothes. Here she managed to get hold of a jacket and a decent pair of shoes that 'lasted' through the winter.[93]

For another, help came from a friend who worked in *Kanada*. She 'risked her life to bring me pieces of clothing to cover my feet because I kept losing my wooden shoes and had to walk around barefoot because my feet were very small and the shoes were very big. Once your feet touched the limey soil in Auschwitz you could get trapped, like in quicksand, and she saved me from that.'[94] For the teenager Ruth Krautwirth Meyerowitz, the privileged role of working in *Kanada* afforded her an advantage in this fight against the mud. While sorting clothes, she found a belt and leather shoes – shoes that were 'very, very uncomfortable' because they were 'much too small for me' but were still 'preferable to the clogs' that kept getting 'stuck in the mud'. The significance of finding a belt emerged in an oral history interview, in which she explained that the dresses prisoners were given:

> were very long. The mud in Auschwitz was . . . clay and it stuck to the dresses, to the hem of the dresses, and when it dried it was very heavy and very difficult to remove. And it dragged us down. Of course, we didn't have much strength to drag ourselves around let alone a muddy dress, so most prisoners found some pieces of string, tied it together and pulled up their dresses and we were allowed to do this. I found a belt.

Ruth assumed that the belt – made of blue felt with 'yellow and red flowers sewn on it' – was 'Greek handiwork'. This lent it even greater significance. It was not only a way to pull up her dress and keep it out of the mud, but also a memory of the 'Greek girls' who she was 'so fond of'. Indeed, such was the significance of this material object to Ruth that she kept it after the war and donated 'this raggedy, dirty old faded belt' to the United States Holocaust Memorial Museum.[95]

Ruth's 'raggedy, dirty old faded belt' makes us 'pay attention to dirt,' as environmental historian Ellen Stroud urged historians to do in order to uncover 'new questions and new answers about the past'.[96] Adopting this perspective is not to downplay the murderous landscape of Auschwitz, but rather to extend it. Taking the mud of Birkenau seriously suggests that this was a place where individuals had to engage in a life and death struggle with the elements themselves – with a sticky mud that seemingly threatened to suck prisoners down into the earth. In Birkenau, not only the guards but the omniscient mud was yet another enemy to be outwitted, and due to this mud shoes and belts assume central roles in stories of survival.

We also need to move far beyond the mud of Birkenau, and even beyond the view from the guard tower or Allied plane. In the museum in the former camp of Auschwitz I there is a map that seeks to do this. It is a map of Europe centred on Auschwitz showing rail lines from north, south, east and west that converge at this most international of camps whose prisoners came from all corners of occupied Europe. However, the map only shows the journeys into Auschwitz, from transit camps and collection points across Europe. What it does not show are the journeys out of Auschwitz, not only of Jewish goods but also emaciated Jewish individuals still deemed fit for labour who were then transferred to camps both near and far. Of the close to 430,000 Hungarian Jews who arrived at Auschwitz-Birkenau in May–July 1944, an estimated 10–30 per cent on each of the individual transports were selected for labour and sent on to over 300 camps in the SS system. The largest number were transported westwards at this point in the war to the camps of Bergen-Belsen, Buchenwald, Dachau, Gross-Rosen, Mauthausen, Neuengamme, Ravensbrück and Sachsenhausen.[97]

There are paradoxes about Auschwitz. On the one hand it was a place of tightly drawn and guarded boundaries – both external and internal – that the inmates experienced as a site of terrible confinement and separation. On the other hand it was also a – highly selective – site of transit. People and goods were constantly on the move in and out via the rail (and later road) network, where national boundaries became erased within a transnational network of exchange in an imperial system. These paradoxes reflect the role that Auschwitz played as not simply a place of murder and incarceration, but also a node in the concentration camp system.

What those multiple experiences meant for one family can be felt in the example of the Bergmans, who arrived on one of the Hungarian transports in the summer of 1944 when Auschwitz was its busiest. For this Orthodox Jewish family from a small town in the Carpathian mountains that was either part of Czechoslovakia or Hungary (depending on the date and the balance of power in central Europe), Auschwitz was a site of separation. Stumbling out of the railway carriage onto the ramp after a journey of a couple of days, David Bergman found himself separated from his grandparents, mother, and younger brother and sister, remembering that he 'didn't even have a chance to say goodbye to them, this all happened so fast'.[98] His father told the guards that his twelve-year-old son was fourteen. This meant that David joined his father in the line of adult men selected for labour, rather than being sent to the gas chambers with his younger siblings.

David Bergman and his father managed to stick together in Birkenau, a place where they were only briefly incarcerated. After only 'five or six days', he and his father were back on a train heading for Plaszów concentration camp just south of Kraków. It was here at Plaszów, rather than on the ramp at Birkenau, that David was finally separated from his father. After six weeks working here as a bricklayer, David was moved on to another camp, further west. Taken by train to Gross-Rosen, he spent about six weeks in the main camp, followed by six months in a sub-camp where he worked most days 'in the city building air-raid shelters'. From here, David was evacuated westwards to Dachau at the end of the war, finally ending up in Austria where he was liberated.

The Bergmans were like so many other Hungarian Jewish families arriving at Auschwitz-Birkenau in the frenetic months of early summer 1944 that left little by way of a trace of their presence. After being divided into 'useful' and 'useless' members on the basis of age and gender, those deemed 'useless' – David's grandparents, mother and younger siblings – were quickly disposed of in the section of the camp that comprised gas chambers, crematoria and large burning pits. Those deemed 'useful' – David and his father – were quickly moved into the wider slave-labour system. The Bergman family's suitcases and bags, carefully packed when they had first been told that they had to leave their small town a few weeks earlier, ended up in Birkenau's *Kanada* complex where they were emptied and sorted. After less than a week, nothing of the

Bergman family remained at Auschwitz. David's grandparents, mother and younger siblings had been gassed and cremated and their ashes dumped in the ponds in Birkenau. David and his father were gone, transported by slow train to Plaszów and another camp in the SS system. The family's goods had been sorted and were headed west to the Reich.[99] All their goods and the two remaining male bodies of this Jewish family were destined for the German war economy.

Auschwitz was never solely a death camp like Chelmno, Belzec, Sobibór and Treblinka, where the traffic was only one-way. In large part this was about time more than space. The year 1944 – when David Bergman and his family were brought to Auschwitz – saw the massive growth of the camp system to provide labour for the war industries gearing up for one final – ultimately futile – push at military victory. In a marked switch in policy, Germany, which had been more or less made free of Jews in 1943, became a temporary home for Jewish labourers in 1944, which is the year when the number of foreign labourers in Germany reached its peak.[100] This 'change' was witnessed by Felicia Hyatt, who remembered how 'late in the spring of 1944 . . . civilians began arriving in Auschwitz to select workers for factories', and Auschwitz 'became an abundant supplier of slave labour for factories'.[101] At this point in the war Auschwitz operated as what Donald Bloxham terms 'the hub of an obscene labour exchange' that connected it with hundreds of camps and sub-camps serving the German military-industrial complex.[102]

Quite apart from the family separation and losses, David and his father were the victims of 'labour exchange' at Auschwitz in 1944. None of the family were registered or tattooed in the camp. In the case of David's grandparents, mothers and younger siblings this was because they were destined for a rapid death. In David and his father's case it was because they were merely transit prisoners en route to other camps. Another deportee from wartime Hungary, George Havas – who was also quickly removed from Birkenau, in his case to Mauthausen – felt as though Auschwitz was operating like a revolving door, such was the speed of victim turnaround. George explained, 'as my father's group got moved out, others moved in, then somebody else got again moved out, so it was rotation and mixing and all that and then on Friday they emptied our entire building or barracks and they marched us to the same railroad platform or station where we were unloaded except now we were on the other side of it'.[103]

Being put back on trains so soon after getting off them was a common experience for those Hungarian Jews like George Havas or David Bergman who were selected for labour in the German war economy. The sites of incarceration of that war economy stretched across Europe. The sheer size and scale of the continent-wide camp system was something that none of those arriving at a place like Auschwitz could imagine. With the benefit of hindsight, it is possible to map out the growth of this vast network that saw a proliferation of sub-camps during 1944.[104] Yet its extent was of course unknown to those initially entering into it through one of its nodes. Recollecting her mother's and later her sister's deportation from Germany, Gerda Schild assumed that she would see both of them again. When Gerda herself was deported she thought that there were a very limited number of places where these trains were being sent, and so she would most likely find one or both of her family members who had already been deported east. Arriving at Theresienstadt (rather than Riga or Auschwitz where her mother and sister were sent), Gerda remembered thinking that 'I would find my mother. I would find people again.' 'We didn't know there was such a widespread transport system, *Lagersystem*,' Gerda explained. 'We thought, well, you know, everybody will see each other again.'[105] However, that *Lagersystem*, which separated out families – in particular along gendered lines – stretched across occupied Europe and was rapidly extended in the last year of the war. Critical to the functioning of this dispersed network of camps were the rail lines that connected the nodes within the network. Trains brought David Bergman and George Havas to Auschwitz in the early summer of 1944, and trains also quickly took them both away again.

Train

Like others arriving at Auschwitz, the Laks sisters were taken there by train. The European rail network connected this place in southern Poland with towns across the continent through miles of track that traversed national borders. This technology that had dramatically shrunk both time and space in the second half of the nineteenth century enabled the emergence of the strange multilingual world that the three sisters found themselves thrust into in 1944. Victims could be taken by train from stations and sidings across a connected continent to the killers in a handful of central locations. In 1942, Jews from Warsaw were taken from the *Umschlagplatz* to be killed at Treblinka a few minutes after their arrival at the fake railway station adjacent to the death camp. In 1943, Jews from Greece were taken on an eight- or nine-day journey northwards to Auschwitz.[1] In 1944 more than 430,000 Jews collected together in around 150 ghettos dispersed across Hungary were deported – the vast majority to Auschwitz – in only 147 trains.[2] An estimated three million Jews were deported to the death camps in around 2,000 trains during three years between late 1941 and late 1944.[3] It seemed to the late Raul Hilberg that railroads were 'a live organism which acted in concert with Germany's military, industry, or SS to make German history'.[4] For one survivor, the memories of what wartime train travel entailed and meant were so painful that 'it took me years before I wanted to take a train any place'.[5]

While trains were critical in bringing Jews from across Europe to the camps and then taking those selected for labour from one camp to another, these journeys were not quintessential experiences of rail travel as a beacon of modernity.[6] Far from it. Prisoner transports were given a low priority among crowded military and civilian timetables, and so the journey to Auschwitz was painfully slow.[7] Asked how long she remembers the journey taking, Hania Laks remained uncertain as to how many days and nights she and her sisters were in the cattle car. 'I would say that at least we travelled two nights because I remember a day and then a night, and I remember another day and another night. So, it's possible that we came on the third day', was her best guess. The length of the journey was something that the sisters still discussed among themselves years after the end of the war. 'I was talking to Renia about it,' Hania explained, and 'she thinks we went there faster, but those trains didn't go fast. The train didn't go on a regular route. The trains were going on side roads and they were very slow, very slow, and they stopped from time to time for crossing, for different things.'[8] Prisoners did not speed through the European landscape. These were staccato journeys interrupted by frequent stops and starts.

Hania and her sisters' uncertainty about how long the journey to Auschwitz took is widely shared by survivors as days and nights merged into each other within the sealed confines of the wagon.[9] It was part of a much wider disorientation that took place during and through these journeys that transported individuals and families away from home, or from a place close to home, to an as yet unknown destination the details of which were a rich source of speculation in the wagons. 'We were not told where we were being taken to, nor did we know what direction we were going in,' Fritzie Weiss Fritzshall explained of her journey from Czechoslovakia to Auschwitz. To try to counter this unknown-ness, she recalled that 'they would lift a child up that could read' to the small opening at the top of the wagon 'as the train would pass a station, so that the child could read . . . what stations we passed. And that would give us a clue where we were going.'[10]

This was easier with the first set of stations close to home, but became harder as national borders were crossed and strange names appeared on station signs. Deported from Munkács in north-east Hungary, George Havas remembered how at first the names of familiar villages and towns were spied through the crack in the railcar door. Further on into the journey these were replaced with 'the names of Slovak villages' that 'we did not know'. The mental mapping of their route that had been easier at the beginning of the journey started to break down as the prisoners were taken further and further away from home. What these unfamiliar names did make clear was that George Havas had left Hungary. This prompted heated discussion among the mobile community he was part of about 'why would they take the Hungarian Jews to Slovakia?' A little further into the journey Slovakian place names gave way to Polish names, and finally the station at Kraków. Now the questioning turned to:

> why Kraków? We did not know anything, we had no idea what was going on or where or why and the train stands there and then it's being shuttled from one track to another track, to another track, to another track and shuttled back and what was front is now moving back. In the morning we end up someplace and the train stops and there's no more movement.[11]

Journeying from home to an unknown 'someplace' several days and nights away, it seemed to those locked inside the wagons that they could literally be anywhere. As Madeline Deutsch, who was also deported to Auschwitz from a town on the Hungarian-Czech border, explained, 'after about three days and three nights of travelling . . . we had no idea where we were'.[12] Disoriented in both time and space, it was impossible to be sure just how far from home they had been brought, let alone to map their place of arrival with any degree of precision. But transportation by rail across the European continent did more than simply disorientate people in time and space. Madeline Deutsch was quick to spell out to her interviewer what travel to Auschwitz meant, in case there be any mistaken assumptions of what a train journey entailed. 'These were not regular railroad cars in which normally people travel,' she explained, but rather 'box cars, you know, in which normally animals are being transported.'[13]

As Madeline went on to detail at some length, the experience of deportation in cattle cars went far beyond simply the dehumanizing treatment of humans as cattle. 'Normally when animals are being transported in such manner,' she explained, 'they just put them in sparsely so they're comfortable for whatever journey they are taking.' In contrast, it seemed to Madeline that they were being treated worse than living animals, as 'we were packed in like herrings or sardines in a can. There was no room to move. We were practically on top of one another . . . we were so tightly packed that if a person wanted to reach over to somebody else, that person had to climb over several other people in between.' She continued, 'Let's say a father and mother were sitting here with their children, but a child wants to reach another child a little further down, a friend perhaps, that child had to climb over adults to reach that person because there was just no place to move.'[14] George Havas struggled to find the right words to capture what the lack of space in the closed cars felt like for those being transported – 'the people crowded together, squeezed together, you couldn't lie down, you could only sit on your haunches'.[15] It seemed that humans had been reduced not simply to animals, but to commodities or 'cargo' that was being shipped en masse.[16]

This was neither simply, nor primarily, an experience of being taken from a known to an unknown place, resulting in the spatial disorientation that poses the question 'Where am I?' More fundamentally, this was an experience of terrible overcrowding and a reduction to a subhuman existence that provoked a more profound attack on self, prompting the question 'Who am I?' The cattle car was moving in slow motion through the European railscape, but rather than these journeys being about an opening up of the world, they were experienced as a closing down into the gloomy space of a locked freight car. It seemed that the universe was 'shrinking' in terrible and terrifying ways that breached everyday norms and challenged a sense of self.[17] It was an experience radically at odds with visions of international train travel as the high point of European modernity. Rather than stories solely or even primarily of movement, these are stories about the difficulties – indeed the impossibilities – of undertaking the most basic of human functions.

The sense of existential challenge posed by these journeys emerges powerfully in the reduction of the interior world of the gloomy cattle car to a story of two buckets in survivors' narratives: 'one was a bucket of water, and the other was an empty bucket for personal elimination for the whole car full of people'.[18] Whereas one bucket was quickly emptied, the other was soon overflowing, meaning that the slow days in the cattle car were remembered as days of thirst and shit. One bucket of drinking water for a wagon packed full of eighty or more people was completely inadequate for a journey that lasted several days, even on the rare occasions when the train stopped for the bucket to be refilled. 'We were travelling in this train for about 3 days and 3 nights with just a drop of water that we were all each able to get,' Madeline Deutsch recalled, 'because there were probably about a hundred people so one bucket of water, all you could get was just a few drops . . . no food and just a little drop of water which went the very first day.' The situation was made worse by the fact that 'during the day it was very, very hot because we were so crowded in and just the little bitty windows that we got some fresh air in'.[19] These days packed into overcrowded, closed cars were remembered as being dominated by an overwhelming sensation of thirst. After describing in some detail how they tried to work out where they were going when they left Hungary and journeyed through Slovakia and into Poland, George Havas summarized the experience in a handful of words: 'the ride and the thirst, without water, the crowding'.[20]

While the bucket full of water features in many survivors' stories, it is the other bucket – the empty one – that looms larger and in more troubling ways in survivors' retellings of the shrunken universe of the cattle car. Still empty, this bucket represented a shocking and shameful overturning of social norms of privacy.[21] Fighting to find the right words, George Havas told his interviewer of 'people more or less urinating in front of each other, defecating in front of each other, the smell, horrible feeling, it just, kids crying and little ones'.[22] Asked 'What was the trip like?' by her interviewer, another survivor started with the overcrowded conditions – 'well, you hardly could sit down in the wagons'. She moved on to the hunger – 'I don't even remember having any food. We must have some food with us but, uh, I don't really recall recall it.' She then described the noise of her fellow travellers – 'and, uh, some people were sick, really out of their mind, old people, senile people and they were crying and yelling all night long' – before honing in on the humiliation of using the empty bucket. As she explained, 'If somebody had to go to the bathroom, then there was a little, uh, little pail there, and everybody, men and women together, everybody, uh, seeing that you're going to the bathroom . . . it was just so humiliating, humiliation and, and, uh, horrible.'[23] A few attempts were made to organize the interior of some of the cattle cars to make the most of the space or offer limited cover to those using the bucket.[24] One survivor remembered trying to cover her grandmother with a coat because she 'was embarrassed to go in the bucket',[25] while another recalled how they used their bodies to shield someone on the bucket.[26]

The shame of sitting on the bucket in public emerged as a recurring motif in Alex Braun's memories of his wartime experiences. Deported from Transylvania in May 1944 along with other members of his Orthodox Jewish family, Alex saw continuity between the shame of exposure in the cattle car and his experiences during the previous days when his family had been taken from the ghetto to a brickyard where Jews from the region were gathered prior to deportation. Here, as Alex explained, the only latrines were 'outside in the open' and he struggled to convey the deep shame he and others felt using them:

I as well . . . you know, when . . . when you privacy when you . . . when you have to . . . uh, when . . . when nature calls you. And . . . uh, I would have never ever even dreamed to do anything in presence of . . . of somebody who's not only is a stranger, not even friends. In fact, even our parents, let's say, we would be not exposing ourselves openly. That's somehow strange, but that's the way it was.

Such was his sense of shame that Alex remembered that during that week. 'it's very, very unbelievably; but it's true. I couldn't possibly . . . uh, do what . . . what nature calls. And that . . . that caused a terrible problem, because we were in the open.' Instead he watched as others were humiliated by their guards, who 'would be laughing and . . . and enjoying that terrible shame that we had, to do our duties in the open and during the day. At least, if it was night or darkness . . . you know? But it . . . it just terrible.'

This sense of terrible shame continued in the darkness of the cattle car, joined now with the stench of human waste in the enclosed space. As Alex explained:

> there were also no facilities where one can go to the bathroom, if that's the way you want to call it, you know . . . And we . . . we boarded the train. And I can tell you, the worst thing yet to come, in that specific cattle car was no sanitation facilities. Was no air, no water . . . When we arrived a few days later . . . Now in the cattle cars, there were a lot of older people and children. They couldn't stand the heat. They couldn't stand the . . . the terrible scent, or . . . Or what do you call it? That's the terrible smell. And we have to do our duties right in there. So, many of them died right in the car as we went. We . . . we didn't know then, but we were going destination Auschwitz.[27]

With one bucket emptying and the other filling, a handful of survivors talk of their desperate breach of a taboo as they drank their own, or other's, urine.[28] Retelling this is difficult. As Rose Warner, deported from Majdanek to Auschwitz in the autumn of 1942, explained:

> we were in the train about four days without water. We begged them for water. They didn't want to give us. Many of us died. They were jumping

over the dead people to the window to scream out for water, please water. Nothing was more important than water. They didn't give us any. So, we used to make number one and we used to drink it. What could you do? Maybe people don't, I don't know how many you interview don't tell these things, but this is the truth. So, we had some water, it was salty, but water.

Rose is unusual in her frank discussion of the importance of urine to her survival, first as a source of water in the train and then as a means of washing in the camp. As she later explained of life in the camp, 'we used to make pee – excuse me I had to say it and wash our body. The salt, they didn't like the salt, the bugs, and we put it on the body. I did it every night. I put it on the body.'[29] The subject of urine and latrines run as a thread through her interview, albeit in a different way than in Alex Braun's narrative. For Alex, the difficulties of defecating in public provided a continuity between ghetto and train connecting both sites as places of shame, which he fought by refusing to humiliate himself in front of others. For Rose, the continuity ran from train to camp, and was simultaneously evidence of her desperation as well as her successful adaptation to the terrible conditions that she faced in a world where urine had to replace water for drinking and washing.

In the first set of recorded interviews undertaken in the post-war displaced persons' camps in the autumn of 1946, David Boder was surprised, indeed shocked, at the stories of drinking urine that a number of survivors told him. 'Was that really so?' he asked after one survivor explained 'that people drank their own urine'.[30] 'Is it really true?' David Boder questioned another who had explained that 'mothers were giving the children urine to drink'.[31] In a lengthy exchange with Benjamin Piskorz, David Boder was incredulous at just what Benjamin's story of drinking urine in the train meant, something that Benjamin himself was reluctant to recount in detail. 'So there was there an acquaintance, a comrade of mine whom I begged, from the terrible thirst, that he should for me even . . . nu . . . I don't know how to say it, because urine,' Benjamin struggled to tell his interviewer. Pushed to explain, Benjamin told how 'he made urine into my mouth'. 'How? Directly?' David Boder probed. 'In the wagon, directly,' Benjamin evasively replied, but his interviewer pushed him further, asking 'What does it mean, he made directly into . . .' 'He made into my . . . directly,' Benjamin offered, repeating his questioner's words, adding the word 'my' but going no further. Still pushing him for more details, Boder asked whether 'He urinated?' 'Urinated,' Benjamin confirmed. 'From his . . .' asked David Boder, with Benjamin cutting him off and replying 'From his . . . yes.' Stepping in to save him, his interviewer euphemistically offered, 'From his body?' 'Yes,' Benjamin responded, with neither man willing to say the word 'penis'. 'Into your mouth?' Boder asked incredulously. 'Straight into the mouth, because of the terrible thirst,' Benjamin responded, not only seeking to explain (and justify) the seemingly unimaginable but also shifting the focus from himself to a shared (and normalized) experience, which he explained 'wasn't the first case, because all the people drank this way'.[32]

Over the course of the journey, memories of shame – of nakedness and defecating in public – were replaced by memories of the stench of this particularly problematic bucket. Whereas the bucket of water was finished by the end of the first day, the makeshift toilet quickly began 'overflowing',[33] and as one survivor recalled, 'we moved in human waste'.[34] Asked what they did once the makeshift toilet bucket was full, another responded, 'I really do not recall and cannot really imagine now . . . what happened with this one bucket', focusing instead on the overwhelming smell of human waste that built up in this enclosed space:

There was stench. I must say I personally wouldn't recall that I used it. I don't recall. I don't recall, and there was stench. There was dirt. There was . . . you know, the, the excrements were all over. Also, when you're in a lot of stench, you become insensitive to it. You don't . . . I don't think you, you, you don't feel it anymore. Uh it was hot. It was depressing. Also physiologically de . . .

depressing. Uh you were not very active, not very alert, but I must say . . . that's a very good question . . . I do not really know what people did after the bucket . . . and I myself . . . after all, as I say, I think it was between three or five days . . . I myself don't recall, and after all, after three or five days you have some need to go somewhere. I don't recall.[35]

It was a progressively worsening situation. With one bucket empty and the other full, 'the stench became unbearable'.[36] What Terence des Pres termed the 'excremental assault' of the camp was first experienced – and most intensively experienced – in the trains taking prisoners to the camp, trains that were themselves sites of what Simone Gigliotti calls 'olfactory trauma'.[37]

In the gloom of the wagons, with little to look at aside from fellow passengers crowded together, people's senses other than sight were heightened.[38] What they smelt, what they heard, what they touched, and how they felt overwhelmed the visual register of what they saw. These freight wagons were not primarily visual landscapes, but olfactory, auditory, haptic landscapes that smelt, sounded and felt terrible. After telling her interviewer about having to go to the toilet where they were, on the floor of the wagon, because there was no bucket in their car, Hania Laks responded to her interviewer's empathetic response – 'this must have felt horrible' – by shifting the focus to the smell, recalling that 'the stench was unbelievable'. With this sensory shift, the interviewer then asked her about the soundscape of the cattle car and specifically whether people were 'crying and screaming?' Hania confirmed this impression of noise, but extended the terrible range of noises from 'crying and screaming' to the sounds of utter despair and a wish to die coming from those who decided it was better to jump from the slow-moving train than to end up where they were being taken. As she explained, 'we heard shots and we heard moans and we heard screams. We heard it all, all the time, and I mean, you know, it was – that was a very traumatic time.'[39]

A similar shift from sight to the other senses can be seen in Fritzie Weiss Fritzshall's account of her transportation by train. Earlier in the interview she dismissed her interviewer's questioning about this space by saying simply 'I don't need to describe to you. It was a cattle car, you know. No windows and no seats. No toilet.' Describing what she saw in the sparest of ways, she then spent minutes honing in on what this space smelt, sounded and felt like:

> How do I tell you about a train ride like that? About the dignity that is taken away from you when you need to use a bucket as a toilet in the middle of a compartment on a train, in front of everyone? About sharing water with every single person? About the mothers holding on to hungry children. The crying. The stink. The fear. It's strange, fear gives out a certain smell and that mixed with an open bucket – it's a smell I don't believe one can ever forget. It's, it's not to be described.
>
> Q. How long were you in that train?
>
> A. I believe, two and a half days. I believe we were there two and a half days in all, with the stopping and going. I can't tell you exactly. I believe if I live to be 100, that smell will stay with me. And I will always hear the crying of the babies; and in particular, the young mother trying to feed an infant, breastfeed an infant and not having any milk to feed this infant. These revisionists that don't believe, I would like to take them all and put them into a compartment like that and show them what it feels like.[40]

As people were unable to see the landscape through which they were slowly making their way, they experienced the freight wagons not primarily as confined visual landscapes but as experiential landscapes or felt places. There was, after all, not a lot to see aside from bodies and buckets. And those bodies and buckets smelt, felt and sounded terrible.

On their arrival at Auschwitz, people quickly became aware of the unusual smells and sounds, especially those who arrived at night in the absence of visual markers: the smell of burning, the sound of dogs barking, of guards shouting orders. 'So after about three days and three nights of travelling, we stopped,' Madeline Deutsch recalled:

> The train had stopped. It was night time. Couldn't see anything except flames in the distance. The odour that was coming in through those little windows into those box cars were horrible. We didn't know what that was. It was burning . . . like burning flesh, but who would . . . whose mind would enter something like this. It was a horrible odour, and just flames in the distance and howling of the dogs. We didn't know where we were.[41]

For Michael Kraus, the 'stench' of the train wagon was replaced by 'a strange smell . . . in the air' once they reached Auschwitz.[42]

But looking out of the wagons through the cracks or once the door had been opened, Auschwitz was also a terrifying visual landscape of barbed wire that indicated continuing confinement. In a post-war 'diary' that sought to capture his wartime experiences during the German occupation of Czechoslovakia and his imprisonment in a series of camps, Michael Kraus wrote of the moment when:

> finally, on Dec 17, 1943, at 11:30 at night, the train reduced its speed and slowly came to a stop. Through the slats near the door powerful rays of lights entered the dark car. I looked out. I was frightened by the sight that presented itself to me through the narrow slats, but I saw enough that I paled and felt goose bumps on my back. I saw so little and yet it was so much! Barbed wire, prisoners in striped suits surrounded by SS men; it could only be a concentration camp![43]

George Havas, looking 'through the cracks in the train' when he arrived at Auschwitz in the daytime rather than at night, recalled how 'we see barbed wire compound there, and we see these things. And within me, wondering what is this. I had no idea. I never was in a camp before. And then, all of a sudden, the train came to a stop. And they opened the doors. And that was . . . when I saw hell . . .'[44]

Whereas George first glimpsed 'hell' on arrival at Auschwitz, for others it seemed that they had already spent the last few days there. Ernest Koenig, originally from Austria but deported from France, struggling to describe the 'indescribable' interior of the cattle car, settled upon drawing an analogy with Dante's *Inferno*. The cattle car wasn't just a place of thirst and excrement. It became a place of death when one of the men transported with him attempted suicide.[45]

Ernest was not alone in seeing the train wagon as a site of death itself, and not simply a vehicle heading towards death. There are frequent references in interviews with, and memoirs written by, survivors to the deaths of fellow passengers. Nina Kaleska, recalling the train journey from Grodno to Auschwitz in January 1943, simply stated that:

> the train ride was probably one of the worst things that I can possibly remember. The train ride was utterly horrendous. People died. There was no water. There were no sanitary facilities. There was no food. Whatever was had gone very quickly. It was about three and half days. And then we stopped and we saw Auschwitz.[46]

Meyer Adler retold his experience of deportation from Chust to Auschwitz over a year later in almost identical terms: It was a journey of extreme overcrowding; there was only a bucket for 'bathroom facilities'; a number of his travelling companions died en route.[47] As Simone Gigliotti perceptively suggests, it is perhaps no surprise, given these conditions, that the cattle car became the principal stand-in for the one deadly place survivors never experienced – the gas chambers in the death camps.[48] That the cattle cars play this role in retellings of the events of the Holocaust powerfully signals that these journeys were more than simply a form of transport to the camps. Trains did not merely take individuals from a known world to an unknown world. They were themselves the site of a radical rupture of norms.

But there is also a counter-story of cattle cars as a site of escape and these train journeys as one of a number of liminal landscapes – or places in between – during the Holocaust that presented opportunities that some seized upon. The mass movement of prisoners – from ghetto to camp, or between camps – was a moment when fixed boundaries were replaced by more fluid boundaries. One man who took advantage of this was Leo Bretholz, who was deported from Drancy to Auschwitz in 1942 after failing in his earlier attempt to make it across the Alps to the Swiss border. In the train car Leo remembered 'a whole gamut of emotions running their course' from 'resignation' through 'despair', and 'a young man . . . attempting to make love to a young woman in the train . . . call that an expression of life'. Leo and his friend 'had decided to make our getaway'. Dunking their 'sweaters . . . in human waste' to make 'them wet, to create a tensile cloth', they tried to budge the bars blocking the small window on the side of the wagon. 'And we twisted and twisted and then finally we saw that glimmer of hope where the bars in the frame started to move ever so slightly,' Leo explained, before using 'our hands to move them apart again, so that they should start loosening' to the point that by 'the late afternoon, those bars had moved apart . . . enough where we could see our way squeezing through'. Under the cover of darkness, they jumped from the train as it slowed to take a bend. 'We heard whistles and shots fired', but Leo and his friend lay 'in the ravine' in 'wet, tall grass, holding our breath together' and heard the train moving off after the hunt for the jumpers was called off. 'For the first time in so many weeks, we were what you might call free,' Leo recollected, 'if not entirely free, at least away from the train that was taking us to certain death.'[49]

While the train journey in cattle cars to the death camps assumes a dominant position within both survivors' narratives and contemporary iconography, for those who survived the initial selections at Auschwitz this was neither a train taking them 'to certain death' nor generally their last journey by train. Rail lines did more than simply connect ghettos with camps. They also connected camps with other camps and sub-camps. They played a critical role in bringing the victims to the killers as the policy of dispersed shootings was replaced in 1942 by one of constructing a handful of purpose-built killing centres. But rail lines also played a vital role in bringing prisoners deemed fit enough to survive the initial and subsequent selections to sites of labour. These became a greater priority, in particular during 1944.

The mass movement of prisoners across the European continent to the sites where labour was needed (and away from those places in the direct line of the Soviet advance) meant that vast distances were covered during this phase of the 'final solution of the Jewish question'. This contrasted so markedly both with the concentration of Jews in Polish ghettos in the early years of the war and the radicalization and killings close to home that characterized the years immediately after the occupation of former Soviet territory. While some like the Laks sisters experienced both a Holocaust close to home and a Holocaust far away, those relative latecomers to the programme of genocide like David Bergman and George Havas, who arrived at Auschwitz in the Hungarian transports in the summer of 1944, primarily experienced mass dislocation and movement on a continental scale. They arrived at a camp that was a connected space within a much broader network of the SS camp system, which extended at its height across a vast swathe of central and eastern Europe and kept on growing with the opening up of hundreds of sub-camps for labour in the Reich during the final year of the war. These needed a constant supply of labour given the high mortality rates caused by the appalling conditions to which prisoners were subjected.

Travel between these camps tended to be by rail. It was only in the last months of the war that the road network was utilized, as bomb damage to the rail network worsened and the pressing demands of military transport became overwhelming in the context of defeat, retreat and the final counter-attacks and defences. Before this, prisoners within the SS camp network experienced multiple journeys by train. Prisoners being transported 'over hundreds, even thousands of miles in answer to labour needs' were, Daniel Blatman notes, 'almost an everyday event from the end of 1942'.[50] For those who survived selections and were deemed fit to work, trains represented more than simply Jews being taken to their death. They also pointed to the ways in which individuals had been reduced to a resource that was shipped wherever labour needs were seen to be greatest within the military-industrial complex.

Retelling his wartime story, it seemed to David Bergman that it could be reduced to a 'story of trains, trains, travelling'. During 1944 and 1945, David was someone constantly on the move. Trains were central to a series of journeys as he went first north-east, then south-east, then west, east, and west again over the course of a year of criss-crossing the continent. What is particularly striking about David's story, and how he told it, is that he pushed the landscape of railroads far wider than solely, or mainly, being about one-way transport to a camp like Auschwitz. Rather, trains played a wider role in David's wartime experiences and point to the bewilderment and disorientation of being a body shipped hither and thither across the European continent in the final years of the war.

The train journey to Auschwitz was not David's first, or only, journey by rail in 1944. His first was the much shorter journey by 'passenger train, instead of a cattle train'. This was from the synagogue in Bochov, where he and his family were confined with their neighbours for a few days just after Passover, to the nearby larger town of Mátészalka, which was a rounding-up point for Jews from the region. A few weeks later, in the early summer of 1944, he and his family were on the move again. This time the numbers were larger. They were not simply 'enough for a train load' from his small town, but 'enough people . . . for a large . . . transport'. As well as being part of a much larger group made up of Jews 'from all of the shtetl around in that area', the journey was far longer – 'and this time', as David told his interviewer, 'instead of a passenger train there was a cattle train'.

David retold this second journey – to Auschwitz – much as other survivors have. It was overcrowded – 'they put us in, packed us very tight and there was hardly room to move' – and disorienting both in terms of time and space. David knew neither where 'we're heading', nor could he remember 'the exact amount of time' they were travelling for. This train journey, like the earlier shorter journey from synagogue to rounding-up point, included 'the whole family there – my grandparents – they were still together'.[51] However, for David's grandparents, his mother and younger siblings, this second train journey was to be their final journey. Auschwitz was quite literally the terminus for those seen to be too old or too young to work. 'When they opened the doors,' David told another interviewer of his arrival at Auschwitz, 'it was like walking into hell.'[52] There this extended family, like so many others, was fatally and finally separated along the lines of age and gender at Birkenau. Like other older teenage boys, David survived the first selection, along with his father who was on the cusp of middle age and just about young enough, in the early summer of 1944, to be considered of some labour value to the Reich.

Over the next half a year or so, David was on the move again and again. These were no longer journeys with 'the whole family there', nor journeys made wearing his own clothes. Subsequent journeys were with an ever-decreasing number of familiar faces, in single-sex prisoner groups, and wearing the thin cotton-striped uniforms of camp inmates. This radically different form of transportation – they were now quite clearly marked out as prisoners within a prison system – came fast on the first journeys. 'After about 5 or 6 days' in Auschwitz, David was on the move again as part of a single-sex group of '13 people, 13, 15, or in that range', which included his father and other men from his community who celebrated his bar mitzvah as they travelled from Auschwitz to the camp at Plaszów on the southern outskirts of Kraków. After 'about six weeks' David was once more on the move, westwards to Gross-Rosen. This time, however, his father was no longer a fellow traveller.

David's separation from his father was a consequence of the separation of prisoners arriving at Plaszów into flimsy categories of different skilled or semi-skilled workers. On arrival at the camp, different trades were identified. For David's father, who had worked as a tailor his whole life, there was a clear group of skilled workers to join. For David it was less clear, although he knew that he needed to possess some kind of skill of value. When they called for bricklayers, David raised his hand. 'I never laid a brick or a stone in my life,' David recalled:

> I never even touched one. But I was in the camp, I saw how people laid the bricks and the stones, how they mixed the cement. And so I figured, 'Well, I could do that.' They said, 'OK fall in line', and they put me in the work group and I . . . in their eyes I was a professional bricklayer.

Retelling this story of becoming a bricklayer, David laughed at how ludicrous and arbitrary the division of labourers into different groups was, when all it took to become a bricklayer was to raise your hand.[53]

Now identified as a bricklayer and tailor respectively, David and his father were soon separated when the need for bricklayers on construction projects elsewhere meant that David was soon back on the train and heading west. As he came to realize, his body was 'just a machine' within the Nazi labour system that could be redeployed elsewhere.[54] Retelling leaving Plaszów for Gross-Rosen, David explained how:

> all of a sudden, without any warning they yanked me out from the work group . . . there's no such thing as sitting down like you would say, 'Well, tomorrow you're going to go someplace else, or do that.' Just, 'Come!' And they yanked me and said, 'Tonight, uh, you're going to a different camp.' And fortunately, I looked all around and I was able to find my father. And

we said goodbye through the fence. And it was a very, very sad moment, too; knowing that I would never see him again . . . you had that feeling. I didn't give up hope, but it was a very strange feeling. Then they put me on a train, and uh, was like an overnight travel. And I found out after we arrived that it was a camp called Gross-Rosen.[55]

As with the earlier journey to Auschwitz, there was no knowledge of where the ultimate destination might be, although David and his fellow bricklayers knew that it would be another site in the labour camp system. Over the summer and early autumn of 1944, David Bergman was reduced to a gendered body capable of labour that was shipped where the need was greatest. At this point, the construction of new sub-camps within the Reich meant that David was one of many labouring bodies dispatched westwards.

Gross-Rosen turned out to be simply a staging post or 'processing camp', where after another six weeks and another selection 'they put me in a train again'. Retelling his story, David joked that 'six weeks, it seems like an average cycle . . . I'd become a professional traveller at that time . . . with all this moving'.[56] However, this was to be his final journey for a while. David spent the next six months in what seemed to him to be his 'first concentration camp'. This was Langenbielau I, one of the sub-camps in the Gross-Rosen system, and here he continued with his laughable identity as a bricklayer.[57] Narrating this year of his life, David laughed at the thought of being both a 'professional bricklayer' and 'professional traveller'. Both seemed equally ludicrous to him. Both were connected within and to the strange economy of the labour camp system.

As David was aware, that economy was fatally flawed. It was one in which a teenager who had never handled a brick could become a 'professional bricklayer' by raising his hand at the right moment. It was one in which the 'little wall' they built at Plaszów 'was useless work' that served no obvious purpose. It was one in which, as David explained, a fellow prisoner who had 'committed a crime' could be freed while he himself seemed to be 'virtually sentenced to life'. It was an economy in which food and shelter were terribly inadequate, and after being marched 'several miles to work' each morning David would arrive 'half dead' and far from being a productive labourer.

There were thousands and thousands of weakening bodies like David's on the move in 1944, redeployed across Europe within the camp system. Each journey was a dislocation, first into single-sex groups, which then fragmented still further. Individuals tried to stay together with family members, friends or neighbours of the same sex, but this was not, as David experienced, always possible. He ceased to have human agency about where he went, but was a 'machine' to be picked up, moved around, and redeployed within the vast network of camps. He had been reduced to merely a labour resource within the military-industrial complex. But worse was yet to come.

As David Bergman retold his story of multiple journeys, it was not the early journey by cattle car to Auschwitz that was the most troubling and difficult to tell, but the central journey in his narrative as David was taken in what seemed 'like a half-open cattle train' from Langenbielau I to Dachau early in 1945. He quickly realized that this journey was different from his earlier journeys to and between a series of work camps. Gathered together with those who were clearly no longer fit to work, he had the sense that this was 'going to be the final journey' and they were 'not being taken to a work camp'. His body – and those of others around him – had weakened to the point where this bricklayer was no longer useful in the strange economy of forced-labour construction.

'They packed us in the train so tight, I mean, like standing up, there was no room to move. It was like sardines,' David recalled. But this journey was an experience of overcrowding, thirst and hunger on an entirely different scale from that of the crowded cattle cars that brought David and his family to Auschwitz less than a year before. Before leaving the camp for Dachau, each prisoner had been given 'a piece of bread', which was entirely inadequate for a journey that lasted about a week. But it was thirst not hunger that stood out in David's memory of this long journey. As he struggled to explain 'what happened' on this journey dominated by memories of thirst, David remembered:

> well, the journey . . . my thirst . . . they didn't . . . they just gave us a piece of bread. We couldn't even eat because we were very thirsty. And the thirst pains were so bad that I even tried to use the urine from my body, just to wet my lips. And I pretty much, as it went down, uh . . . And when we arrived, I have already passed out virtually.[58]

Without even a single bucket of water in their open wagons, there was nothing to drink aside from urine.

This week-long journey westwards to Dachau was the source of 'the most gruesome, gruesome nightmares for many years'. They were to occur not because of the lack of food and water or shame of being forced to drink urine, but because of the coexistence of the living, half-dead and dead in these open trucks. Exposed to the elements and 'packed in . . . so tight' that there was standing room only, this journey to nowhere became murderous. David described how 'some people start getting weaker, and they could no longer stand anymore. Then they would fall down; and they'd be trampled on, because there was no room to move. And soon as they were trampled on, they died.'

As he went on to tell his interviewer, this experience of falling, being trampled on, and dying was not just something that happened to others but something that he was personally involved in. 'When I fell down,' David recalled:

> there was somebody fell on top of me. And I felt like, I actually felt like I'm dying already. I could uh feel like it was a feeling like I just wanted to go to sleep. It was not a painful feeling. Just going to sleep. And there was inside this . . . like an electric shock I kept getting. 'Don't fall asleep! Don't fall asleep! Wake up! Wake up, because this is gonna be your last sleep!' And I didn't know how to get the body off me, because I was so weak. And yet

I knew that if I don't push him off that it'll be the end. So that little voice saying, 'Come on! Muster all your strength, and you got to push him off.' So all of a sudden then I just got on and uh the last strength and I pushed him off and then I fell on top of him. And now he was trying to struggle to survive. And I couldn't move, I just, I didn't even have the strength to move. And he was trying to push me off, and he didn't have the strength. And I didn't have the strength to move, and we, neither of us wanted to hurt each other or anything, but the bodies were all around. There, nobody moved. It was the most awesome, gruesome thing that ever human beings can do. And we would uh travel by . . . like a bridge overhead, where trains go by, and it stopped. And people would look down, and look at us like uh, 'What's going on? It's kinda strange.' And they had no idea what it was all about. And then all of a sudden, when I finally did push him up out of the way and I, he fell down and I, I fell on top of him. Now he was struggling to push me off. And I was holding there, and all of a sudden he got up and his final moment of breath and he bit my leg, right in here. And then he fell back and died.[59]

It is a story almost too terrible to tell. At the moment when he recalled the life and death struggle between himself and this man who was first on top and then underneath him, David shifted his gaze – and that of his listeners – to one of the bridges that the open cars passed under that provides some distance away from this dreadful space where 'falling' meant dying and killing.

This death, which David was intimately involved in, was not the only one on that journey. David recalled one man being shot by one of the guards, and others dropping down dead in mid-conversation. For David, this was 'the first time I was really confronted with death'.[60] It may seem strange that it was only at this point, on this journey to Dachau in the last months of the war, that David was surrounded by corpses. Corpses were a common sight in the Warsaw ghetto, however they were not part of David's mental world, even after boarding a cattle car to Auschwitz, then being taken less than a week later on to Plaszów and then on to Gross-Rosen and its sub-camps. In part this was because the Hungarian deportations came at the very end of the war and telescoped into a matter of weeks events that in Poland had spanned years. It was also due to the separation of functions at Auschwitz, where the living and dead did not coexist aside from the *Sonderkommando* who were given access to the killing zone. A labourer in the SS camp system like David Bergman lived without seeing death up close through the second half of 1944. However, that changed in 1945 when death – and the dead – came horribly close in this open rail car.

The coexistence of the living and the dead in the rail cars during the journeys westwards in the final months of the war is something that shocked William Lowenberg's interviewer as William retold his journey by box car from Zychlin to Dachau. 'There was no water and no food. I remember that,' he explained, before adding 'but I know we used the dead bodies to sit for seats or benches alongside.' His matter-of-fact recounting of corpses being used as benches was too much for his interviewer, who interrupted with the horrified question, 'Who did?' This question remained unanswered as William started to move on to the next part of the story. Not getting an answer, his interviewer intervened once more, asking, 'So was that the worst experience in those boxcars?' 'That was, yes,' responded William. 'That was the last time I was in a boxcar. And I remember when they opened the doors it was Dachau, and very few got out of the trains. I believe only maybe 200, 300, 400 at the most.'[61]

Like David Bergman, it was this later journey by train that was remembered as the 'worst experience in those boxcars'. William had first been transported as a fifteen-year-old in a cattle car in the spring of 1943 from Westerbork to Birkenau. On that journey he had travelled with a girl he had met in Westerbork. It was a journey that he confessed 'I don't remember anything about', neither recalling whether they had received food nor how long it had taken. Pushed by his interviewer who asked, 'Do you remember noise, smells in the boxcar?', William responded:

> Well, obviously the human, there were no toilets . . . I'm sure. But no one died on that trip. Subsequent of course I have other stories to tell you. But on that trip no one died that I knew of in our boxcar at least. Maybe in others', older people. And there's very little that I remember.

However, the lack of a toilet on the first train to Auschwitz paled into insignificance compared with the journey to Dachau, where drinking river water meant that his fellow travellers had 'dysentery so everything there was just horrible'. But more markedly, sitting holding hands with a girlfriend on the floor of the cattle car was a world away from the surreal experience of sitting on corpses.[62]

In William Lowenberg's and David Bergman's descriptions of these evacuations by train westwards in the late winter and early spring of 1945, there are echoes of the kind of contrasts between the camps cited by survivors, which I turn to in the final chapter. If there was one thing worse than the 'final solution of the Jewish question' being efficiently enacted, it was that moment towards the end of the war when everything was unravelling. Worse than being carted around the Reich to work in the military-industrial complex was being put on a train to nowhere with the dead and the dying as everything was in a state of chaotic collapse.[63]

The nightmare journey from a sub-camp of Gross-Rosen to Dachau, a journey that was so difficult to describe, was not David's last. After 'about six weeks' in Dachau, 'all of a sudden, again, I was yanked out without any warning and put on a train again,' he recalled, joking again that he was a 'real professional' traveller:

> They took the few of us that could still walk, and they marched us out. And we had no idea why they were marching us out. This was about three days

before the Americans came. And they put us in a passenger train. And I learned, years later, what actually their main purpose was. But at that time, I didn't know. And we travelled for about a couple of hours or so and then they told us to get off the train . . . And as we were . . . marching . . . off from the train station, I remember that I saw . . . a couple of women in a group there . . . were staring at us, that they were crying. And within me, I sensed that something is going to happen to us. And after we marched out of the station into the forest, they started shooting at us. They massacred many of them.

David managed to escape and stayed in hiding until he was liberated by American troops, who took him to recuperate at Garmisch–Partnekirchen. 'And within three weeks,' he joked, 'I was ready to travel. Again!' This time his journey was back east, heading home in 1945 through Czechoslovakia to Hungary to see whether anyone had survived. 'I would have to wait, because there were so many people who wanted to go home. Those who had survived. And that the only way to get home was to travel on top of the train, one of those cattle-type trains. Can you imagine the experience? Travelling overnight when I had nothing to hold on to. And just swinging there, going through tunnels. I was so anxious to get home.'[64]

David Bergman was part of a much larger movement of survivors eastwards in search of news of family members and friends, a subject that I return to in the epilogue. This heading home, using trains to cover the vast distances involved, was his attempt to unpick the previous years of forced journeying or find some sort of meaning in them. Being a body with labour value in the SS camp system, David was, as he was well aware, moved at will where his labour was needed. In order to reverse those frequent forced relocations, he headed home, back to Hungary to the place where he and his family had first started their journeying a year earlier, when a passenger train had taken them from the synagogue in their small town to the nearby town of Mátészalka. That had been only the first of a whole series of journeys. The forced mobility that characterized David's wartime experience, multiplied thousands and thousands of times over, meant that people like him were scattered across the continent miles from home. For David, and he was not alone here, heading home was the logical first step in restarting an autonomous life, back to the last place where his family had been together before the German state began moving them – and separating them out – by train around the continent.

But, as David quickly realized, home was no longer home. His family's journeys had come to an end much sooner than his – either in Auschwitz or in his father's case in one of the camps along the way. Not only was David now alone, but the political mood was changing. He decided to leave Hungary with a number of friends who 'formed what we called a "kibbutz" to go to Palestine'. The group never got there. They found out:

> that the only way we'd be able to get out from Budapest is to go on cattle train, like we went to Auschwitz; because the Russians were not allowing legally. So they had to . . . whatever arrangements, whoever made it didn't explain anything to me other than get on the train. And . . . and I remember we were travelling at night, and the train going through just like in Auschwitz – cling, cling, going; cling, cling, stopping. And just wondering if we'll ever be discovered, because we went illegally. Finally morning came; and they told us that we were in Austria, in American zone. So we knew we were finally free. So when we got to Vienna and we stayed there about two or three days . . . And they said we will not be able to go directly to Palestine, because the British were blockading it. Uh, that we'll have to go to Germany and wait. Talk about depression [laughing] setting in!
>
> Q. So then you are now on the move again.

A. Back on the train again! [Laughing] This is why I had done this story before. I called 'To Hell and Freedom'; and this is a continuous story where I superimpose the sounds of the trains. Because that's what this is all – the whole story of trains, trains, travelling.[65]

Although most marked in this story of illicit people-smuggling out of Soviet-controlled Hungary into the American zone in Austria, border-crossing characterized many of David's wartime and immediate post-war train journeys. Crossing the national border for the first time, as the train left Hungary on its journey to Auschwitz in the spring of 1944, was a highly significant moment for David and his family. During the initial days of travelling they could hear their guards talking in Hungarian, but a new language was introduced when the train:

came to a stop. And we didn't know what it was. Then we heard talking. All of a sudden we heard Hungarian, we heard German talking. And then the Hungarian voices disappeared; and then German guards had taken over. So that put fear in us, knowing that we're not going to Hungary anymore. That this was . . . And from there on in, it was the beginning. I'd say the beginning of the end, for a lot of people.[66]

Once David was in the SS camp system for the purposes of labour, he was transported by train across national borders from one camp to another before being taken further and further into the Reich. The train as technology that covered vast distances and crossed borders was critical in the period when the radicalization of policy and practice in the east shifted to become the continent-wide practice of murder and forced labour that tore apart David Bergman's family.

These border-crossing journeys to which victims were subjected during the transcontinental phase of the Holocaust were both mirrored by, and countered by, quasi-voluntary movements across borders. During the war,

Jews were not just being transported across borders but were also making those journeys themselves. As they crossed borders, Jews sought to answer the question that dominated conversation: Where will we be safe? Moving towards, or into, neutral territory, they imagined safety – as Joseph Elman's father did – to lie in a place.

Attic and Cellar, Mountain and Sea

Gerda Blachman's attempts to flee Germany in 1939 did not succeed quite as she and her family had planned. Turned back first from Havana, and then from Miami, Gerda and her family disembarked in Antwerp and settled in Brussels. They might not have made it to Cuba, but Gerda recalled with satisfaction that at least 'we were not in Germany'. That was what mattered most to her and her parents at that moment. Brussels might not be Havana, but neither was it Breslau. A year later, however, the situation changed. In May 1940, Germany invaded Belgium, during a westward push into Belgium, Luxembourg, France and the Netherlands that saw Jews living in western Europe coming under German control. In the aftermath of the German occupation of Belgium, a growing number of anti-Jewish measures were enacted that Gerda described as a tightening of 'the screws'. In 1942, Jews in Belgium were ordered to wear a yellow star and had to register with the authorities. Gerda's mother – along with thousands of other Jewish immigrants – decided to ignore this demand. As Gerda explained, 'from the lists that had been registered they went from house to house and you know, they had the addresses. They had the people. It was very easy. They went and picked them up.' Those picked up were among the close to 25,000 Jews deported from Belgium to Auschwitz between 1942 and 1944.

Gerda's father had been arrested by the Germans. To avoid deportation Gerda and her mother first looked to local solutions and briefly went into hiding in Belgium, 'only we didn't have that much money and it was very expensive'. However, what they did have were friends with contacts with the French underground, and so they were able to follow the route of others making their way through France to the Swiss border with the help of false papers. Travelling with dollars sewn into a loaf of bread, Gerda and her mother crossed into France by train and then were taken to the border in a hay wagon. They walked into Switzerland and were discovered by a border guard, ending up spending the remainder of the war in refugee camps in Switzerland.[1] They were not the only ones trying to make it into neutral territory. Italian Jews were heading north to the Italian-Swiss border in the Alps, while others were heading south through France to cross the Pyrenees into Spain.[2] Several hundred miles away, another border between occupied and neutral territory was also breached. Denmark, occupied by the Germans in April 1940, became the site of a major rescue action in the beginning of October 1943 when close to 6,000 Jews were moved from the capital to the northern coast, and then across the Öresund – the strait between Denmark and neutral Sweden – to escape threatened deportations.[3]

Deciding that home was no longer safe – whether in Breslau in 1938, Brussels in 1942, Copenhagen in 1943, or in the case of families like the Baumans, their home in the Warsaw ghetto in 1943 – Jews faced the challenge of where to go. From 1938 onwards, a series of measures – placing Jews in ghettos or sending them to the camps – were acts of quite literally putting Jews in their place. Within a world where Jews were being separated, confined, moved around and ultimately murdered, individuals and families faced stark decisions about where to go. Deciding where might be safest, individuals and families worked with whatever inadequate information they could get hold of and a hunch of what was possible and preferable. All of this took place in a context of severe limits over what could and could not be done.

There were broadly three options if individuals sought to evade German-controlled space. One was to try to take on a new identity and pass as a non-Jew living on false papers in the anonymous space of a large city or a rural area far from where anyone knew you. Another, and the initial option that Gerda and her mother briefly pursued in 1942, was to lie low and go into hiding in what was in effect a non-place. A third, and ultimately the strategy that Gerda and her mother successfully undertook after their failed attempts some years earlier, was to leave occupied Europe entirely and seek refuge across national borders in neutral territory. Steve Paulsson estimates that roughly equal numbers of Jews – perhaps as many as 400,000 in each category – sought to hide from or flee the deportations and killings, excluding the much larger flight eastwards into the Soviet Union from Poland first in 1939 and then also in 1941.[4] Oftentimes individuals and families – as Gerda's story shows – pursued more than one of these strategies as they adjusted to new circumstances, new information, new opportunities and new threats.

Passing as a non-Jew was seen to be harder or easier for some than others, depending on their sense of how they looked or talked. It was also certainly gendered. For those who felt that they could not survive passing as a non-Jew outside the ghetto or camps, there were two options left: flight or hiding. Both presented different challenges. In the case of flight, the major challenge was simply the difficulties of getting to one's destination. Oftentimes a guide was required with a means to traverse the mountains or sea that stood between occupied and neutral territories. Once those who had decided on flight had made it, there were no guarantees about the kind of welcome that these illegal border-crossers would receive. They might, as Gerda was well aware, simply be turned back. For those who went into hiding the challenges were different, but just as real. While the journey in many cases might not pose such a challenge, finding a safe hiding place and most crucially a helper willing to bring food from the world outside was extremely difficult, especially when this meant putting that person at risk of arrest, imprisonment and in many cases death. Once in hiding in occupied territory, there was always the chance of discovery or betrayal and so even the most ingenious of hiding places never felt completely safe.

Flight – literally getting out of there – was something that characterized both pre-war and wartime responses to anti-Jewish measures. In the aftermath of *Kristallnacht* and the *Anschluss*, many German and Austrian Jews, like Gerda's family, sought safety beyond the borders of the ever-expanding Reich. As Germany moved first east and then west, Jewish families like Gerda's continued to seek out safety through border-crossing in order to escape from German-occupied territory. At its simplest level, these attempts to evade arrest and deportation were about moving from occupied territory to neutral territory. Sitting in the Proushinna ghetto, Joseph Elman's father longed to be closer to Sweden or Switzerland, two neutral countries that promised safety. However, while Joseph's father imagined Europe as an ever-changing political map shaded into either neutral, Axis or Allied powers, many viewed the continent's political geography as a little more complex. Wartime Europe was made up of a patchwork of differing degrees and natures of occupation and alliance. Europe could be – and was – mentally mapped out as a series of more or less safe and dangerous countries rather than the binaries of occupied or neutral – dangerous and safe space – conjured up by Joseph's father.

Many worked with this more nuanced understanding of shifting degrees of control or persecution and moved from countries they reckoned less safe to those seen as safer. For Jews living in western Europe, for example, there was broadly a southward movement, as Jews fled the Netherlands for Belgium, and went from Belgium and Luxembourg to France, and moved within France from north to south and in particular towards those zones in southern France under Italian control.[5] This southward movement from those countries seen as particularly dangerous – such as the Netherlands – to others deemed a little less so – such as France – was also often about getting closer to ultimately making it to the safety promised by a neutral country such as Switzerland on the other side of the Alps.

This movement from those places seen as more dangerous to those seen as less dangerous did not happen simply on a continental scale, but also much closer to home as individuals and families moved from place to place at the local, regional or national level. This can be seen earlier on in the war in the experience of Dov Cohen, who decided to leave his home city of Novogrodek for the smaller town of Karelitz about twelve miles away after the first massacre of Jewish men in his city shortly after the German occupation in 1941. 'We talked things over,' he later explained, 'and assuming that young men were in greater danger than others and that small towns might be safer, decided that my uncle Yankel and I should try to reach my grandmother's home in Karelitz.'[6]

Even with somewhere to go, and someone to go to, getting there was still a problem. Dov and his uncle decided that travelling during the night would be safer than travelling during the day, that they would avoid using 'the main road in order to avoid German troops', and instead walk through the fields. The choice of both time of journey and route taken was calculated to make traversing the space between one place – Dov's home – and another – his grandmother's home – as safe as possible. Once they arrived there, Dov and his uncle discovered that they were not the only men in their extended family who had had the same idea. A cousin – Idel – had also reckoned that their grandmother's house was a potential place of safety and they found him already there when they arrived at dawn. At first things went well and this seemed to have been the right decision. 'Karelitz was relatively quiet,' Dov later wrote, so 'we helped our grandmother and hoped for calmer times.'

However, things soon changed. There were not only shifting micro-geographies to sites of perceived safety and danger but also shifting micro-chronologies. When men aged over sixteen were called to report to the market square in Karelitz, Dov realized that this place was no longer safe.

'I was terrified. I wasn't a resident of Karelitz, and I knew that if the Germans found out, I would be questioned, tortured and finally shot,' something that did happen to a number of Jewish men. 'This horrid event convinced us that Karelitz was as unsafe as Novogrodek,' Dov explained, and so he and his uncle decided to return home so they could once more be with their families. He also reckoned that having the right, rather than the wrong, papers might be the difference between life and death. Therefore, passing as non-Jews, he and his uncle 'left Karelitz early in the morning, taking the main road this time, and reached Novogrodek a few hours later. We encountered German troops on the way, but they suspected nothing because we were dressed as peasants, and we got safely back to our families.'[7]

If journeying the twelve miles between Novogrodek and Karelitz was difficult, the challenge of making it to a safe or safer place was magnified at the continental scale when these journeys involved considerable distances and international borders. These journeys oftentimes necessitated the aid of a guide who generally charged handsomely for their services to navigate the difficult terrain of mountain or sea. For those Jews attempting to make it through the Alps into Switzerland, the services of a guide with local knowledge was essential. Johanne Hirsch Liebmann recalled that a contact found her someone who 'would literally take me across the border'. Meeting him in the French border town of Annemasse, Johanne was part of a group of six who were led into Switzerland and given directions as to where to go next to make it to Geneva just a few miles away. Her border-crossing involved little more challenging terrain than a stream that her guide carried her across.[8] However, her future husband, Max Liebmann, faced a much more arduous climb through the French Alps, led by a ten-year-old boy 'who knew . . . these mountains like his back pocket'. After one day of climbing, Max and the group of four others slept 'under an overhang'. The next day they continued climbing 'well above the tree line' before their guide returned home, explaining how to make it down into Switzerland. Turned back by a Swiss patrol on their first attempt to make it across the border, Max and another man tried again. Crossing glacial streams and negotiating narrow paths, they finally made it to the border village of Finhaut, and eventually on to Lausanne.[9]

A similar story of being led on a long, arduous walk through the mountains was retold by Leo Bretholz. It was very tough to make his way with a small group of other Jews through the Alps in October 1940 in 'heavy shoes', walking 'forty-some hours there or maybe even more'. Sleeping the night out in the open, they woke with a covering of light snow. The next day their guide left them with instructions of where they should go, but, like Max, they were turned back at the border, ending up being returned to Vichy France. There Leo spent the night in a police cell where he 'had to peel my socks off my feet' made 'bloody . . . from walking in the mountains'. Unlike Max, Leo's next destination was not a successful attempt to make it into Switzerland, but deportation to the internment camp in Rivesaltes in southern France.[10] For those who failed to make it into Switzerland, the view from the mountains during an unsuccessful attempt had echoes of the 'Israelites looking at the Promised Land. It was so near. You know, we could almost touch it and yet it was so far and we wondered if we would be denied like Moses . . . you can look at it, but you can't go in.'[11]

That safety seemed so near, yet was so far once Jews had made it through the Alps, was because the long journey there was only half the battle. After funding and making the journey, gaining admission into neutral territory generally relied on matters well beyond their control. Max Liebmann put his ultimate success at making it into Switzerland down to a Swiss soldier who he realized was telling him 'exactly how to go back to Switzerland' as he seemingly 'tiraded me for about 15 minutes' on 'what I'm not permitted to do'.[12] If anyone knew the weak spots in the border, it was one of those patrolling this long mountainous border, who clearly took pity on Max and his group. However, as Leo Bretholz discovered in October 1942 and Gerda Blachmann had discovered three years earlier, border guards could, and did, turn individuals and families back at the border. It is estimated that Switzerland turned back as many Jews as it admitted during the war. For those seeking to enter Switzerland illegally through the Alpine border, the situation was one that changed over the course of the war. Gerda thought that she and her mother were not turned back because 'public opinion' was on their side. So by the time they attempted to cross over into Switzerland, they were taken into a Swiss refugee camp rather than simply turned back into German-occupied territory by the border guards, because of a shift in the official position towards these illegal border-crossers.[13] Their gender may also have been significant, for another successful border-crosser reported that her male companion was sent back while she was permitted to stay in Switzerland.[14]

As Gerda saw shifting attitudes on the part of the Swiss authorities to be critical in explaining the welcome that she and her mother received when they crossed the border, the same was true in neutral Sweden. The journey from Denmark to Sweden was considerably shorter than that from Belgium through France to Switzerland. 'We were lucky that Sweden was so close,' one policeman who participated in the mass rescue of Danish Jews recalled.[15] However, it was not simply the relatively short distance across the sea boundary that meant larger numbers of Danish Jews escaped. Flight was as much about ease of entry as it was about ease of exit or the journey between the two. By the time that Danish Jews were threatened with deportation, Swedish government attitudes towards Jews had softened so that it was made clear in 1943 that Jews arriving on the Swedish shore from Denmark would not be turned away.[16] This was de facto an open invitation to make the journey across the Öresund strait, and thousands did. However, crossing a sea border presented its own set of challenges. Most obviously there was a need for boats and sailors with knowledge of these waters to ferry Jews fleeing Denmark for Sweden.

The journey by boat across the Öresund was generally only the final stage in a series of journeys. Recalling his role in the Danish resistance,

Frode Jacobson explained a two-stage process to the rescue. Once rumours of planned German arrests circulated, the initial priority was evading arrest and so Danish Jews were simply warned to leave home because this was the place where they could most easily be picked up from. Once they had left the most immediate place of danger, plans shifted to moving Jews to a place of safety, which meant arranging flight to neutral Sweden.[17] Niels Bamberger, a German Jew who had fled to Copenhagen in the 1930s, remembers being warned not to go home in the first days of October 1943, so his family made arrangements to stay for a few days with their grocer. After a week with him, they took a taxi to one of the coastal villages that were the departure point for passage to Sweden. Their precise destination was arranged through contacts in the resistance that their grocer had. Hiding under blankets, their family was taken by taxi from Copenhagen to a house where several hundred people arrived each day. From there, they were taken on foot by 'somebody from the resistance movement' to 'the pier at night' and then by boat across the Öresund. Their boat was met 'in the middle of the ocean' by a 'Swedish torpedo boat', which Niels and his fellow passengers boarded, 'and they gave us coffee and candy or whatever and then we went into Sweden and we were saved'.

Niels' journey from danger at home in Denmark to safety in Sweden took a little more than a week, and involved two stopping places – one in Copenhagen and the other in a fishing village on the coast – and what he remembered as a thirty- or forty-minute taxi ride and an 'hour or so' by boat, although in reality the trip was generally a little shorter.[18] Preben Munch-Nielsen, who was a schoolboy at the time and had grown up in a fishing village on the Öresund, recalled working on one of the boat services arranged by the resistance that made up to two or three trips per night, shuttling between Nazi-occupied Denmark and neutral Sweden.[19] One of Preben's main tasks as ship's boy was cleaning up the cabin between trips. As he explained to his interviewer, 'if you can imagine how the boat is when a dozen of refugees afraid, what they leave after in the . . . cabin was, well, I can still recall the smell'. But it was not simply the vomit that came from sea-sickness that Preben smelt. Describing the cabin, as a dozen Jews were being ferried across to Sweden, his overwhelming auditory and olfactory memories were of complete silence and the 'smell' of 'fear'. There was only a short stretch of water between the Danish shore and Swedish shore, but this was patrolled by German boats. As well as avoiding interception by German patrols, the success of this maritime mass movement of Danish Jews depended on the local knowledge of captains who 'knew every inch of the beach and the shore' and where the 'shifting sand reefs' were. These men were critical to the undertaking.[20]

Local knowledge – whether crossing the Alps or Öresund – did not come cheap. The sums paid for the less than half-an-hour journey across the Öresund could be exorbitant, in particular in the early days of the action. Niels Bamberger remembered how their first attempt to cross was thwarted when 'the boat we were supposed to go with had been taken by somebody else who paid more money for it'. The next day they were able to get on board a larger boat arranged by the resistance. 'First we paid them money,' Niels recalled. Two thousand krone per person 'was the going rate which was a lot of money at that time, but we were told if you come to Sweden the money is worthless. You can't do anything with it. You might as well leave it here . . . whatever money you give now will help those people who are poor or sick and can't afford it. They will also get out.'[21]

If flight was challenging both because of the journeys and the expense entailed, going into hiding was arguably even more difficult. As she told her story of evasion through flight, Gerda Blachman suggested that hiding simply was not something that they considered as a viable long-term solution. Feeling that the net of deportations was closing in, she and her mother did initially go into hiding. However, as she explained, 'we didn't have that much money and it was very expensive. People didn't do it just for the love only, you know . . . they wanted to be paid and they wanted to be paid for the food at least and for the room.'[22] While Gerda explained their decision to flee from

Belgium, rather than to hide in Belgium, as primarily an economic decision, this no doubt also owed much to their refugee status. For relative newcomers to a city or country, going into hiding was rarely a viable option. Newcomers tended not to have the necessary network of established contacts that were so important for those deciding to go underground, nor the money or source of money through the sale of furniture and other valuables that was needed, having lost these as they fled from their original homes, in Gerda's case in Germany. Another newcomer in western Europe – a German Jew who had crossed into the Netherlands in 1936 – William Lowenberg, recalled how their relatively recent arrival, combined with their lack of wealth, meant that going into hiding close to home was simply not an option. As he explained:

> we were relatively newcomers in the town because we had only gotten there. You know, we weren't born there, my father wasn't born there . . . So we knew . . . my father knew people, I knew that, but he wasn't, I don't know, there weren't these connections like if you were born and raised with the same people. And then I think the other issue was finances. I mean the people were hiding people. Most people had to, most people, if not all, but most people had to pay, there had to be some resources. My father didn't have resources . . .[23]

As Raul Hilberg suggested, it was 'more problematic to approach strangers than old friends, more frustrating to seek help without money than with some means'.[24]

Without an established network of local contacts and a lifetime of possessions to sell to fund a long period in hiding, Gerda and her mother headed south, crossing first into France and then on to Switzerland. Fleeing to a neutral nation was about heading to an anonymous site of potential safety. Individuals and groups helped them on the way, but their ultimate fate in Switzerland depended on agents of the Swiss state – the border guards – and the attitude of that state towards Jewish refugees at this particular point in the war, an attitude that Gerda saw as softening. Hiding much closer to home, by contrast, was a less anonymous experience that generally meant staying, often for weeks, months or years, within someone's home. That person was generally paid for their services, but the nature of the threat they faced if it was discovered that they were helping Jews in hiding, meant that their role was oftentimes built on pre-existing relationships, or a set of political or religious convictions.

But as she retold their decision to flee south, rather than try to lie low in Brussels, Gerda explained that there was more to this decision than simply economics or their status as relative newcomers. Having 'spent one night' in hiding, Gerda explained:

> I said 'Mother, that's not right. We're going to go crazy. We can't stay here the two of us until the end of the war you know, alone and we don't have enough money to pay her', so we came out of hiding the next day.[25]

In some ways, going into hiding shared something with flight. By hiding at the periphery in an attic or cellar, individuals and families were in a sense removing themselves entirely from the world. The most famous group of Jews in hiding in the Netherlands, the Frank family (originally from Frankfurt), entered the secret annex in 1942 spreading the rumour of their having fled the country. In a sense they may as well have. Otto Frank's family had effectively disappeared.[26] However, as Gerda appears to have been aware, going into hiding meant in a sense going nowhere, as much as going somewhere. Going into hiding was akin to a kind of imprisonment where movement was severely restricted and freedom curtailed. In the Netherlands the term widely used during the war for those who went into hiding was '*Onderduikers*', or literally divers who had gone under and were no longer living on the surface. As far as Gerda saw it, going under the surface seemed very much like being drowned.

A strong sense of claustrophobia pervades the diary, memoir and oral history accounts of those who went into hiding. While going into hiding did spare individuals, either initially or more completely, from arrest and deportation, the weeks, months and years living in cramped quarters was far from easy. Reading through Anne Frank's diary, the sense of overwhelming claustrophobia is palpable as two families and an eighth man lived together in a confined space for day upon day over nearly two years. In particular, tensions brewed, as when some of Anne's housemates were not on speaking terms for days at a time.[27] It was impossible to escape the tense atmosphere, much as Anne and her fellow dwellers in the secret annex wished they could, leading to a sense of being imprisoned.[28]

The Frank family were just four of the perhaps as many as 20,000–25,000 Jews – and a larger number of non-Jews called up for labour service – who went into hiding in the Netherlands during the Second World War.[29] However, their experience was far from representative. It was very rare for an entire family to hide together and stay in the same hiding place for close to two years. Much more normal were experiences of being split up into smaller groups to hide and frequent moves between a number of hiding places. As many realized, the largest-sized group that anyone was willing to hide was most likely to be two, or perhaps at a push three, but certainly generally not more.[30] This meant that going into hiding in most cases also meant deciding to split up the family, often along lines of age and gender. Moreover, while the Frank family remained together in one place, it was not unusual for those in hiding to have to move to a series of multiple addresses for longer and shorter stays. Steve Paulsson estimates that in Warsaw those in hiding moved on average over seven times.[31] In the Netherlands, hidden children lived in an average of just under five different hiding places, but some had more than double or quadruple this many separate addresses.[32]

More typical than the Frank family's story is the story of the Schwarz family, also originally from the Frankfurt region of Germany, who moved to the Netherlands in 1933. When Susie Schwarz's father began to make plans for the family to go into hiding, he was in no doubt that this would inevitably mean splitting up the family. He had found one place for himself, another for Susie, and a third for Susie's mother and elderly grandmother. 'Of course I was hysterical at the thought of having to part with my mother,' Susie recalled. However, in the end she went into hiding with her mother rather than on her own because of the sudden illness and death of her grandmother. One day in the spring of 1943 her father left on his bicycle to go to one hiding place 'early in the morning' while Susie and her mother were taken by two contacts to the other hiding place in the evening.[33]

Many children, and this was the original plan in Susie's case, went into hiding without their parents. The Frank family were unusual in making careful plans to fit out their own hiding place in father Otto's office, which meant that they could and did hide together as a family unit. Most were unable to take this DIY approach to hiding, but were reliant upon underground contacts that knew of a network of safe houses. In this case, they were completely dependent upon contacts who determined how many could go into hiding where, and generally found it easier to place children without their parents.[34] Hiding usually meant separating families, which was, as one survivor recalled, 'so painful'. It was something that a child hiding in the Netherlands, Hetty d'Ancona de Leeuwe, sought to convey to her interviewer as she told of the day when she 'left home myself without anything. I just walked out of the house, and a lady came to pick me up, and I had nothing with me when I left.' For Hetty, 'it's impossible for people to understand how hard it is to just leave your home, your parents, and know that you most likely never see your parents again'. Shifting from narrating that terrible day from her perspective, she tried – and failed – to put herself in the shoes of her parents who made this choiceless choice. 'I don't know how my parents could have done it,' Hetty stated, 'it's so painful to say goodbye to your one and only child, and don't know where she is going.'[35] One survivor who sent her child into hiding recalled how her husband – 'who was very far thinking' – decided in 1941 that 'we should prepare our child that she's not depending on us'. So they were 'less warm with her' – 'no hugging, no kissing' – so that 'it should be easier for her not to miss us'.[36]

The separation and loss of knowledge of where family members were, which was experienced by many who went into hiding, paralleled the gendered division within the camp system. Parents and children, both in hiding, did not know where each other were, and often this was entirely intentional. One woman who put her daughter into hiding knew neither the name of the couple she was placed with nor 'where they were living'.[37] One hidden Dutch Jewish child discovered after the war that her parents were living, 'unbeknownst to me and unbeknownst to them because it wasn't safe for them to know where I was', only ten miles apart. As she explained, if they had known where she was, her parents would, no doubt, have tried to find her, so endangering the hiddenness of both her and themselves.[38] Those ten miles of separation in hiding may as well have been the hundreds of miles of separation experienced by those Jews seen to be of labour value to the German military-industrial complex who were deployed to gendered camps dispersed across Europe. In both cases, knowledge of where the other was – and whether they were alive or dead – remained unknown throughout the war and often into the post-war period.

But going into hiding alone, as Hetty and many other Dutch Jewish children did, involved more than simply separation from parents and leaving home without one's possessions. It was a threat to her sense of self and a feeling of utter aloneness that Hetty sought to convey as she remembered that 'it was very scary because I had no name. I had no papers. I didn't know who I was. I didn't know who the man was that was taking me. I didn't know the child that was with me. I didn't know anything. I was a nobody.' These feelings of insecurity were heightened by the sheer unknown-ness of where Hetty was going and who she would now live with. Hetty recalled going by train to 'a little town that I had never heard of' where she was told 'to stand there and wait' by her unknown chaperone, who first took away the boy who had travelled with them. 'Maybe he was back in an hour,' Hetty recalled, 'I don't know, but that lasted forever for here I was, all on my own. I didn't know where I was going. I didn't know where I came from. I had no idea. I was so scared.'[39] Going into hiding arranged by others within underground networks tended to mean entering into a frightening unknown.

When Susie Schwarz and her mother went off on the back of two bicycles ridden by 'this man . . . and his son' they did not know, their ultimate destination was similarly unknown. 'I did not know where we were going,' Susie explained, 'all I knew is we would go to a farm.' They were first taken to what Susie called 'a halfway place'.[40] These places in between tended to be known underground spaces that were used as a temporary site to rest for one or a few nights while another more permanent hiding place was being sought out. They were sites used for the constant comings and goings of Jews.[41] This rhythm of moving between sites was recalled by Julia Schor, whose mother hid Dutch Jews in her home when Julia was a child. Writing of this period, she remembered both a rapid series of temporary guests and more permanent inhabitants of the attic rooms. There was the long-term group of twelve who undertook the necessary roles of living as normal a life as was possible in this wartime community in hiding – from keeping watch, through child-minding, to preparing food or doing the washing. Additionally, her mother's contacts in the resistance knew that here they could 'stow their charges for a few days', as they were moved from the city to more permanent hiding places in farms out in the countryside.[42]

After moving through one such temporary stopping place, Susie and her mother 'ended up somewhere' that 'was really very country, very desolate' and utterly alien. Waiting in a barn in the dark to meet their new hosts was, Susie remembered, 'really very frightening'. Led into a crowded farmhouse kitchen, Susie recalled one of those around the table questioning why a child, and not an old woman, was with her mother. 'That was a very frightening moment,' Susie explained, when she thought, 'Oh, my God. I have to go.'

However, she was permitted to stay. After spending the first night in the parlour, the next morning they moved to a hiding place in the barn so their presence in the house would be kept secret from the youngest children in the family, who it was thought might innocently blurt out the presence of strangers in their home.

For several months Susie and her mother's new life consisted of lying on top of hidden bags of grain in a gap underneath the floorboards in the barn that was just about 'wide enough to hold the two of us'. This 'hot', airless space, which was only opened up 'once or twice a day' when it was safe to bring them food, was 'simply ghastly'. It felt to Susie that she had been buried alive. It looked 'like . . . a coffin', Susie recalled, 'and it was just about that'.[43] Her description of their first hiding place as like a 'coffin' parallels the description of some who went into hiding in the woods and slept in what they saw to be graves dug into the forest floor.[44] Going into hiding meant entering a narrower and more restricted place that was almost a non-place, literally submerged beneath the surface. In some cases it felt like entering into a place that was not quite the place of the living.

Living conditions for Susie and her mother eventually improved marginally. At first they were able to leave their hiding place under the floorboards in the evening to walk around the attic. Later they moved into a newly built hiding place next to the barn that lay beyond a secret door in the wall. Crawling through the narrow opening, Susie and her mother found themselves in a space that was five or six feet wide, 'high enough so you could sit and long enough so you could lie'. Normally pitch black, there was a 'roof pane' at one end that could be moved to 'let a little air or light in'. Each morning they received 'a bucket for our needs' and then 'two or three times a day' they were brought food. 'We knew that was it for the duration,' Susie recalled with a sense of resignation – 'at that point . . . I was reconciled. I had no choice.' Compared to what they mockingly referred to as their 'palace', her father's 'living conditions were better', given that he not only had his own room where he could move around, but he also took his meals with his host family who had older children who were aware of this stranger in their midst. 'He had a little more cushy arrangement than we did,' Susie remembered, whose one and only experience of the world outside during her two years in hiding was a day in the summer when she lay outside among the tall sheaves of wheat in the sun.

While Susie and her mother stayed hidden both day and night within two hiding places camouflaged beneath floorboards and a false wall, many others – like her father – had more freedom of movement by day or night. In Susie's case, she and her mother were engaged in a double hiding – firstly from German search parties, members of the Dutch Nazi Party and neighbours, but secondly from the youngest children in the family who could not be trusted to inadvertently let on about the presence of these two strangers. Where all in the house were aware of those in hiding, there was not the same need for constant disguise. Rather, what tended to happen was that a secondary hiding place within the house was reserved for those moments when there was a knock on the door. This was the signal for a rapid retreat into a pre-arranged place within the safe house. One hidden child remembers rushing to hide with 'two other undergrounders' through a trap door in the hayloft.[45] Another remembers being able to make it into 'a marvellous hiding place in the house' under the floor within two minutes of the sign being given that a search might be imminent.[46] In the commercial premises where they hid in Warsaw for a time with others, Janina Bauman and her family had to practise heading quickly to a crawl space between the loft ceiling and roof if 'a suspicious-looking stranger appeared at the gate'.[47] In her 'Mamma's ark', Julia Schor remembered those in hiding in her mother's house having thirty seconds to get to the hiding hole in the eaves of the attic if the alarm was sounded.[48]

For Susie and her mother, this kind of inner hiding place within a safe house was where they stayed day in, day out. Confined to this tiny place, Susie remembers falling into a 'routine' of storytelling and reading that mirrored Janina Bauman's experience of her first three to four months in hiding as hours of conversation and reading.[49] Susie's mother 'did whatever she could to occupy the time' as she told her daughter stories and taught her 'innumerable songs', but she found 'that was hard to do, because there was a lot of time'. While her mother darned socks, Susie started copying out recipes 'of wonderful things to eat which I didn't get' from magazines into a 'little notebook' that also served as a diary of sorts. Later a local teacher would occasionally 'crawl in the hole' and do 'what he could to teach a 13 year old'.

Susie and her mother eventually had to share their 'palace' more permanently with others. The first new arrival was her father, who had to leave his hiding place because it was no longer deemed safe as the Germans retreated in late 1944. 'Well that was good and that was bad,' Susie recalled. The family was reunited again, but 'now there were three of us in the hole, so basically when one turned, the others had to turn too'. Worse was to come when another couple joined them in their hiding place. 'We had to really squish ourselves to . . . let them get in,' Susie explained, and the single bucket that served as a makeshift toilet was shared by the five of them in this terribly confined space where the others tried to look away. 'I don't really remember how we managed in that time,' Susie reflected, but manage they did.

Susie's experience of staying in one farmhouse for the entire duration of her two years of hiding was unusual. Although the house was searched, Susie and her mother were not discovered behind their false wall in the attic of the barn. Susie recalled being 'always frightened' while in hiding, but her anxiety levels were heightened during a search when it was clear that had she been discovered, 'that would have been it'.[50] Going into hiding was never completely safe. The possibility of discovery was ever present. Janina Bauman, her mother and sister were forced to leave their first hiding place after their presence was discovered by a gang of blackmailers, rendering their 'shelter' no longer 'safe'.[51] A series of short-lived shelters were arranged either together or apart, before the three of them were reunited in a large hiding place in commercial premises. After being discovered again by blackmailers, they were on the move again to a further short-term shelter for 'people on the run', one of the sites that made up what Steve Paulsson has dubbed the 'secret city' of wartime Warsaw.[52] On the move once more, Janina spent time staying in the city suburbs alone. She then rejoined her sister and mother with a family outside Warsaw for six months that were 'the longest and least eventful spell of my life on the run'.[53] More run-ins with blackmailers, followed by moves and separation, continued this pattern of weeks or months spent in one place followed by a number of rapid moves before a period of some stability again.

In each hiding place, they were entirely dependent on others. Janina later reflected on how 'humiliating' their 'dependence' on their hosts was, as she set about gaining 'the knowledge and skills which paying guests of a large, well-settled Polish family needed and were expected to have', and learning 'the rules we were supposed to comply with'.[54] 'Hiding in other people's homes,' Janina wrote:

> meant not only losing touch with the world outside, but also putting up with irksome restrictions and constant danger. Confined to a limited space, doomed to idleness, we seemed to have no life of our own. The men and women who sheltered us, even their children, wrestled with their daily problems, had their minor miseries and major dramas, their successes or failures, spells of joy or sadness. Our existence was blank, we just marked time. And having no life of our own, we lived the lives of others, sharing their joys, and sorrows. Our concerns changed from one shelter to the next, according to what was important in the lives of our successive landladies and landlords.[55]

Dependence on others could verge on exploitation. Recalling her mother giving money and jewellery that was demanded by their reluctant host, one survivor reflected 'it was all very strange, but we were so powerless that we did everything they asked us to do'.[56] Individuals could be moved from one place to another seemingly at will, and effectively made a prisoner within the home. One girl in hiding became de facto 'the maid' in the house where she ended up hiding. Here she 'had to clean the house . . . was not allowed to talk to anybody . . . was not allowed to go open the door ever . . . was not allowed to go out of the house' and 'didn't get much to eat'. Not surprisingly, her memories of this hiding place are of a 'very awful time for me to be there alone'.[57] Others were sexually exploited within the unequal power dynamics of host and hider.[58] While things were not easy for those who went into hiding, neither was it easy being the host. Although those providing food and shelter were often paid, this was not always the case, and with food in short supply for everyone, one Dutch survivor remembered that 'there was a lot of tension around food'.[59] More significantly, those who hid Jews put themselves and their families in considerable danger.

To be in hiding was to be far from free. It was a form of control, albeit by your hosts rather than German guards, and a form of imprisonment, although not in the camp system. It was also full of unknowns, in particular with the constant fear of discovery that necessitated frequent moves. For some, it all proved too much and it seemed that somewhere else must be better than being subjected to the restrictions that going into hiding entailed. Menachem Katz and his group finally decided to leave their hiding place to go into the forests. Before heading there for the final time, Menachem lived with a handful of others in a couple of different hiding places provided by family friends, close to his home in Brzezany in eastern Poland. The first was in the attic of Piotr and Hanka Kmiec's village home, but the sound of the group's footsteps in the rooms below threatened to give away their presence to their hosts' children who knew nothing of these secret guests. For a while they stayed hiding in the attic, where they had to remain in 'total quiet' and 'the days passed slowly and were laden with boredom and unending worries,' Menachem later recalled, as 'day after day, week after week, they held soundless conversations'.[60]

When German troops came to the village in the autumn looking to seize crops after the harvest, the attic hiding place seemed too vulnerable to discovery and so Menachem and his group moved underground into their second hiding place, or bunker, in the cellar. Here, Piotr had carved a hole out of the earth underneath the living room of the cottage. This dark, dank and crowded hiding place was, Menachem later explained, 'not much more than a pit'.[61] At one end was a small ventilation shaft 'camouflaged . . . with rocks, twigs and dry manure', and 'across from the opening, level with the benches' was 'a niche a bit wider than a human body' complete with a 'large bucket with a lid to be used as a toilet'.[62] The idea of using this bucket in front of the other seven bunker-dwellers was too much. In the end they took the bucket into the adjoining cellar and used it 'one by one' in there and emptied it onto the heap of manure in the farmyard.[63] At night a kind of 'mattress' of 'twigs and straw' was suspended from two poles slotted into the earth walls of the bunker, giving everyone 'his or her small place' in this makeshift bunk-bed arrangement.[64] During the day, they sat on the benches carved out of the earth – four on each side – in complete darkness unless the door to the main cellar was open where a tiny window let in some light. In such cramped conditions, 'new rules and different conduct and solutions had to be decided on'. At first they decided to move between the bunker and adjoining cellar in a shift system, moving between the two 'after about an hour or two, when everybody was stiff and sore with immobility'. This 'changing of the guard' that was 'accompanied by short exchanges of words, took place several times during the day until suppertime and before it turned dark'.[65]

Later, as the fear of German raids increased, Menachem's group were confined to the dark bunker where 'they sat close together, for sixteen hours a day'. 'It was terrible,' Menachem recalled, 'and got worse by the minute', as the toilet bucket 'filled' the cramped quarters 'with an unbearable stench' and 'due to a shortage of oxygen, the lamp was kept lit for only short periods of time. The darkness increased everybody's sensitivities to others' conduct, on the one hand, and to lack of consideration, on the other. Irritability and immense suffering were everyone's lot.'[66] It seemed to the eight crammed into the bunker under Piotr's living room that they had quite literally gone underground.

But worse was to come. After Piotr was shot by Ukrainian nationalists, German soldiers were billeted with his widow, Hanka. Now, the stone separating the bunker from the cellar 'was opened very rarely, only once every 24 hours, and sometimes only once every 36'.[67] It seemed to Menachem that they were now 'buried alive' in a 'congested grave' where they were 'slowly dying of suffocation'.[68] The conditions proved too much for first one of those in hiding, and then the rest, and they all headed to the forest to get away from 'the congested air in the bunker, the unbearable crowdedness, the stench of the faeces-full bucket'.[69] It seemed to Menachem and his fellow pit-dwellers that anywhere must be better than staying in their dark and airless hiding place. They abandoned their bunker in the cellar for first one bunker, and then another, dug into the soil of the nearby woods. In the final years of the war, the forest was a safer place than it had been a few years earlier. However, Menachem and his friends did not leave primarily because they decided that the forest was a safer place to go, but more because they could not stand their dark hiding place anymore.

It would seem that this overwhelming sense of imprisonment that generally accompanied going into hiding was part of what motivated Gerda and her mother to eschew hiding in Brussels and instead head towards neutral Switzerland. The journey was challenging, but Switzerland offered a promise of freedom away from Nazi-occupied territory. However, as Joseph Elman's father made clear to his son, the problem with flight was getting there and safe places seemed an awfully long way away. If Jews could not get out of occupied

Europe to make their way to neutral countries, then what if those neutral countries came to occupied Europe? In a sense, that is what happened in the winter of 1944 on the Danube shore in Budapest. However, it was not entirely clear to Budapest's Jews whether the houses in the city under the protection of Sweden – and other neutral nations – were safe places or not.

River

In the spring of 1944 another large national group of Jews came under German control. Although a member of the Axis powers since 1940, largely in order to get back territory lost after the First World War, by 1944 Hungary was busy trying to extricate itself from the war. In order to prevent this, Germany occupied Hungary in March, installed a pro-German government led by Döme Sztójay, and sent Adolf Eichmann to Budapest to oversee deportations. Hungary had passed a series of anti-Jewish laws during the interwar period – laws in 1938, 1939 and 1941 sought to remove Jews from economic life and to prohibit marriage between Jews and non-Jews. It also had the dubious distinction of being the first country in the interwar period to enact anti-Jewish legislation. But the Hungarian government had consistently refused German demands for deportations, arguing that it was dealing with its Jewish 'question' in its own way through primarily economic restrictions. Jewish men had been called up to separate unarmed labour battalions that suffered terrible losses alongside regular Hungarian army units fighting on the eastern front from 1941 onwards. However, close to 600,000 Hungarian Jews lived in something of an island of safety during the bloody years 1941–3 when Jews to the north, east, south and west were being murdered.

All of that rapidly changed in the spring of 1944. Hungarian Jews were marked with a yellow star, moved into ghettos, and deported from across the country. Some 430,000 were sent to Auschwitz-Birkenau in less than three months over the summer – among them David Bergman and his family. Although also placed into ghettos – in their case a highly dispersed ghetto made up of nearly 2,000 apartment buildings and houses spread across the city in June 1944 – Budapest's large Jewish population of close to 200,000 was ultimately spared deportation to Auschwitz when these were halted in July.

The strange shape of this ghetto owed much to the fact that the beginning of Allied bombing coincided with the introduction of ghettoization and in Budapest the two became intertwined. As ghetto plans were being discussed in April 1944, officials voiced reservations about the wisdom of creating a single closed ghetto in the city. To do so would, it was claimed, open up the remainder of the city to Allied bombing. Underlying such thinking was an assumption that the city's Jews were a fifth column or internal enemy who were in league with the Western Allies. There were rumours that Jews signalled to the Allied bombers to show them where to drop bombs and not drop bombs. On the flip side, it was assumed that the Western Allies – seen to be pro-Jewish – would avoid bombing where Jews were housed.

These rumours and assumptions – misplaced as they were – seem to have carried some weight in the spring of 1944, and they certainly cropped up in interviews with officials, across the press, and in the writings of ordinary Hungarians. In short, it seems that plenty of people bought into this linkage between Jews and allied bombing. In this context the ghetto plans being developed in May and June 1944 for the Hungarian capital were characterized by multiple, dispersed ghettos rather than a single ghetto. The degree of dispersal increased radically. In May there were plans for seven ghettos spread across the city. In June there were plans for 2,500 mini-ghettos literally almost everywhere. In the end, after a week of petitions and surveys, a final number was adopted of just under 2,000 mini-ghettos – the majority on the Pest side of the Danube. The greater dispersal seems to have owed much to fears about displacing non-Jews, but the broader context in which all these plans were being sketched out does seem to have been one of assuming that

Jews could form a human shield of sorts to be utilized to render the city if not safe, then at least safer.[1]

In an odd way then, Jews were being used in 1944 to seek to make Budapest safer for non-Jews. They were being strategically placed in an attempt to limit bombing or certainly to limit the impact of bombing. However, Jews were no longer seen as a resource that needed to be retained. The mass deportation of Jews from across Hungary that began in May 1944 was certainly intended for Budapest Jews also. The plan was that they would be next on the list. But diplomatic pressure from the neutral powers, internal political battles, combined with the shifting fortunes of the war – not only was the Red Army continuing to advance from the east, but Germany was now threatened with being squeezed from the west after the Allied landings in Normandy in June – meant that the Hungarian Regent, Miklós Horthy, halted deportations at the suburbs of Budapest. In the summer of 1944 there was something of a lull when a new and more moderate government led by General Géza Lakatos meant that Budapest's Jews felt safer, if not entirely safe.

But this sense of things getting better was short-lived. On 15 October a bungled attempt by Horthy to extricate Hungary from the war resulted in the native Hungarian fascist party – the *Nyilas* or Arrow Cross Party – assuming power, supported by Germany. Jews were once again targeted, with Jewish men and women being called up for labour. Thousands were marched westwards to build fortifications aimed at halting the Soviet advance. Those left in the city were placed into a single closed ghetto around the main synagogue in the traditional Jewish quarter. However, another place for Jews was also being developed in the city during the autumn and winter of 1944.

Dubbed the 'international ghetto', this cluster of apartment buildings in Pest emerged from the attempts of the neutral powers to offer protection to Jews in the city in the second half of 1944. If Jews in Budapest could not get to Sweden in the way that Danish Jews had in 1943, then Sweden – in the second half of 1944 – would have to come to them. The result was the creation of a so-called international ghetto on the banks of the Danube where a little bit of Sweden, Switzerland, Spain, Portugal and the Vatican City came to the Hungarian capital. It was an unusual territorial solution to the overarching problem facing Jews in occupied Europe of where to find a safe place, but the international ghetto operated with the widely shared sense that safety ultimately lay outside German-controlled territory in one of the neutral nations.

In the summer of 1944 when Budapest Jews began living in the dispersed ghetto that spanned the city, news spread of protective paperwork being offered by the neutral legations that was quickly seized upon, as one survivor put it, as 'the key to life'.[2] In July 1944, Raoul Wallenberg – who had been recruited by the American War Refugee Board and given the role of First Secretary of the Swedish Legation in Hungary – arrived in Budapest to 'more or less . . . organise . . . in Budapest for a peaceful sort of . . . immigration to Sweden of Jewish people', as his former boss Per Anger explained in a post-war interview.[3] After negotiations with the Hungarian government, it was agreed that the embassy could issue protective paperwork for 4,500 Hungarian Jews. This paperwork was not entirely novel but emerged out of the practice of giving provisional passports to Swedish citizens who had mislaid their original passports. What was new about this paperwork was that Swedish papers were being given out to Hungarian Jews whose connections to Sweden were far looser than citizenship. While, as Per Anger explained, provisional passports were given to Swedish citizens, the new paperwork of the *Schutzpass* was given to those 'under the protection of the Swedish embassy' until they were 'able to travel to Sweden'. As he recalled, 'we gave the provisional passport to these persons with very, very close relations to Sweden, and the others who came who had more vague relationship we gave these visas . . . more or less based on instructions from Stockholm, where all who had relatives in Stockholm approached the Foreign Office and asked for help'.[4]

This initial stipulation of at least a 'vague' relationship with Sweden through family, friends or business, was seen by some as rather limiting. Eugenia Szamosi remembered hearing that the Swedish embassy was giving out papers to those with relatives or business contacts in Sweden, but for her Sweden was a place 'very far from' Hungary. It was not a neighbouring country where it was relatively normal to have contacts just over the border, but a distant place that felt very much out of her reach. With no relatives in or connections with Sweden, Eugenia's attention turned, initially, to the Swiss, who had developed a similar scheme of offering protective paperwork, and her husband's Zionist connections.[5]

However, over the course of the late summer and into the autumn of 1944, the nature and extent of the connections to Sweden that Jews applying for protective paperwork needed to have 'became thinner and thinner' and ultimately almost non-existent, in this 'bureaucracy built up to help'. Although Raoul Wallenberg 'had officers who were scrutinising this man's background, how close is his relationship with Sweden, and so on, and they made notes to send it to another bureau and said, well this man is so-and-so, and they had other people who looked at it and said, "oh," and it went around like that,' Per Anger reflected, 'that kind of paperwork was fantastic.'[6] The question of how far some kind of proven relationship with Sweden was essential for getting hold of this paperwork led to a disagreement between István Schalk and his interviewer in a post-war oral history interview. The interviewer's assertion that, in order to limit the number of applicants, it was necessary to produce 'a confirmation letter from Sweden' was roundly rejected by this survivor who had gained Swedish paperwork without anything of the sort. 'Well, we didn't produce anything, that's for sure,' Schalk responded, before recalling that it seemed that Wallenberg's office on the Pest side of the city operated as a production line generating paperwork for whoever lined up to get it. As he explained to his disbelieving interviewer, Wallenberg's office was a place where 'a few people constantly typed the *Schutzpasses* and stuck the photos, stamped and signed the papers. Who knows what was signed by Danielsson [the Swedish ambassador], Wallenberg, the secretaries or the doorman. Nobody was interested in that, the important thing was that there was an illegible signature, a stamp, and the *Schutzpass* was ready, you could take it.'[7]

However, the question of how much paperwork could and should be given out was a moot one and a constant topic of discussion between Per Anger and Raoul Wallenberg. In one sense the sky was the limit. It was simply a question of how quickly papers could be printed up, signed and handed out. Producing paperwork did not have to grapple with the problems of providing transport to Sweden, or places to stay once there. However, there was agreement among Swedish officials that there was a tipping point at which such paperwork would become valueless – literally not worth the paper it was printed on. As Per Anger explained, 'you can't go too far, you can't give 100,000 people. That's impossible to, they will lose their value. So . . . we agreed on maintaining these criteria or having close relationship with Sweden . . . we tried to keep it within a reasonable number'. However, he admitted to a relaxation of the numbers during the late autumn of 1944 when, after the Arrow Cross rise to power, the Swedish legation were more willing to give out papers with 'no limit . . . because then we had nothing to lose'. In order to maintain an impression that only the number of passes agreed with the Hungarian authorities had been issued, numbering only went up to that figure – and then officials began issuing passes again from the start. While the Hungarian authorities had stipulated that slightly fewer than 5,000 Swedish passes could be issued, it seems that in the end roughly four times this figure were typed up and distributed.[8]

The number of passes in circulation was a cause of concern not only to the Hungarian authorities and neutral legations but also Budapest Jews, precisely because this was something the authorities had an eye on. As an array of protective papers emerged during the summer and autumn of 1944, Jews began to rank those seen to offer more potential protection on the basis of how many were thought to be in circulation. Eugenai Szamosi was

typical in thinking that Swiss-issued papers were the least valuable. She had
a clear ranking in her head with Spanish papers listed at the top, followed
by Swedish, with Swiss at the bottom of the pile. Whereas the Spanish
paperwork was something of a rarity and therefore more 'exclusive' and
'valuable', the Swiss paperwork was widely considered to have been produced
in far larger numbers, including by forgers.[9] Survivors recall in the autumn of
1944 a situation where Swiss papers became 'almost worthless because there
were so many forgeries'.[10] Although the Swiss followed the Swedish practice
of numbering and then renumbering passes to create the impression that only
the agreed-upon number of 7,800 had been issued, estimates of the number
in circulation – given the extent of forgery – reach the astonishing figure
of 100,000 or more – enough for one in every two Jews in the city.[11] No
wonder, then, that while one survivor remembered the Swedish *Schutzpass*
as 'the first class one', the Swiss paperwork was something that 'the Arrow
Cross Nazis tore . . . apart in seconds'.[12] It was not that Spain, then Sweden,
then Switzerland, in that order, were deemed safer places for Jews to live. It
was simply that fewer papers were being issued by Spain and there was not a
plethora of forged Spanish papers in circulation (in part because those papers
were considered harder to forge). This meant that Spain and Sweden emerged
as the nations of choice to Budapest Jews seeking safety in another country.

However, the disconnect between paperwork and place that characterized
the Jewish search for refuge during the summer and autumn of 1944 was
narrowed in the late autumn as the protection offered by the neutral legations
assumed a territorial dimension. As early as July and August 1944, it is clear
that plans to protect Jews with bricks and mortar and not simply paperwork
were being actively discussed in Budapest.[13] In late July it seemed that Raoul
Wallenberg was using the extraterritorial status of Swedish legation office
space to house a small number of leading Jews.[14] But more ambitious plans
for separately housing protected Jews were also being discussed.[15] On 29 July
1944, Wallenberg reported that 'negotiations with the foreign ministry' had

led to agreement over 'repatriation' and 'that it is prepared to secure special high-quality housing for our Jews'.[16] A week later, plans that Jews scheduled to emigrate to Sweden would be housed separately appeared more advanced.

On 6 August, Wallenberg reported on his conversation with the Minister for the Interior, who 'told me that he would welcome an even greater number of Jews leaving for Sweden and confirmed that they might be allowed to stay in special houses under Swedish protection before their departure'. He informed his superiors that 'this coming Wednesday or Thursday we will probably be able to empty the rental property Pozsony[i] utca [street] 3, a Jewish house, of its present occupants and replace them with the same number of Jews under the embassy's protection'. Furthermore, 'the adjoining houses in the same street will eventually be transformed into Swedish collective centres' holding 'an average of about a hundred people per house'.[17] It seems that these plans continued to develop.[18] In the middle of August, Wallenberg explained that the deadline for the separate housing of protected Jews had been moved forward to 26 August, leaving him with the 'extremely difficult' task of finding 'suitable houses and apartment houses in such a short time'.[19] It was reported that Wallenberg 'urgently' needed money to lodge '2,000 people in the houses rented by him'.[20]

In the end these plans for separate housing were abandoned, for the time being at least.[21] In a report from mid-September, Wallenberg confirmed that plans for a 'Swedish ghetto' on Pozsonyi Street were 'never carried out due to the changes in the general situation',[22] although it is also clear that there was also vocal opposition from non-protected Jews.[23] As Wallenberg made clear to his superiors, he and his colleagues were operating in a situation very much in flux.[24] But this situation was soon to worsen. By late October, Wallenberg reported that 'since my last report the situation regarding the Hungarian Jews has deteriorated considerably'.[25] This deterioration came as a result of the dramatic political changes, which meant that the neutral powers in Budapest were now negotiating with the native fascist Arrow Cross government.

For the new Arrow Cross puppet government, there was a sense of diplomatic credibility to be gained through their discussions with the neutral powers.[26] Therefore, when plans were unveiled over what to do with Jews remaining in the country, six categories – each receiving separate treatment – were delineated and one of these was Jews under foreign protection.[27] Rather than living in apartment buildings spread throughout the city, Jews remaining in Budapest were concentrated into two ghettos. Jews with protective papers were to move into a loose collection of around 120 apartment buildings scattered over a small number of streets in the Ujlipótváros district of Pest by mid-November. Jews without protective papers who remained in the capital were to move to a fenced ghetto established in the heart of the traditional Jewish quarter in Pest at the end of November. Reporting on these new circumstances in his final 'Memorandum concerning the Situation of the Hungarian Jews' on 12 December, Wallenberg explained that 'the Jews are collected in a central ghetto intended to house 69,000 Jews, but which will probably house more than this number, as well as in a ghetto for foreigners for 17,000, already containing 35,000 of whom 7,000 in Swedish houses, 2,000 in houses belonging to the Red Cross, and 23,000 in Swiss houses'.[28]

Jews were housed in separate Swiss, Swedish, Spanish, Vatican, Portuguese and Red Cross buildings according to the 'proportions' of Jews officially permitted to receive protection from the different neutral powers. In part at least, it seems that the decision to create protected houses was designed to put limits on the mass production of protective paperwork.[29] While paperwork could expand endlessly through bureaucratic renumbering or forgeries, apartment buildings simply could not. It seems that the Hungarian authorities were well aware of the spatial limits of a ghetto and creating protected houses was in part at least an attempt to check the inflation of protective paperwork.

The precise status of these protected buildings was just as nebulous as the precise status of the earlier protective paperwork. It does seem that the idea of extra-territorial sovereign space given to an embassy building was already being stretched and applied to other buildings in Budapest. As Per Anger explained, the building where Raoul Wallenberg worked over in the Pest side of the river on Üllői Street, 'we considered that to be ex-territorial, and right or wrong, I mean, that was the way to do it'.[30] In November the notion of Swedish territory seemed to extend to the thirty or so apartment buildings rented by the embassy in the international ghetto area. Asked directly whether the notion of extra-territoriality was transferred to these buildings as well, Per Anger struggled to answer definitively:

> Well in a way . . . we maintained of course this theory which is I mean it's quite an impossible situation, you can understand that when you come to an embassy you can't just go around and put on signs all over saying this is our territory. How would that end, so to say? And there are also different degrees of ex-territoriality. You have for instance the hundred per cent ex-territorial is of course your main office where you work and so on. And the ambassador's residence. But then you have all the other staff's houses where they live. I think the ex-territorial sort of value diminishes, of course.[31]

However, while the precise legal status of these buildings was hard for an established career diplomat like Per Anger to pin down, they tended to be seen by survivors in much more clear-cut terms as 'Swedish territory'.[32] To all extents and purposes, it seemed like a little bit of Sweden had come to the Danube shore in northern Pest. In November 1944 protected Jews may not have made it to Sweden, but they had made it to a 'Swedish House' with a notice on the door announcing that 'these premises and inhabitants possess extraterritoriality'[33] – and in one survivor's memory, a Swedish flag fluttering in the breeze.[34]

As the neutral legations shifted from issuing paperwork to housing people, the question of the ethics of dividing the city's Jews into two groups – those with and those without protection – was asked with a new urgency by the neutral legations. When discussing how many papers to give out, there was a recognition that in setting a limit to ensure that this paperwork meant something, the implication was that not everyone would get hold of protective paperwork. As the notion of protective paperwork shifted to protected houses, it was clear that there would not be enough room for everyone. More problematically, and something that Raoul Wallenberg was well aware of, the buildings identified as Swedish houses in November 1944 would need to be emptied of those Jews without protected papers who had been living in these houses that made up part of the dispersed ghetto. Back in August, in the early days when the potential separate housing of protected Jews in Budapest was being discussed, Wallenberg was well aware that this would inevitably mean moving unprotected Jews currently living on Pozsonyi Street. He therefore suggested that 'it would be greatly desirable to be able to pay moving costs and limited damages to those Jews who have to in this way suddenly leave their homes'.[35]

In the vast number of cases, the apartment buildings that became Swedish houses were not in a sense simply regular apartment buildings but part of the dispersed ghetto that had been set up in the city in June 1944. The status of these buildings was now shifting, from Jewish house to protected Jewish house. The shift in status necessitated evictions. Here was one downside of Sweden coming to the Danube shore, rather than Jews being taken to Sweden. Whether the Jews living in the buildings that were now under Swedish control had the right paperwork or not was the critical question. If they did, they could stay. If they did not, they had to leave. Unprotected Jews were evicted from their homes and sent to another world: the crowded Pest ghetto, which was a place that, as one survivor recalled, 'everybody who had any means avoided'.[36]

This division of the city's Jews into two separate ghetto areas – one the closed Pest ghetto in the traditional Jewish quarter in the heart of the city, and the other a cluster of interwar apartment buildings in the newly developed middle-class suburb on the Danube shore – was a hardening of a broader division. It was a division between those who had and those who did not have the protective paperwork issued by the neutral legations in Budapest in the second half of 1944. But beneath that division lay an even more troubling one that contemporaries picked up on. It seemed that this was also a division between two broadly different groups of Jews.

In her reflections on the creation of these two ghettos in Budapest in the winter of 1944, Judit Brody – an eleven-year-old girl living with her parents at the time – saw some 'reason in the madness' of placing the two ghettos where they were. Describing the Swedish protected house where she lived with her family, Judit explained that it was one of 'a handful of buildings interspersed among other blocks of flats where gentiles could stay put and it was in a newer part of town, home for many middle-class non-religious Jews'. In contrast, she described the Pest ghetto where 'those with no protection were ordered to move' as sited 'behind the big synagogue, the area of town where mostly religious Jews lived. The few gentiles who lived there had to move out. There was some reason in madness.'[37] For Judit, there were broadly two different groups of Jews living in Budapest – 'middle-class non-religious Jews' and 'mostly religious Jews' – who were placed into two different ghettos sited in effect where these two distinct groups already lived. Judit was not alone in her thinking. Contemporaries made connections between the locating of the international ghetto in one of the wealthiest parts of Budapest and the assumption that those protected were a privileged elite.[38] In short, it seemed that the two ghettos in Budapest in the winter of 1944 came to represent two different groups of Jews.

Judit's hunch is borne out by looking at the largest surviving list of Jews under Swedish protection – a 447-page bound volume with the names of 6,686 Jews.[39] This list does not contain all the Jews rescued by Raoul Wallenberg, let alone all the Jews rescued by the neutral powers in 1944. However, it is suggestive in pointing to the very high numbers of Jews rescued by Wallenberg who came from the city's fifth district. This was the neighbourhood where the international ghetto was created and a place that had emerged as an area 'where mostly well off Jews lived',[40] in what one survivor dubbed 'the rich part of Budapest'.[41] Not only was the Swedish list dominated by Jews from the fifth district – they make up over four out of every ten names on the list – but the single street from that district that appeared on the list again and again was Pozsonyi Street, which had been the centre of Wallenberg's focus in August 1944 and formed the heart of the international ghetto in November 1944. Reading through the Swedish list, it is striking how many family names and first names are Magyarized or Germanized. This was a list dominated by assimilated middle-class Jews. It appears that Judit Brody was right in her sense that there was method in the madness when it came to choice of location for the international ghetto. It was sited where the majority of protected Jews already lived.

That Jews with protective papers were not a representative sample of Jews living in the city but represented a middle-class elite was no doubt in part a reflection of the fact that, initially at least, a connection with Sweden – for example through business links – was a reason for getting hold of this paperwork. According to Laura Palosuo and Attila Lajos, Jews of higher social class and with connections were more likely to get hold of documents from the neutral powers, although Palosuo suggests that 'during the autumn, the neutral legations differentiated less between individuals seeking help, and the social background of the protected became more diverse'.[42]

But there was also a flourishing market in protective paperwork. Wallenberg himself became aware that Swedish papers were being bought and sold.[43] He reported to Stockholm, 'We have been told that people have sometimes made financial sacrifices to secure a protective or provisional passport', pointing in particular to 'unscrupulous lawyers' who 'have taken advantage of the precarious situation of the Jewish population and exacted large fees to handle the application for a protective passport', with unwarranted claims that they 'have connections among the staff'.[44] Some survivors certainly recall money changing hands as protective paperwork – whether forged or real – was secured.[45] Rumours were circulating that people were paying 10,000 pengö to be sheltered in Swedish embassy buildings.[46] One child survivor who had received Swedish papers through her uncle remembered being told by her father in 1945, 'Dear children, you should know this eleven months cost me over a million American dollars.'[47]

By the time that the international ghetto was set up there were a lot of Jews with protective paperwork to fit into these houses, indeed too many. As one explained, 'there wasn't any room for us in the protected house, it was so overcrowded', and so with that 'house . . . full, we couldn't go there', and it felt that having a 'pass' was 'in vain'.[48] For those who did manage to get inside they found that conditions were extremely cramped.[49] 'It was literally wall to wall people at night,' one survivor recalled, with 'something like 70 people in the apartment'.[50] With so many people, the line to get to the bathroom was 'two hours' or 'perhaps even more'.[51] 'So many documents had been printed and issued,' one survivor later wrote, 'the interior of the building looked like rush hour on the subway,' where he and his family made their 'home' on a 'stair between the second and third floors'.[52]

Jews in Budapest had got used to a certain amount of overcrowding as a result of the introduction of a dispersed form of ghetto in the city in June 1944, where the norm was that each family received one room to live in. Agnes Aranyi's experience was fairly typical of other Jews living in the dispersed ghetto in the city. The apartment building where she lived was not one of those designated, so they had to move in with her aunt in another building. This two-room apartment now housed Agnes, her mother, her grandfather and grandmother along with her aunt and her two cousins. Agnes slept in one room with her mother and grandmother. Her aunt slept in the other with her cousins and grandfather. There was not a lot of space.

However, this sense of overcrowding was nothing compared to their experience after they received Swedish papers and moved into one of the Swedish protected houses. Getting in was a struggle. Despite having the correct paperwork, the caretaker was not keen to allow anyone else into what was already an overcrowded building. When the caretaker was finally persuaded, Agnes and her mother found themselves in a two-room apartment that seemed to house sixty people already. 'It was just a horribly busy place,' Agnes recalled, and she and her mother spent six weeks sleeping on the floor in the corner of the room. Over the weeks, they were joined by other family members. Once her grandmother arrived, space was made for her – as the oldest person in the apartment – to enjoy 'the prime place' to sleep: the bathtub, which was the closest thing to a 'bed' in the place.[53] The move from Jewish house to Swedish house was a move into less and less space. As another survivor recalled, 'the Jewish houses were not over-crowded, but the protected houses were crammed with people. I, for instance, shared a tiny room with six other people.'[54]

The Swedish houses may have been more crowded than the Jewish houses that people moved from, but the critical question was whether they were safer because they were under the flag of one of the neutral powers. How safe they were, was a moot point. In their retelling, it is striking that survivors oftentimes add a caveat when talking about these so-called protected houses. Agnes Aranyi clarified that it was a 'safe, quote safe unquote place'.[55] Another explained that these houses did not offer 'full protection'.[56] Asked directly 'how safe' was the Spanish 'safe house' that she lived in, another survivor replied immediately 'it wasn't safe. It wasn't safe', before nuancing her answer somewhat:

> it was safe because it was protected by the Spanish flag, so maybe some Hungarians or some Germans maybe respected or respected not. But because we didn't know this, whether they would respect us, we were in constant fear . . . So we . . . we were protected by them, it's true. They risked their lives, but we didn't know whether we were protected. Why? Because we heard the rumours that the Hungarians . . . uh . . . Nazis, they are going to even to the protected homes and try to take out people.[57]

It seems that some regarded the Spanish houses – like the Spanish paperwork – as the safest of the lot.[58] But even in these houses it is clear that so-called protected Jews did not feel entirely safe. Living in one of the 'safeguarded sections of Budapest', one survivor nuanced this description by adding the caveat that while 'for a long time this worked', the safety offered by the international ghetto was not permanent and certain.[59]

Initially, Lilly Schwarz Gach felt a sense of relief when she and her husband and daughter got hold of Swedish papers. Armed with this paperwork and no longer wearing the yellow star, it seemed to them that they were 'Swedish subjects' rather than solely or primarily Hungarian Jews. However, the safety offered by this newly acquired paperwork and by moving into one of the Swedish houses quickly became seen as more fragile. Arriving in the Swedish house – 'a very beautiful house' over 'four or five floors' – Lilly saw how overcrowded this building was. It seemed to her that 'everything was mattresses', with even the kitchen floor covered with mattresses. She and her husband were unsure of the wisdom of moving in. As she explained, they left in the afternoon and 'never came back because we decided . . . this is a collection for only Jews'. Such sentiments were shared by others. As one survivor reflected, 'I felt that a place where there were so many Jews together was more dangerous than the Jewish house of which there were a lot scattered all over Budapest.'[60] In this overcrowded Swedish house where people slept on every square inch of floor space, the earlier sense of safety – if not a new identity – offered by Swedish paperwork dissipated one mattress at a time. It seemed to Lilly and her husband that this was little more than a gathering point for Jews that could and would be raided, rather than a safe refuge. Instead of returning to the Swedish house, they went to an apartment building that they owned where one of her husband's former employees was the caretaker.[61] Pre-existing social networks and hiding places seemed to offer more safety than Swedish paperwork and the claims to extraterritoriality stretching across a section of apartment buildings close to the Danube shore.

An almost identical story can be found in Eva Brust Cooper's recollections. Like Lilly, Eva and her parents got hold of Swedish protective papers and made their way to one of the protected houses. However, after one night in this overcrowded house, filled with what seemed to Eva to be 'hundreds and hundreds and hundreds of people', her parents decided that 'there were just too many Jews under one roof' here and they would be safer somewhere else. They spent the next few nights in different houses before, like Lilly, moving into an apartment building they owned where the caretaker housed them. Ultimately, they decided that they would be better off leaving Budapest entirely and fled the capital to hide in the countryside.[62]

The overcrowding within the Swedish houses was not simply experienced or seen as uncomfortable. It transformed these places that seemed to offer protection into what families like Lilly and Eva feared would simply be easy pickings, given the housing together of so many Jews in one place. For both Lilly and Eva, the Swedish houses on the banks of the Danube were not Sweden – a place removed from the reach of anti-Jewish forces. The claims of the Swedish houses to extra-territoriality were seen by both Lilly and Eva as far from secure. However, their decision to leave the Swedish houses was not just based on a reckoning that these were not entirely safe places, but that being with large numbers of other Jews was far from safe. It was the numbers crammed into these houses that made Lilly and Eva question the safety of these places. So many Jews in one place felt to them like being a sitting target. It was better and safer, they thought, to hide elsewhere and hide alone, away from other Jews. They saw that while these houses were international, they were simultaneously a ghetto. The international ghetto was officially a gathering place for Jews with provisional passports prior to emigration to neutral countries at the end of the war. However, what Lilly and Eva feared was that this ghetto might be a gathering place of another sort – prior to deportation or execution.

In the chaos of winter 1944 it is clear that their fears were not entirely unfounded. Protected Jews from protected houses in the international ghetto were being rounded up, marched to the Danube and shot into the river by armed *Nyilas* gangs that ignored the paperwork of protection. Indeed it seems that the international ghetto houses along the northern Pest banks of the Danube were specifically targeted. In part this may have been because these were widely known to be home to wealthier Jews. Certainly robbery was one of the tactics of these gangs. That sense of being specifically targeted was something that Paul Milch – living in the international ghetto in the winter of 1944 – suggested as he explained how 'the Swiss protected house was not protective enough to stop the Arrow Cross from performing periodic raids'. It felt to Paul in the late autumn and winter of 1944 that he and his family were threatened in two ways – by Allied bombing of the city and by Arrow Cross raids. As he explained, the former were feared less, and indeed preferred. 'Often when these raids from the Arrow Cross came,' Paul explained:

> we were praying that an air raid would come. Because . . . once or twice that did happen and that sent them scurrying. We felt that . . . we were safer under the air raids than under the raids of the Arrow Cross because they were seeking you know us particularly, whereas the Anglo-American bombers were just dropping bombs perhaps indiscriminately. We had better chance against that, by being down in the cellar . . .[63]

In contrast to indiscriminate bombing, it seemed that Arrow Cross raids were targeted at Jews gathered in the protected houses.

There was something incongruous about 'people from the Swedish protected houses . . . also [being] taken to the Danube embankment to be executed'.[64] This sense of how things changed was something that Per Anger himself noticed and acknowledged. As he explained:

> taking them under a kind of diplomatic protection, of course, was very much a bluff. But the Hungarians, they . . . sort of accepted it mostly to start

with. It wasn't till . . . the *Nyilas* the Arrow Cross people took over, when everything was violated. Everything. But as long as the first Hungarian government . . . was in power, and the Germans also, they never violated . . . our premises.[65]

Compared to negotiations with the Hungarian government in the summer of 1944, when the idea of mass issuing of provisional passports was first raised, 'October was very difficult,' Per Anger admitted. It was a time characterized by:

ghastly stories about how they were lined up along the Danube and shot and thrown into the Danube afterwards. One or two of them managed to save their lives because they were not that wounded and managed to swim and come back and told the stories from those who had saved their lives a few of them not many, what happened and so on.[66]

Giorgio Perlasca, working for the Spanish embassy, went as far as claiming that 'after the middle of November until the arrival of the Russians, the Swedish embassy didn't count anymore'. He continued, 'all the deportations from Szent Istvan Park were in connection with the Swedes or the Swiss. They were the only ones raided. Raided. Raided means that they were taken away . . . any time I saw a column of Jews march, encircled by the police and *Nyilas*, I asked who they were. And 80% were Swedes, and the rest 20% were Swiss, some people from the Vatican or something else.'[67] His reflections sound a little like one-upmanship, but it was clear to all that the international ghetto was far from a safe place.

Not all protected houses were targeted. But many were. Agnes Grossman Aranyi discovered that the 'protected environment' where she lived was only 'a seemingly protected environment'. Her Swedish house was entered and the inhabitants were taken to the closed ghetto established in the traditional quarter around the main Dohány Street synagogue, where they lived in the cellar until liberation by the Soviets. This round-up felt to Agnes like the invasion of a neutral country. She 'could not comprehend' how the *Nyilas* gangs could 'invade us' and 'round us up . . . in a protected house'.[68] In many ways Agnes was relatively fortunate. She was taken from the Swedish house to the main ghetto set up in the city. Others were marched just a couple of streets away to the Danube shore for – as the *Nyilas* guards mockingly phrased it – 'a good swim'.[69]

As they were being marched away from these Swedish houses in the winter of 1944, the city's Jewish inhabitants were well aware of the two places that were their most likely destination – either the Pest ghetto or the Danube shore – and what these destinations meant. Because they knew the city well, individuals were attuned to what taking a left here, or a right there, might mean in terms of which of these two places they were being marched to. As one child survivor from Budapest retold his family's experience of being taken through the fraught geography of the city's streets:

> We're being escorted slowly toward St Stephen Boulevard. Once on it, we'll find out which way the Arrow Cross will make us turn. Right, and we'll be facing the bridge. The river. Left, and they'll be taking us to the ghetto. No one knows which way we are going to turn.[70]

It is hard to put accurate figures on how many Jews were taken down to the river and shot into the Danube. No records were kept during this chaotic winter. However, it does seem that this was a mass phenomenon undertaken by as many as 4,000 armed *Nyilas* members.[71] In the winter of 1944 large numbers of Budapest Jews were killed by their neighbours in mass shootings into the river, which washed them downstream. It was not the first time that the Danube had been used as a disposal site for Jewish bodies. In January 1942, Jews were shot into the frozen river at a 'bathing spot' in Novi Sad on the southern border of Hungary.[72] However, the killings in 1944 were on a far larger scale and in the centre of a capital city rather than at the periphery in the borderlands.

When Jews were marched to the banks of the Danube and shot into the river in the winter of 1944, this marked the extension of the so-called 'bloodlands' into the very heart of a European capital city. This was not mass killing at some distant site, far removed, but killings much closer to home. In some ways it seems that things had come full circle, including some parallels with the first waves of shootings from 1941 onwards on the edge of towns and villages in former Soviet territory. Those killings close to home were, by and large, replaced by the relocations that characterized mass deportations to the Operation Reinhard camps in 1942 and 1943 and finally to Auschwitz-Birkenau in 1943 and 1944. Jews living in provincial Hungary – like David Bergman and his family – were taken by train to Auschwitz in the summer of 1944 in what was the final large-scale mass deportation of a nation's Jews. Six months later, the situation had changed. Rather than taking the Jews to the killers, the killers came to the Jews in Budapest – this time the more ad hoc mass shootings of Jews by native fascist gangs. The Danube was the backdrop to these mass shootings. It could both assist in the killings – one person could be shot, dragging all those tied to him into the river to drown – and the disposal of the corpses.[73] The river could, quite literally, cleanse its own city of its Jews – taking them away downstream, out of sight and out of mind.

As with the earlier killings in and around towns and villages across former Soviet lands, the sites of these killings were very much in the locality. They took place under the gaze of neighbours. They took place at the hands of neighbours. The site of killing persisted like a sore in the heart of the city. The river provided a constant reminder to survivors in the post-war period, who lost relatives during this wave of killings in the winter of 1944–5. Adam Biro tells of the murder of his grandfather and uncle who were shot into the Danube close to the Chain Bridge, which he lived nearby for the next decade. While his parents would go each year to throw two red roses into the Danube, his grandmother refused to go anywhere near the place. Forced to cross the river to go to a hospital in Buda, she averted her gaze so that she would not see the water that had been, and still was, her husband's grave.[74]

These killings were part of the end game of the war, when the 'bloodlands' were pushed westwards. During these last months of the conflict, the 'bloodlands' was a space on the edges of Nazi control, an area in flux with the ebb and flow of the war and territorial gains followed by territorial losses. In the winter of 1944, Budapest was briefly a space at the very edge of German-controlled Europe – close to the advancing Red Army – and this buffer zone became a site of opportunity for *Nyilas* gangs to rob and kill. In this narrow space between the advancing Soviet army and the retreating German army, a European capital city was turned, for a couple of months, into a massacre site. Here, all notions of Sweden and the other neutral legations coming to the banks of the Danube, which had seemed to promise so much in the summer of 1944, were cruelly threatened and undone in the chaotic winter of 1944 when Budapest briefly became a war zone.

The 'bloodlands' continued to be pushed westwards. In 1945 the roads (and railroads) of Germany became a deadly space as prisoners from the camp system were evacuated westwards on so-called 'death marches'. This westward movement of prisoners on foot is something that took place out of Budapest in the winter of 1944 as thousands of Budapest Jews – largely women – were taken towards the Austrian border. Men and women from their teens into their forties and fifties were mobilized for labour and marched west, not sure of their final destination, pausing to sleep in whatever buildings were to hand.[75] After a week or more marching, they were put to work building fortifications in an attempt to halt the Soviet advance. As the Soviets pushed westwards, these prisoners marched out of Budapest in November and December 1944 oftentimes found themselves on the road again in the spring of 1945 walking 'from village to village' and camp to camp, as the road network of Europe became a key Holocaust landscape.[76]

Road

In the final months of the war, prisoners were marched on the roads of the shrinking Reich. As the Soviets advanced westwards, camps were rapidly closed down and in some cases destroyed. Entire camp populations – prisoners and guards – were on the move. In mid-January 1945, Auschwitz was evacuated and close to 56,000 prisoners took to the roads. These 'death marches', as survivors generally refer to them, were neither the first nor last mass evacuations. In the summer of 1944 there had been a small number of early evacuations on foot further east in the Baltic States and Poland ahead of the Soviet advance.[1] In the late spring and early summer of 1945 there were a larger number of evacuations further west in the ever-shrinking territory of the Reich.[2]

In the first half of 1945, Nina Kaleska experienced both waves of hurried evacuations. In January she left Auschwitz on foot, before being taken by train to Ravensbrück. After a few weeks dominated by vague memories of 'masses of people, death, terrible starvation, no work', Nina was taken to a labour camp in Retzoif-am-Richlin. But at the end of April she was on the move again. Nina and her fellow prisoners were hurriedly evacuated in the middle of the night, and the days that followed were ones of relentless walking:

No idea where we were walking . . . at this point here, Germany was combined of a tiny little spot where the Americans and the English and the

Russians and the French on all sides. They kept going with us. Of course, they the guards were much more relaxed. They knew that this is the end. There was just no way, but they kept walking us, for week . . . a lot of people couldn't make it and went by the wayside . . . we went on and on and on, finally we couldn't really walk anymore.[3]

The evacuations in January 1945 saw thousands marched through the snow of a particularly cold winter. Marching was perhaps not the best word to describe the scene of hundreds sliding along the icy surface of snow-covered roads. A Jewish woman from Vilnius who had moved westwards through a series of camps, Lily Margules, explained how 'you couldn't walk on the snow with the wooden shoes' that she and her fellow prisoners wore, and so she ended up looking like 'a circus performer', slipping and sliding along.[4] For one survivor of several evacuation marches, it came as something of a relief once spring came, and with less cold weather it was more 'comfortable walking in our wooden slippers', although they had to be 'careful not to step into the many puddles that the mild weather had created from the melting snow'.[5] In summer it was not snow that posed the greater challenge to those being marched along miles of Europe's roads, but rather the dust kicked up by the hundreds and hundreds of other feet.[6]

However, there were more significant differences between the two times that Nina found herself on the road than simply the temperature and conditions underfoot. In January 1945 there were still camps in the west that prisoners could be sent to, although these were quickly becoming overcrowded as Nina discovered when she ended up in Ravensbrück. Her experience of being evacuated – by a mixture of road and rail – from Auschwitz to Ravensbrück was one shared by the Laks sisters, who made the same journey from one fixed site of incarceration to another. By April 1945, however, as the Allied advance continued and picked up pace, the number of camps operating was rapidly shrinking and those few still functioning were horribly overcrowded. At this very late stage in the war it was not uncommon for columns of prisoners to be turned away from overcrowded camps and sent back on the road in search of another camp. One survivor left Wattenstedt in early April 1945 and recalled a list of aborted destinations – 'we came first to Belsen, where luckily for us there was no more place, then to Sachsenhausen, they did not want us there either' – before 'finally we came to Ravensbrück on the 14th April in the middle of the night'. Here they spent the next week or so. On 25 April they were marched 'westwards' for three days, 'doing 20–25 km daily, with very little to eat', before stopping at 'a small concentration camp, near an ammunition factory' in Malchow. After 'one day and one night' there was 'another hurried departure caused by the approach of Russian troops' and so they hit the road again. Two more days walking brought them to Lobs, which is where they were liberated on 1 May 1945 when they 'met American light armoured vehicles and our guards run away'.[7]

This experience of being shuttled back and forth in an increasingly narrow corridor of land between the Allied advance from both east and west in the final weeks of the war was relatively common. Rather than there being a clear plan, survivors had the sense that their captors 'didn't know what to do with us', except to keep on the move. With 'the place . . . overrun by the Allied armies . . . they didn't want us to fall into their hands, so they kept us away'.[8] After 'going from here to there by foot, by train' during March and April 1945,[9] it seemed that their guards 'didn't know where to put us anymore'.[10] Kitty Hart reflected that when she and her mother left one of the Gross-Rosen sub-camps on foot, it was not only the case that they had 'no idea where we were going', but it also seemed that their guards were 'not . . . much wiser'.[11] Her sentiments were echoed by another survivor who was sure that 'the Germans themselves hardly knew what was going on'.[12]

Those who survived these final 'completely senseless' journeys saw themselves caught up in the chaos of the final weeks of the war during which their guards' chief concern was keeping away from the Allied advance.[13]

Although this was particularly marked in April 1945, the priority given to departure from soon-to-be-liberated camps can also be seen in the earlier waves of evacuations such as those from Auschwitz a few months earlier in January. That these were primarily journeys away from somewhere meant that this mass movement of prisoners was radically different from the earlier experiences of prisoners being moved around the camp system, as characterized by David Bergman's constant redeployment within the slave-labour economy. Rather than relocating a labour force across the continent, these were mass evacuations that involved emptying out an entire camp population – or at least all those deemed fit enough to walk. Rather than simply being a group of prisoners on the move, this was the camp itself on the move. In January 1945 it was not simply a case of Nina Kaleska or the Laks sisters leaving Auschwitz, along with tens of thousands of other prisoners. Auschwitz itself took to the road, complete with both prisoners and guards. And this experience of the whole camp in motion was one that was repeated again and again over the following months as first one camp and then another took to the road.

As the entire camp was placed on the road, the rhythms of camp life were adapted to the new environment and experience of movement. The rhythm of work details and sleep punctuated by roll calls was replaced with a new rhythm of marching and trying to get some rest before 'in the morning', Lily Margules recalled, 'we had to . . . straighten ourselves, put ourselves in a column. They will count us. And we will go forwards.'[14] Without the infrastructure of the camp on the road, requisitioned barns were turned into makeshift barracks where prisoners collapsed exhausted. Miriam Farcus Ingber, a Jewish woman from Czechoslovakia deported to Auschwitz and then Stutthof, remembers the entire column of what she estimated to be 5,000 women being shoved into a large barn for the night. Feeling cold and hungry, she recalled scavenging for 'potato peels' or anything left behind in the 'cans that the soldiers throw away' in the 'garbage', given that prisoners were no longer being systematically fed even the meagre rations of the camp system.[15]

Miriam's memory of something like 5,000 women crowded into one barn is a powerful image of the breakdown of the architecture of the camp as it took to the road. Gone were the rows of barracks. Also gone were the demarcated zones that kept prisoners apart from others. With the disappearance of the internal boundaries between sections, which was so characteristic of a place like Auschwitz, the strict segregation of distinct prisoner populations was replaced by a mixing of bodies within what one survivor described as a human 'snowball' that gathered 'a lot of people' from different camps, sub-camps or parts of camps along the route of the march.[16] As lines of prisoners came together, the strict gendered divisions of the camp began to fray. Leaving Auschwitz in January 1945, one woman remembered, 'as we walked out we met the men, who had been separated from us by barbed wire, and we started to march together'.[17] Bela Blau, who also left Auschwitz in 1945, recollected that after a few days on the road 'we collided with the women' who 'came from a different way' at an intersection. This coming together of prisoners who had been separated in gendered zones or camps for months or years was seized upon as an opportunity to try to find out what had happened to family members. 'The women, they looked for men,' Bela remembered, and:

> the men looked for women, if somebody's there – relation, friend or something . . . the girls went to the SS woman asking for permission, if they could give them a permission to talk to us because somebody recognized me there from one of her friends and told that 'Bela is there. Try what you can do.' But meantimes a big crowd started, because such a mass of people, two or four SS woman or men couldn't keep uh back even if they would start to shoot or whatever. So they started a big crowd; and we somehow came close to each other and we spoke a few words . . . to each other.[18]

It was not unusual for lines of prisoners to come together on the road, separate out again and head along different tracks before coming together again. Mapping these shifting journeys as groups shrank and grew, and then shrank again, posed a challenge to post-war investigators from the International Tracing Service. They quickly became aware that while marches might have the same start point and end goal, this did not mean that the march took a single, shared route between a and b. In their paperwork, there are plenty of cases of marches dividing and going off on different routes and then coming back together, but with many fewer prisoners than a couple of days before.

The sheer number of casualties on these evacuations – and hence the reason that survivors dub them 'death marches' – meant that prisoners' encounters with family members of the opposite sex on the road or in cattle wagons were not always with living people. For some, their encounters were with the corpses of prisoners who had been marched before them and shot by the roadside. One woman described her experience of walking along the snow-covered roads away from Auschwitz in January 1945, where:

> on the sides of the streets we saw bodies of men who were evidently taking the same road before us. They were chased out before us and many of them, a lot of them did not survive. And we saw a leg or a hand or a nose sticking out . . . from the snow and we realized that this is what happens. So it made our journey that much worse because we wanted to see when we saw somebody if it was not anybody, my father, my brother or somebody else, whatever.[19]

On these roads that 'were littered with dead prisoners all the way', evacuated prisoners were aware that among those corpses might be family members or friends.[20]

The presence of corpses along the roads was evidence that while the incarceratory architecture of the camp had been disrupted, it had not entirely disappeared. Both internal and external barbed-wire fences were left behind as the camps took to the roads, but this did not mean that all boundaries had disappeared. Far from it. Instead, the camp fence was replaced by another moving and arguably more deadly boundary – the intersecting sightlines of armed guards who accompanied the columns of prisoners. In the camps, throwing yourself onto the electrified fence was a choice – albeit something of a 'choiceless' one – to commit suicide rather than be killed. However, when the camp took to the road, something as simple as falling down or lagging behind as a result of their terribly emaciated state meant that prisoners were ruthlessly disposed of with a shot to the head.

Writing of the death marches, Daniel Blatman tends towards a rather literal reading of the camp boundary and argues that 'the moment the prisoners left the camps, the spatial dimension of the murders changed, as did the circumstances and reasons for their liquidation'. For Blatman, the killings on the death march took place 'outside the fence perimeters . . . when the prisoners were no longer under detention', and so he argues that these 'murders had different motives and were perpetrated by different people'.[21] However, both guards and prisoners clearly saw these marches to be bounded spaces. The electrified, barbed-wire fence was gone from these camps in motion. It had been replaced with a new boundary where the idea of what constituted escape had been reworked to mean not only an active choice to flee, but failing to remain within the shifting boundaries of the march.

Given that something as simple as falling down now meant a death sentence, the condition of prisoners before, and as, they set out was critical. Because they had managed to find privileged work sorting clothes in Auschwitz, the Laks sisters had managed to get hold of 'warmer clothing, better shoes'.[22] Shoes and clothes had been vital in order to navigate the mud in Auschwitz. They were equally, if not more, important when Auschwitz took to the snow-covered roads. This comes through in an oral history interview with Edgar Krasa – deported in 1944 to Auschwitz from Theresienstadt – who retold in considerable detail finding 'a piece of wax cloth' in a barn where they slept for the night during the evacuation march. His discovery of what appeared to be something of little importance was, for Edgar, no minor matter. He used this fragment to patch a missing piece

from the shoe where 'two sharp corners were digging into my foot'.[23] This
meant he could keep marching, which during the evacuations was critical
for survival. No wonder that, like in Auschwitz, one of the first things to go
from the bodies of the dead were their shoes and clothes.[24]

But as well as recognizing the importance of their footwear, marchers also
adopted spatial strategies as they sought to survive the evacuations. Although
they were surrounded by guards on all four sides, it was clear that the greatest
danger lay at the rear of the column where the boundary created by armed
guards appeared particularly fast-moving and deadly as they pushed the
prisoners westwards. As a result, prisoners sought out a place of greater safety
towards the front of the long line of marchers.[25] Magda Blau explained that
her 'aim was, "Girls, we in the front" because in the back they was shooting
everybody'.[26] Lily Margules recalled that 'we had like a kind of coalition, and
we knew the only way we can survive if we will stay in the front. Because if you
were staying in the back and you couldn't walk with the column, you were just
shot.'[27] For William Luksenburg:

> the way you march is when you look around you find yourself to be the
> last one in the column. You don't want to be the last one because you get
> the last one, you mostly get shot, so you push forward. You constantly
> without anybody prodding you, we were moving fast because nobody
> wanted to be the last. The minute you look around and you find yourself
> the last in the column, you go beyond everybody, push forward, till you
> fall back again, and me being so emaciated and couldn't walk anymore,
> every time I heard a shot, you heard shots all night long . . . I felt it's going
> to be me next.[28]

The sound of shots at the rear of the march crop up again and again in
survivors' accounts. If transport by train was characterized by the appalling
stench, evacuation from the camps by road was accompanied by the sounds of
shots being fired.

In order to try to keep away from the rear of the march and to keep going despite their emaciated state, prisoners sought to be part of what Lily Margules called a 'coalition'. Because falling down in the mobile camp meant summary execution by their guards, prisoners became increasingly dependent on each other for their survival. Chris Laks recalled that on the march out of Auschwitz she and her sister Hania 'had a problem with Renia because she just could not walk. She was very sleepy and we knew that no sooner will she sit down at the edge of the road . . . whoever sat down or bent over or ran into the field to relive themselves or whatever were shot to death.' In order to keep Renia moving, Chris explained that 'Hania and I grabbed her under her arms and we dragged her . . . Renia didn't have to walk. She was just sliding along.'[29]

Renia could only vaguely remember this experience of movement through the Polish countryside when it seemed to her that she had been 'sleepwalking', as 'Chris and Hania were dragging me'.[30] Carola Steinhardt also recounted sleep-walking as 'one helped' her on one side and another 'on the other side'. 'That's how we went on,' she explained, with the group being the agent on the move.[31] This sense of commingling of bodies on the crowded roads that was seen as essential to survival extended to those moments when the march was paused and prisoners were herded into a barn or church to rest. One man who was marched through Germany in the winter and early spring of 1945 recalled a 'horrible night' spent sleeping on the 'cold stone floor' of a village church 'totally exhausted and shivering with fever. The blanket offers no protection from the iciness under me, nor from the freezing air coming through cracks in the door and the windows. We move close together to warm each other.'[32] Miriam Farcus Ingber remembered how when they were trying to sleep at night, 'we pulled ourselves together, you know, like this, and we was like this, you know, one on top of the other warming up and we tried to sleep a little bit till they came out and took us further'.[33]

Those who survived the death marches described their survival (and explained their survival) in terms of these being profoundly communal events.

This was not an experience of hundreds and thousands of men and women marching on their own, but rather an experience of a commingling of bodies, so it was hard to say who was doing what and where one body ended and another began. Hania Laks was sure that she had been carried by her sisters, rather than doing any carrying herself.[34] Retelling the march, the three sisters with their limbs intertwined appear as a kind of three-person unit pulling and sliding along the snow-covered road, such that it was unclear to each of them exactly who was doing what.

The importance of intertwined micro-communities on the move was one thing when all survived the death march, as was the case for the Laks sisters. It was a much more problematic story to retell when one part of what seemed almost a single organism did not survive. Even when agency lay with the guard doing the shooting, these are hard stories to retell. Lily Margules was reduced to tears as she explained that 'we started to walk and we were a group of young girls that were very close . . . together', and so:

> we actually supported ourselves . . . One of my friends started to feel bad and we took her and I was from one side and another of my friend and we were dragging her, practically dragging her. She couldn't help. Legs were frozen. So the guard noticed it. He he he told the column to stop. He took her to a certain field and we heard the shot. He shot her right there.[35]

In other tellings, agency lay with the fellow marcher who could continue no longer. The German Jewish survivor James Bachner described how his friend Wally 'began to complain that he couldn't keep up with us any longer and, even with support from Peter and me, he tripped and fell often'. 'Finally,' James wrote:

> Wally could no longer hang onto us. He pushed us away, lowered himself to the ground, and refused to listen to us any longer. Weakened as we were and blocking the road for others, there was nothing we could do to save him as

we were being pushed forward. I turned and waved to him one more time, and his last bit of strength, he lifted his arm for a final good-bye.[36]

A similar sense of agency lying ultimately with a weakening friend can be seen in the Czech-Jewish actress Hana Pravda's description of how:

On the march all the horrors caused her [Anča] to lose her mind and she refused to carry on. Three of the girls and I tried desperately to lift her from the ground, but again and again she lay back on the snowy road – she fell from our hands. Her eyes were calm, as if made of glass, and she was looking beyond this world and simply refused to go on. We had to leave her to walk in the snow on the frozen road. They were chasing us to go on. In about two or three minutes we heard a shot and Anča didn't live any more. Altogether they have shot about 15 girls on the march.[37]

More difficult were those narratives where the survivor felt a sense of guilt for what felt like an act of abandoning one member of the group on the road during the march. Edgar Krasa was evacuated from the labour camp at Gleiwitz, which was on the route for many evacuated from Auschwitz. Like others, he walked with those he knew beside him – two 'kids' who had latched themselves on to him during the original deportation from Theresienstadt to Auschwitz. Their sheer physical closeness during the march meant that limbs entwined as they helped each other along. Edgar and 'one of the kids' half-carried someone who was struggling to walk. 'And we could do it as . . . long as he could move his feet his legs forward,' Edgar explained. 'But then he became totally heavy, we had a dead weight, and we ourselves were already weak. So we just couldn't continue to drag him.' Holding the man's upper body, Edgar and his partner could just about keep the man moving when his legs were also moving. Once they stopped, this became impossible. They had to let go of what was now 'a dead weight', who (or in Edgar's telling 'that') was dispensed with a single shot. 'When we heard the shot it was like it felt like I was shot,'

Edgar explained, confessing that he 'felt guilty that I didn't try more'.[38] In his retelling, Edgar moved from describing a friend and human being to an object – and a negative object at that – that they had little choice but to rid themselves of. However, even this narrative strategy failed to completely assuage a sense of guilt. Getting rid of the 'dead weight' was the logical thing to do, but Edgar continued to wonder whether it was the right thing to do.

Roadside shootings feature time and time again in survivors' recollections of these 'death marches', shifting between brief references to the anonymous victims of the guards and much lengthier descriptions of the killings of named friends. Marchers were clear that 'as we went along, the number was coming down by . . . people dropping down from exhaustion, fever, from whatever' and as 'more and more couldn't go – they were shot'.[39] The detailed recounting of specific acts of violence contrasts with what one survivor described as something of a 'blank' when it came to trying to remember being evacuated from Auschwitz.[40] Renia Laks' experience of 'sleepwalking' or being moved through an almost dream-like or 'fantasy' black and white landscape – literally whited out by snow – is one shared by others.[41] Susan Silas, a Jewish-American photographer who rewalked the route of one of the death marches and produced a series of photographs of the landscape of the road, was struck by this recollection of the cold when she spoke with a survivor. When Susan asked her what she remembered of the landscape the marchers walked through, the survivor told her that she could recall the cold, the cruel guards and her friends, but nothing of the 'scenery' that they marched through.[42]

This sense of almost tunnel vision that characterizes most recollections of what one called marching 'almost mechanically'[43] makes sense given that, as Tim Ingold notes, marching:

is the form of pedestrian movement that approximates most closely to transport. Unlike the wayfarer whose movement continually responds to an ongoing perceptual monitoring of the country through which he passes, the pedestrian on the march notices nothing. Before his steadfast, unswerving gaze, the country passes unobserved, while his straightened legs and booted feet beat out a purely mechanical oscillation.[44]

The contrast between walking and being marched was one that struck Susan Beer, who had been taken to Auschwitz during the Hungarian deportations in 1944 and was evacuated on foot from the camp in January 1945. After Susan and her mother had been liberated, they left Neustadt-Glewe in search of Susan's father. In early May they walked to the town of Ludwigslust. Retelling this journey, Susan reflected on how it differed from her earlier experiences of being marched along roads. 'We got on this highway and there were woods on both sides of this highway,' Susan told her interviewer, while admitting:

> Actually, we really enjoyed this walk because it was for the first time that you walked and no one said, 'Schnell' and 'Raus'. You didn't realize what it is, just to walk and no one chasing you. And then we saw the woods, which until then, you know, Auschwitz had absolutely nothing of nature, and we heard birds that . . . it's so delightful when you haven't heard it for such a long time, just a nice voice instead of those harsh, horrible voices.[45]

As Susan's distinction between these two journeys makes clear, the evacuations from the camps were marked in her memory by the hurrying and harrying presence of guards who were 'chasing them'.

The murderous boundary that seemed to be pushing prisoners along was personified. It was no longer simply an inanimate electrified fence, but a group of human beings who acted in violent ways for a host of reasons. The mobile camp on the road brought prisoners and guards into a new relationship with each other. There were continuities. Guards could and did shoot escaping prisoners in the camp, but the terms had changed. Failing to keep up with the moving column of prisoners now equated with escape and so guards shot prisoners in increasing numbers. There was an escalation of guard to prisoner violence on the roads, which meant that camp guards who had not previously killed with their own hands became murderers. Daniel Blatman gives the example of Wilhelm Genth, who was in his late forties when he accompanied the column of prisoners being evacuated from Hanover-Stöcken to Bergen-Belsen in 1945. In his post-war retelling of events, Wilhelm explained how he had begun shooting marchers who collapsed en route. Initially, he explained that he did this on the advice of an accompanying doctor. Later he did it on his own initiative, referring to the widespread order that prisoners should not end up in enemy hands alive. 'And thus,' writes Blatman, 'a middle-aged musician from Mannheim . . . became an accomplice in the murder of camp prisoners toward the end of the war.'[46] And it is clear that others became even more trigger-happy, as evidence of massacres emerged in the immediate post-war period.[47] Blatman is right to point to a widening here of the circle of killers, which included men such as Genth who had not killed before. This was a moment when, as Blatman notes, 'the extermination process was totally decentralized'.[48] At this late stage there was a return to the intimacy of the killings that characterized the early phase, but with a difference. This was not systematic mass killing, but rather a situation where an individual prisoner's fate lay in the hands of the individual guard marching alongside or behind them, who chose to shoot or leave another colleague to do this.

However, in this shift to prisoners on the move and the blurring of the boundaries of the camp in motion, there was opportunity as well as deadly threat. Hana Pravda was well aware that what stood between her and the world outside the camp system was no longer electrified wire but the gaze of the guards. This meant that she was constantly on the look-out for those moments when the guards were not looking. As long as you were seen, you remained imprisoned within the camp on the road, and being 'spotted' while trying to escape meant being shot.[49] The opportunity came when you were unseen – either on the road or one of the stopping places along the way – so Hana and her friends waited for those fleeting moments when the guards were not looking, when the boundary of sight that surrounded them suddenly and temporarily disappeared. Writing of 26 January 1945, Hana explained, 'I want to escape at any price, because there is nothing left to lose now. It is clear that we have lost our lives already. I am looking around for hiding places, but it is impossible. There are some empty water pipes full of snow, but the SS are watching us far too well.'[50] However, a few days later, her opportunity came, when 'suddenly I notice that nobody is watching us'. Hana and her friend Vera walked away from the group and hid out of sight. Later, making their own way on the road, they were seen by a German policeman, 'but he is walking so fast it is as if he wants to escape from us'. Although seen, it seemed to Hana that this particular German chose not to look. It appeared to her that he was intentionally 'not looking back. It's quite clear that he is giving us the chance to escape.'[51] And that chance was seized upon.

Escaping from the march was one thing. Finding a place to go to was another. One woman who decided to escape with another Hungarian woman when the march was near Dresden managed to stay hidden as the march moved off, leaving them behind. However, as she recalled, it was then that 'we started to worry about what to do next'. As she explained, 'we could find no place to sleep and no food, so we started looking for our group', thinking 'maybe it was better there'. Although they 'tried to get information about their whereabouts', it seemed that 'nobody knew anything and we could not trace them'. Feeling alone in an unknown, and potentially hostile, place, they were forced to keep 'walking', finally finding first one household who were willing to help them for a few days and then a farm where they worked in exchange for food and shelter.[52] Unless they could find civilian clothing, escaped prisoners were well aware that their uniforms with a large cross daubed on the back in paint – let alone their shaven heads – were a giveaway as to who they were.[53]

Escape came for others not because they were able to hide from their guards' gaze or because their guards were not looking or chose not to look, but when their guards simply disappeared and, as Nina Kaleska put it, 'nobody looked for us anymore'. With her guards gone, 'that was it,' Nina recalled, and her close to two and a half years as a prisoner in the concentration camp system were finally over. The fences went physically when Nina left the camp. But the boundary that kept her imprisoned only went when the guards were gone. 'The next day, we slept in . . . a barn we found with the cows and the pigs on the bottom, and the next morning very early – the sun was still shining – I looked through a crack and I saw a Russian soldier.' It was 5 May 1945. Her glimpse of a Russian solider between the boards of a barn in rural Germany was her moment of liberation.[54] Nina was not alone in being liberated seemingly in the middle of nowhere, rather than in a camp. Thousands were liberated from the mobile confinement of lines of prisoners guarded – or as in Nina's case, abandoned – on an ever-decreasing number of roads and railroads in an ever-shrinking Reich.

That their guards were slipping away spelt a broader change. It was clear that the fortunes of the war were changing and that the evacuations of the camps westwards signalled German defeat. The whole camp system was on the move. It was not just prisoners being taken from one camp to another, but guards and prisoners alike as part of a wider retreat of the German military. Although Fritzie Weiss Fritzshall did not have a clue about 'where we were going' during the evacuations, this was a different kind of placelessness than during the earlier deportations by train that were also marked by a sense of unknown destinations. While Fritzie did not know where they were being taken, she did know 'that it was the last days of the war. We knew because of the bombings; and we knew because of the way the German soldiers were pushing us and pulling us already, and emptying the camps and whatever.'[55] As they made their way westwards in January 1945, survivors were aware that they were part of a much larger group that included the retreating German military and fleeing refugees.

While they and their guards did not have a shared experience of evacuation, survivors were aware that their guards not only had an eye on their prisoners falling into Soviet hands but also themselves. Their guards were men and women on the run. As Magda Blau explained:

> the SS men was running away, because they knew the Russian are coming close. So they yah, they was rushing us with all the speed possible because they didn't want to be caught by the Russians. Any anyone who, who moved down to fix her um shoes or bend down for something they straight away um put her to death.[56]

It seemed that their guards were pushing them along from behind as they left the camps behind. For Hana Pravda, writing in her war diary about being marched from one of the Auschwitz sub-camps with a thousand other women prisoners, 'the Germans running away from the Russian Army, were chasing us to make us march with them'.[57] Experiencing the evacuations as being pushed westwards not only meant that prisoners sought to stay as close to the front of the line as they could. It also provided a way of trying to make sense of the frequent shootings not as random acts of brutality but as the rational actions of guards fleeing westwards with thousands of prisoners who threatened to slow down their retreat. It was clear that their captors were in a hurry and therefore, as Hana explained in her wartime diary, 'the ones who could not carry on marching were shot'.[58]

As they headed west in January 1945, survivors became aware that it was not simply they and their guards who were heading home. Out of the camps, and on the roads, prisoners saw evidence of complete German retreat on roads clogged with soldiers and civilians alike. The sheer numbers are staggering. One US Army intelligence report estimated that 4,500,000 refugees were on the move in front of the Soviet advance.[59] For Magda Blau, it felt like 'the war was getting closer . . . they was rushing us out from the camp and they wanted to us to go . . . deeper in Germany. And on the way it was the population was moving backwards and forwards with their baskets and with their furniture and everything.'[60] Hiding in a cottage after escaping, Hana

Pravda could see through 'the cottage windows big and small wagons full of escaping Germans . . . rolling by'.[61] At times, there were so many on the roads that it became impossible to keep moving. Describing her evacuation from Retzow, Renia Laks recalled how she and her sisters:

> found ourselves on the road with all the evacuees of every stripe and of every possible persuasion, because you had the Jewish prisoners of war – Jewish – you know, prisoners from the concentration camps, and you had Polish labourers who worked on the farm, and you had German military and German out of uniform, and German civilians with dogs and cars and whatever – we had to carry their stuff. And then when it came to a point where the road was so clogged up we couldn't move, they told us to sit down.[62]

It was here – as everything ground to a halt in the chaos of crowded roads – that she and her sisters were able to escape.

The presence of prisoners on German soil was not only significant for the prisoners and those who saw them as they were marched through villages and towns, but also for the guards who were now back 'home', seeing the same material evidence of the coming defeat. In this context, it was not only prisoners who were looking for opportunities to escape from the more fluid experience of being on the move. Guards were also slipping away, changing into civilian clothes and blending into the background as the Allied armies advanced. After escaping from the evacuation herself, Hana Pravda headed home with her friend and discovered 'in all the big deserted houses . . . SA and SS uniforms lying on the floor, like discarded snake skins'.[63] With Germany on the verge of defeat, the hunters realized that they were about to become the hunted. With this changing of clothing – sometimes discarded German military clothing was taken by ragged prisoners – it was hard to tell who was who, 'because there were civilians and there were the camp prisoners and there were the Germans who were trying, some in uniform and some already in civilian clothes, there was such a commotion, there was so much coming and going, you couldn't figure out what was happening'.[64]

As they were evacuated westwards, for many prisoners this meant entering Germany for the first time. Seeing the evidence of a nation on the verge of collapse all around them was a memorable moment. As William Luksenburg told his interviewer half a century later:

> I want to describe the first time we realized that the Germans . . . are losing the war. We were driving in our open cattle wagons right through the heart of Berlin and we saw all the destruction and we didn't believe our own eyes. Finally we seen that the Germans really are getting what's coming to them and there were big slogans 'we're going to fight to the last drop of blood' and so on. We few people who were left on the . . . freight train were embracing each other who couldn't believe that really Germans . . . got something in return for our pain . . .[65]

A similar revelation dawned on Nina Kaleska, evacuated in January 1945 from Auschwitz to Ravensbrück, who recalled that 'we actually went through Berlin and saw a levelled city'.[66] Seeing the German capital in ruins was incontrovertible evidence that Germany was on the cusp of defeat. Ruth Krautwirth Meyerowitz, a German Jew who encountered gypsies at the camp of Malchow, realized that their 'happy-go-lucky' attitude was based on the visible proof that Germany was in ruins. As she explained, 'we weren't aware of it as much but they had been walking from Auschwitz to Malchow which is I don't know how many miles, hundreds of miles – and they had seen what was going on'.[67] Seeing was believing – believing that the war was finally coming to a close.

The presence of large numbers of prisoners on German soil meant that both the prisoners and ordinary Germans saw evidence of the inevitability of German defeat all around them. The Germans also saw lines of emaciated prisoners and witnessed the violence being meted out on them by the roadside. In the International Tracing Service files there are hundreds of pages of maps, questionnaires sent to German mayors, and investigation notes relating to mass graves scattered across the territory of the former Reich. Some relate to victims of the death marches, shot by the roadside in the suburbs of German towns and hastily buried in mass graves. Other graves were in the vicinity of camps and sub-camps that proliferated in Germany in 1944 and became increasingly overcrowded in 1945 as prisoners were being moved westwards before the advancing Soviet army. Reading through the International Tracing Service files, it seems that almost no small town or village escaped the dramatic escalation in the numbers of Jewish and non-Jewish prisoners being brought to the Reich in 1944 and 1945.

Ordinary Germans witnessed the shooting of prisoners literally on their doorstep. In her affidavit for investigators, thirty-four-year-old Hilde Borodajkewycz from Neuenhammer reported how 'on the 19th and 20th of April 1945, I saw about 10,000–15,000 KZ prisoners march through the village of Neuenhammer. One man was shot near my dwelling-house, loaded upon a cart and brought along with the column by the body of guards. Two men were buried near our house.'[68] With the westward shift in the preponderance of prisoner killings, the 'bloodlands' entered into Germany. Killings were no longer confined to the distant 'east' but were happening much closer to home, indeed right on Hilde Borodajkewycz's doorstep. As described by the writer of a report of the concentration camp convoy Kochendorf passing through Hütten, 'this was the first time that the population became eye-witnesses of the cruelties in the concentration camps', as the camps literally took to the roads. Here in the woods on the outskirts of town, the mayor 'saw a picture of horror' and locals saw 'the spectacle of horror: about 200 sick people, looking famished . . . lying in rows'.[69]

The presence of bodies on German streets was something that survivors also remember. Fritzie Weiss Fritzshall's memories of being marched through

Germany during the spring of 1945 were dominated by death and hunger. As she explained:

> And there was no food, because the Germans were losing the war. Oftentimes, as they marched us through a town, a window would open and a shutter would open, and either a potato or a loaf of bread would come flying out; and the shutter would close after. And we would all pounce on this potato or this – whatever this piece of food was that came at us. And, of course, they would shoot at us; but we didn't care at that point, because we were hungry. The streets were literally covered with bodies. As we marched, we would pass bodies. Body after body after body. People that were dropping dead from hunger, from diseases, from dysentery; because they did not have the strength or because they gave up. So we knew it was towards the very end. We would sleep in the fields. We lived on whatever we could find. If we could find a carrot, a potato, snails, snails! In order to survive.[70]

Fritzie's story of scavenging for whatever food she could find in a landscape dominated by death was one that was replicated elsewhere in Germany, which became the centre of the 'bloodlands' for a few months in the spring of 1945. In April 1945 the overcrowded camp of Bergen-Belsen emerged as a critical Holocaust – or rather post-Holocaust – landscape.

Camp

Fela Warschau, who survived four years in two Polish ghettos before being sent to Auschwitz and then a sub-camp of Neuengamme, arrived in Bergen-Belsen at the beginning of April 1945. Here, her sister found a miraculous potato. That Fela chose to tell this story of a single potato is perhaps not that surprising, given that the challenge of getting hold of food dominates the narrative of her entire wartime experience and potatoes appear again and again. Describing her two years in the Łódź ghetto, Fela remembered that 'first of all we were hungry' and so 'trying to put food on the table' was her overarching priority. To supplement their 'staple' foodstuff of bread, Fela recalled standing 'in line waiting for the potato peelings to be thrown out' at the soup kitchen. 'We brought big sacks home,' Fela explained, and:

> washed these potato peelings, ground them with a meat grinder, and we made potato pancakes out of it. And sometimes, when we didn't get enough, if you happened to have coffee grounds left over, you mixed the coffee grounds with the potato peeling so you had something more to eat.

Reflecting back on her months in the labour camp that formed part of the Neuengamme complex, Fela reduced daily life to a rhythm of work and food, where 'our main concern' was whether 'we got some potatoes in this soup, not just a bowl of water floating around'.

Fela's stories of the importance of getting hold of food were accompanied by her accounts of the need for self-discipline and sharing the very limited supplies that there were. During her brief time in Auschwitz, Fela recalled how she shared a bowl of soup with four other women and given the absence of 'any spoons . . . we had to count swallows and be sure we didn't take too many swallows so it would be enough for all the five of us'. This concern with ensuring absolute fairness continued in the next camp where another 'miracle' took place. There, Fela recalled that the task of dividing the bread ration between herself, her sister and their two girlfriends from Łódź was made easier after the miraculous discovery of a piece of string, 'so we made a measure out of that string and cut the bread accordingly so each one had the same amount'. In the Neuengamme sub-camp they not only divided the bread equally between the four of them, but also further subdivided it to ensure that the bread lasted through the day. As Fela explained, 'some people could not control themselves and they ate it right away and later on they were just terribly hungry. We always divided it in half. One for the morning, one for lunchtime, because we didn't get anything else.' These practices of disciplined self-control in saving and sharing food extended to the story of her sister's miraculous potato in Belsen. Great care was taken to ensure that this potato was 'shared' among the group of four girls with 'every day a slice' for 'each of us just to hold us together'. Using her storyteller's ability to generate narrative tension, Fela described liberation as coming just in the nick of time, with British troops arriving at Belsen on the 'last day when there was no more potatoes' and Fela had retreated into the barracks 'to die'.

But while the story of this potato fits within a wider narrative that runs through Fela's story of the significance of saving and sharing food, it also serves to reveal just how different Belsen was from anywhere – and everywhere – else that Fela had been. This was a unique Holocaust landscape. In the ghettos and camps that Fela had lived through before Belsen there had never been anything like sufficient food, hence the importance of saving and sharing it. However, in all these places prisoners had been given something. By contrast, in Belsen, 'we didn't get any food' and so the discovery of a single potato was miraculous. It seemed to Fela that the previous set of unwritten rules, by which she provided labour and her captors provided (inadequate) food in return, had broken down completely. Belsen in April 1945 was a place where 'we didn't work anymore' and 'they didn't feed us anymore'.[1] Retelling Belsen as a radically different place in the final weeks and months of the war, many survivors hone in on the absence of work.[2] Those interviewed in oral history projects in the 1990s and 2000s tended to survive the camp system – like David Bergman – precisely through their labour. Arriving in Bergen-Belsen in the spring of 1945 therefore was a troubling experience, because this was a place where there was neither work nor food and it seemed that prisoners had simply been abandoned to die from starvation and disease.

Being left to starve to death was about more than simply the breakdown of supply lines and a complete lack of food at this late stage in the war. There was still food around, however it lay outside the camp, where Fela remembered seeing – and smelling – a 'high' pile of rotting kohlrabi just the other side of the perimeter fence. The 'horrible' smell of rotting kohlrabi merged with the stink of 'the dead bodies' to create a terrible 'stench' – one strong enough, Fela suggested, to draw in curious passing troops. Fela's liberators were, in her retelling, accidental liberators, who 'were just passing by, that's what I was told, to a different destination, but they were attracted by the stench that came from this place and they wanted to investigate to see what was going on'. The reality of course was that Belsen was handed over to the British by the Germans in an exceptional act of surrendering a particularly problematic place. However, in Fela's narrative it was the overwhelming stench of Belsen that led to her accidental liberation just in the nick of time. That stench came – in part at least she suggested – from a rotting pile of kohlrabi that, like the miracle of a single potato, pointed to the radical discontinuity of Belsen in April 1945 from the other Holocaust landscapes she had experienced during the previous five years.

There was something cruelly surreal to Fela about seeing starving bodies and decomposing food on either side of the camp's perimeter fence. The tempting proximity proved too much for some prisoners who 'tried to grab that decomposed food and eat, and these guys that was guarding us . . . were shooting at the prisoners trying to grab hold of this'. Witnessing this scene, Fela explained 'that was supposed to be food but they didn't feed us anymore'. She of course recognized the cruel disregard of guards who had long since stopped feeding prisoners and were now shooting at those so starved for food that they had resorted to reaching through the fence for rotten cabbage. However, she explained it as part of a broader issue that she had picked up on when she had arrived in Belsen – the complete breakdown of the camp system.

As Fela became aware, the 'guys . . . guarding us' were primarily non-German – 'Hungarians, Ukrainians, Lithuanians' – with only 'a skeleton crew' of Germans left. This perceived withdrawal of SS camp personnel paralleled a breakdown in the normal patterns of camp life made up of roll calls and work details. 'In the beginning they attempted to count us in the morning,' Fela recalled, but 'soon they abandoned this also.' With no food, no work and no roll calls, it seemed to Fela that all the basic elements of the camp system had collapsed completely. This breakdown extended also to the final act of disposing of the corpses of dead prisoners. 'It was unbelievable,' Fela explained. 'The camp was in disarray. They did not bury the bodies anymore. Dead bodies standing up in one pile like cardboard. The rest of them strewn all over the ground.'³

Discovering Belsen to be a strange place where prisoners no longer worked, 'they didn't feed us anymore' and 'they did not bury the bodies anymore', is something that was repeated across survivors' memories. Lilly Malnik, who like Fela had been in both Auschwitz and Belsen, drew a direct comparison between the two camps and explained how Belsen was 'just the opposite of a camp from Auschwitz'. As for Fela and so many others, the lack of work was striking for those used to years of slave labour. However, rather than focusing on the lack of food that was central to Fela's narrative, Lilly pointed to the collapse of boundaries that had kept the clean and unclean separate at Auschwitz, and honed in on the absence of two spaces in Belsen – the latrine block and the mass crematoria – that were sites for the disposal of excrement and corpses.

For Lilly, Belsen was simply a filthy place. 'In Auschwitz at least there we worked,' Lilly recounted:

> and every once in a blue moon . . . we went into the showers. As much as we were afraid to go to the showers, because we didn't know if the showers would give us water or gas, but we showered once in a blue moon. Over there [in Belsen] we had no showers. We had no toilets. In Auschwitz we had a barrack, which was nothing but a toilet. One long toilet . . . And when we came into Bergen-Belsen and I was looking for the toilet barracks, there was none. So I found out that they had made a ditch, and we had to go in the ditch and do it. The decay and the filth in Bergen-Belsen was undescribable.

Rather than the stench of rotting kohlrabi, Lilly's Belsen was dominated by the stench of human waste. 'Life in Bergen-Belsen was just terrible,' Lilly told her interviewer, 'and the people just died like flies over there because there was nothing. We had . . . no work over there. We just sat around. And we walked around in the decay, in the dirt, between the . . . ditches from the bathrooms. The smell was horrible . . . and people . . . got sick.'

In Lilly's mind, both the filth of Belsen marked this camp out as different from Auschwitz and also the ever-present corpses that surrounded her. As she explained, at Auschwitz:

> they took away the dead people. They gassed them and they burned them; and in the camps we didn't see any dead people. We only saw . . . people being hit or being dragged away, but we never saw any dead people laying

around. In Bergen-Belsen was just the opposite. Bergen-Belsen was nothing but dead people. Skeletons. Skins and bones. They piled them up as they died. Every day, five people would be dead from . . . one barrack. And they just piled them up like a mountain outside . . . the barrack. And the piles got as high I would say . . . six, seven feet.[4]

That Belsen was a landscape dominated by a 'mountain of dead and nothing else' emerges in survivor and liberator accounts alike, and captured the attention of journalists, photographers and filmmakers when they entered the camp and fixed their eyes and lenses on the piles of corpses.[5] Looking through the hundreds of photographs taken in the days after liberation and now housed in the Imperial War Museum photo archives, it is clear that British military photographers were drawn to the dead. The sequence of images taken by four photographers on 17 and 18 April 1945 combines a handful of close-ups of individual corpses[6] with a large number of photographs of piles of corpses.[7] It was the sheer number of the unburied dead that these photographers sought to capture, with accompanying captions positioning individual images as representative of a wider truth. 'A common sight in the camp, where bodies of dead and dying are strewn everywhere', reads the caption for two images, and the title 'In all parts of the camp dead bodies can be seen' extends the claims of representativeness of another set of images.[8] That Belsen was a place littered with corpses was something that struck the first reporter who arrived in the camp, Richard Dimbleby, who described passing 'through the barrier' into 'the world of nightmare' where 'dead bodies, some of them in decay, lay strewn along the road'.[9] The presence of thousands of unburied corpses at Belsen meant that the main camp quickly became known by the liberating troops simply as the 'horror camp'.[10]

When British troops and medics first encountered Belsen, they were struck by the breakdown of the traditional boundaries keeping excrement and death in their place, which had so haunted Lilly Malnik. The coexistence of living skeletons – or 'scarecrows' – and the dead, the huts filled with excrement, and the lack of any water to wash or drink, dominated British attempts to describe this 'filthy' place.[11] But what was particularly shocking to the British troops, photographers and press who arrived in Belsen in the middle of April 1945 was not simply the presence of so many dead, but the cohabitation of the living and the dead. In his wartime diary Major Charles Phillip Sharp, describing his first encounter with the camp, started off with the sheer number of corpses – writing of 'huts . . . packed with dead and great heaps of them lie out in the sun in the camp' – before moving on to describe the terrible conditions in which those still alive existed. Indeed it seemed to him that:

> the living are if anything more horrible. They lie half dead about the place or crawl slowly around. Not a latrine in the whole camp – floors of huts are brown and packed inches deep in excreta. Men and women stand and squat all over the place – they . . . have lost all self-respect and are just existing and dying.[12]

The coexistence of the living with death and piles of excrement continued to dominate Sharp's reportage of this place. After his second tour of the camp, he wrote:

> I cannot describe the horror of the place. The huts – five tier bunks with two people in each bunk and usually one or both dead, dead who have been lying there for weeks and others too feeble to move, flies crawling from the dead to the living, floors swimming with excreta. The women's quarters are its worst if anything. They sit around delousing each others heads and their own private parts quite regardless of everyone – their bodies are covered with spots, bites, scratches and filth – a few still try to wash. They sit about unconcerned amongst the heaps of dead.[13]

His rendering on paper of 'unconcerned' prisoners sitting around 'amongst the heaps of dead' was replicated by the decisions of photographers to frame prisoners living among the dead. To drive their point home they captioned the photographs with titles such as 'Women peeling potatoes, while in the background are piles of dead bodies' or 'Women sitting about the camp showing dead bodies in the background'.[14]

Reading Sharp's diary, it is clear that what he saw at Belsen horrified him. He wrote down relatively little of what he saw. As he explained, 'it is not necessary for me to make notes to serve as a reminder of this experience.' But he also clearly struggled to put into writing what he saw with his eyes as he toured the camp for the first time and saw a place that was impossible to describe.[15] He was not alone in this sense of the indescribability of the place.[16] For Sharp, seeing was believing. 'No one who saw it can ever forget as long as they live,' he wrote, and hence his repeated admonition that all 'should see it'. 'I wish every man and woman in Britain and America and the colonies could see this now,' Sharp wrote after his second visit to the camp, 'if they could just walk round, no atrocity stories to believe, just their own eyes and if they were sick and fainted they could leave but they should see it.' He was heartened that 'the world will probably hear at least something about this place' after the arrival of the press, although he was unsure whether they would 'publish the most revolting scenes'.[17]

However, as they looked around the 'horror camp' at Belsen in April 1945, British troops and journalists did not see quite the same things that survivors saw. Military photographers detected in the blank gaze of surviving prisoners an indifference to the dead. Survivors, however, saw the piles of corpses as evidence that this was not a place of killing but a place of dying, where it seemed that death itself had taken over the role previously occupied by the German authorities. 'Bergen-Belsen . . . was not like Auschwitz,' one woman explained. 'There were no gas chambers. They didn't need any gas chambers. It was really a death camp' where 'people were dying all around us'.[18] For another survivor, 'Bergen-Belsen was a terrible situation, there was no crematoriums, but people were just dying and the typhoid.'[19] Although Belsen did actually have one crematorium, for survivors the sheer number of corpses piled high suggested that it did not. What they realized was that this was not a place like Auschwitz where mass death, following selections, took place through the machinery of gas chambers and crematoria. Instead it was a place of apparently indiscriminate dying where inmates sought to keep their head down, 'just waiting for a transport' away from this place where they sensed you could not 'last very long'.[20]

For survivors, the sheer number of corpses that had not been disposed of at Belsen was something new. Lilly Malnik had first encountered corpses on the journey between Auschwitz and Belsen during a 'death march' along roads 'red from blood'. She recalled walking through a landscape dominated by memories of 'people being shot' and 'laying all over, on top of hills, behind trees', which was 'really like a war zone'. But these corpses scattered across the landscape differed from the encounter with the dead – and death – at Belsen. Along the roads of the 'death march' the bodies were not stacked up in the towering piles that seemed to Lilly to dwarf her at Belsen. Out on the roads, the constant motion of the march meant that Lilly swiftly passed corpse after corpse, rather than spending aimless weeks in Belsen sitting around with the dead. And it was not just the sheer number of dead that was new, but the manner of their death. As she recalled the deaths on the roads, Lilly explained that 'they were shooting people'. It was a world where humans were in control and so there was some kind of twisted logic to the neglect and killing of those who 'fell behind', and 'the Germans just shot them'.

In Lilly's account of Belsen, the German guards were no longer primarily shooting people. They were no longer doing anything. They were not providing work, showers, latrines, bunks, or food. This nothingness meant, for Lilly, the breakdown of the normal order and the emergence of a terrifying new disorder – a chaotic and threatening landscape of 'decay', 'filth' and 'dirt' where 'people got sick' and 'people just died like flies . . . because there was nothing'.

Belsen seemed to be nothing less than a landscape of death where everyone would eventually succumb and Lilly herself simply lay there half-dead 'like a skeleton'.

In the last weeks of the war Lilly saw human agency in Belsen slipping away. This was a place where lice devoured the corpses rather than members of the *Sonderkommando* removing the bodies of the dead to the crematoria. As she retold the death of her friend, Lilly recalled her horror at seeing the corpse covered by lice that reduced her striped uniform to a sea of grey and seemed to be 'eating Christiane up'.[21] But it was not only the dead who were covered with lice. It seemed to Bella Jakubowicz Tovey that the lice had also taken over the living. 'I would get up every morning,' she explained, and:

> I was covered with lice. I wore one of those . . . uh . . . concentration camp uniforms. You know, they were grey and blue. Well in the morning you couldn't see the blue. It was all grey. I was totally covered with lice. As long as I could I used to shake. I used to take this thing off and I used to shake it out. If I could get some cold water, I would wash. Later on, I am sure I didn't wash. I would shake out all the lice. I would put that thing on, and half an hour later, I was covered with lice. I had typhus, then I had typhoid . . . I don't know how I made it.[22]

It seemed to survivors later on that something terrifyingly new had been happening in Belsen during the spring of 1945. This differed from the systematic killing that began with mass shootings during 1941–2 and then reached its height in the Operation Reinhard camps and Auschwitz-Birkenau, where Fela Warschau was sent in 1944. It was also different from the return to the mass killing and individual shootings that characterized both central Budapest in 1944 and the death marches in the first half of 1945. Across 1941–5 people were being killed, en masse or individually, by gas or bullet, by German forces and their collaborators. In Belsen in 1945, with a 'skeleton crew' of German forces and collaborators guarding the external perimeter fence, it seemed now to Fela that dying had taken over killing and 'all you did is just walk around in a daze and make some sense of what is going on here'.[23] Belsen was a place where 'people dropped dead in front of you'. It was somewhere that Fela summed up in a short list of five phrases – 'dead people all over the place, typhoid fever, dysentery, lice, terrible' – that revealed a world that was being overtaken by disease and death.[24]

But Belsen had not always been like this. A little under two years earlier the camp was built on the site of a deadly holding point for Soviet POWs, to house so-called 'exchange Jews'. These were prominent Jews being spared from execution, to be used as pawns in deals that it was thought might be struck with the Western Allies. The first group of 2,500 arrived in July 1943 – although most of these were later deported to Auschwitz. Others joined them at Belsen from across Europe, with larger numbers of Dutch 'exchange Jews' arriving in 1944, followed by Hungarian 'exchange Jews' once deportations started from that country in May 1944. By the end of July over 4,000 'exchange' prisoners were housed in Belsen, living in very basic conditions.

One of those sent here from the Netherlands, from the transit camp of Westerbork in February 1944, was Doriane Kurz. She recalled a place of order rather than the place of disorder that later arrivals like Fela Warschau and Lilly Malnik remember. Doriane, her mother and brother arrived at a camp that she described as 'a very large place' that 'was divided into many different sections . . . by barbed wire', housing prisoners from different nationalities.[25] Doriane's overwhelming memory of the camp in this period was of barbed wire in this highly segregated and zoned space. This was a dominant image shared by another of the Dutch exchange Jews, Abel Herzberg, who mused that 'wherever you stand or go there is barbed wire', which he dubbed the 'macaroni of the Third Reich'.[26]

As she recalled daily life in the camp, Doriane's memories contrasted markedly with Fela's experiences of Belsen just over a year later. In 1944, Doriane remembered the rhythm of being counted during morning roll call and adults leaving the camp to work. Abel Herzberg reduced this to a daily litany of 'camp – roll-call – work – humiliation – slavery – work – SS'.[27] Doriane also recalled that Belsen 'did have crematoria' and she remembered seeing a cart removing the corpses of those who had died overnight. Although 'there was not very much to eat', Doriane recalled daily rations being 'three-quarters of a litre of watery soup made from a variety of turnips' – 'kohlrabi soup' – and 'three and a half centimetres of bread' and 'some kind of an Ersatz coffee'.

In an echo of Fela's own practice in the sub-camp of Neuengamme, Doriane explained how she and her brother spent 'lots of time with our little piece of bread, cutting it for hours into the tiniest, tiniest, little, tiny squares that we could and then eating them tiny tiny piece by tiny tiny piece so we could make it last as long as we could'.[28] Another exchange Jew, Martin Spett, who spent close to two years in Belsen, had a very similar set of memories. Recalling that in the beginning, 'the food was good', Martin had his own story of cutting bread into equal-sized portions using a piece of string. 'They gave us a loaf of black bread,' Martin remembered, 'and we had to cut it, cut portions, appropriate portions for each person in the camp, and we made a scale out of strings and pieces of wood and each crumb, God forbid it fell off . . . that scale.'[29]

In contrast to Lilly's description of Belsen as a place without latrines, Doriane remembered the toilets at Belsen in specific detail, describing how:

> the bathroom facilities were a . . . large outhouse for everybody, quite far from the other barracks . . . You had to walk there and they were composed of . . . a large wooden plank . . . with . . . holes cut into the top of the wooden plank and there was an excavation below it and so . . . when everybody relieved themselves . . . would just fall through the holes into . . . I remember it was a very bad smell and I remember feeling very lucky that I didn't have to worry about going to work because before work there were so many people who went running there and then everybody had to wait for each other and that I could wait to do that until after everybody was gone.[30]

However, in the latter half of 1944, the camp began to expand considerably, first to house sick prisoners from across the labour camp system and then women from Auschwitz. Abel Herzberg witnessed this expansion as 'a symptom of the downfall of the Third Reich'. The construction of a large tented camp in August 1944 filled with women and children, who the other prisoners assumed had been evacuated from the east, was read by him as a sign of 'disintegration' and 'chaos' as much as it was a potential source of hope that the war was drawing to an end.[31] On 28 August he wrote with shock in his diary that he and his fellow prisoners had not been counted during roll call – this seeming staple of the camp system – for the first time in eight months.[32] The next day Abel reflected that the coming of the end of the war seemed to spell fewer food rations.[33] Towards the end of the year his diary entries became shorter and food and sanitary conditions worsened.[34]

Martin Spett, who was evacuated towards Theresienstadt in the final weeks of the war, also witnessed the rapid and marked deterioration of conditions during his time in Belsen. As well as recalling the deteriorating food supply, Martin remembers sanitary conditions worsening. While 'in the beginning . . . the latrine was a building with a big ditch and two benches on each side' with 'a panoramic view of everybody', 'later on we had a barrack with a toilet that didn't work'. Water was rationed, and they 'were . . . eaten up by lice'. By April 1945, Martin remembers that 'conditions were terrible' and 'people were dying'.[35]

The precise number of dead was something that Abel Herzberg kept a careful eye on as he also noted down the increase in the camp population. By December 1944 the camp housed over 15,000 in increasingly harsh conditions. But things worsened considerably as Belsen became a dumping ground for prisoners evacuated from camps further east. By the end of January 1945, Abel put the prisoner population at 30,000.[36] Two weeks later he estimated this was up to 40,000 as there were fewer and fewer camps in an ever-diminishing Reich.[37] By the end of March, Abel estimated around 45,000 prisoners and

17,000 deaths in that month alone.[38] Writing of the expansion of the camp as it seemed to him that prisoners evacuated from across the camp system were being crammed into Belsen, Abel described a scene of 'unimaginable chaos and misery' and the breakdown of the previous zoning of the camp into discrete and separate prisoner groups.[39] Writing in his diary on 1 April – at around the time that Fela was arriving in the camp – Abel Herzberg recorded that there 'are no more roll-calls. Also no work. There is only death. A little flour is distributed and a few people receive some oatmeal. It is all nonsense'.[40] Reading his diary, it is clear that Belsen changed dramatically over the course of 1945 into the place that Fela and Lilly encountered, where it seemed that food had been replaced with corpses and the latrines with excrement lying around everywhere.

This picture was repeated elsewhere across the ever-diminishing SS camp system that nonetheless somehow continued functioning during the first half of 1945. In camp after camp, the influx of prisoners being evacuated from territory coming under the control of the Allies rapidly increased the population. In overcrowded and unsanitary conditions, typhus spread. The death rate sky-rocketed. While Belsen was the place where conditions were probably about at their worst in this final phase of the war, camps like Dachau and Ravensbrück were also sites of terrible overcrowding. In Dachau an estimated 14,000 died in the few months between January and April 1945.[41] When Nina Kaleska was taken to Ravensbrück from Auschwitz, she described conditions there as 'dreadful' and 'horrible' because of the chronic overcrowding, leaving this experience 'a blur because it was terrible'. It seemed to Nina that a camp 'built for . . . maybe thirty-five hundred people' was now stuffed with 'something like fifteen thousand people'. After a few weeks dominated by vague memories of 'masses of people, death, terrible starvation, no work', Nina was taken to a labour camp in Retzof-am-Richlin where they chopped 'wood for war production'. With more space – and work once more – it seemed to Nina that Retzof 'was heaven' – 'particularly after Ravensbrück'.[42]

Ravensbrück was where the Laks sisters ended up, dumped into tents – because the barracks were already overcrowded – after being evacuated from Auschwitz. Like Lilly Malnik, Renia Laks found the terrible efficiency of Auschwitz terrifying, but there was something worse about the seeming 'chaos' of Ravensbrück.

Asked by her interviewer 'How horrible was it in Ravensbrück?', Renia replied 'Very bad – it was the worst.' 'Worse than Auschwitz? Why?' her interviewer asked, surprised at this answer. 'Because it was disorganized,' Renia explained:

> It wasn't in any way planned to contain the number of people that were shipped in. It was in no way organized with a plan for the future, even, because the war was now turning, you know, the war effort of the Allies was now taking shape. So, that the Germans, whatever they were up to, knew only themselves, but the fact is that a place like Ravensbrück that had all these people shipped in – and maybe the decision wasn't yet made what to do with that, with these people, I don't know – but the fact remains that the camp was overrun. We stayed in a tent. There were no more people possible to squeeze into the barracks . . . I mean, this was beyond any setting, especially since they always were so organized in the . . . their genocidal plan included every detail on down the line, and this was, of course, already out of their hands. So, that was rough; that was bad . . . no food and no place to stay in, and just chaos.[43]

Renia's overwhelming memory of Ravensbrück at the tail end of the war was, like Lilly's experience of Belsen, that 'it was total chaos'.[44] She explained the 'chaos' as a result of the disorganization as the Reich collapsed and so planned genocide was 'already out of their hands'. In a sense these last weeks and months of the war were experienced as a time when the genocidal machinery was broken. The planned killings may have largely ceased but these had now been replaced by chaotic dying. If there was one thing worse than the Holocaust, it was its unravelling in places like Bergen-Belsen or Ravensbrück where human agency appeared to have been overtaken. It was not simply that the victims were not in control. It seemed that no one was in control anymore.

The camps that the British and American troops liberated in April and May 1945 were chaotic landscapes that were not primarily genocidal space, but post-genocidal space where planned killings had been replaced by chaotic dying. The Germans were willing to surrender Bergen-Belsen to the British precisely because it was a place and a problem to be given to others to solve. This is what the British – making mistakes along the way – set about doing as they instituted a massive programme of burying the dead, feeding the living, hospitalizing the sick, cleaning the filthy, and burning the entire camp to the ground.[45] The living – like Lilly – were washed in a mass cleaning programme. The dead – like her friend Christiane – were bulldozed into rapidly dug mass graves. There was an attempt to reassert order and control and to reinstate human agency.

The attempt to render order out of the chaos they encountered in this place with 'no organisation'[46] comes through strongly in the diary written by Major Charles Phillip Sharp. For Sharp, the chaos within the camp needed to be controlled because it was so threatening. Explaining the extraordinary decision of the Germans to surrender the camp to the advancing British troops, rather than fight over every last square foot of land, Sharp understood this as an attempt to safeguard Germany and beyond from a typhus epidemic. Before he had seen the camp for himself, he wrote of the 'horrible stories we hear' of typhus and other infectious diseases 'raging' there. 'If they got out it would be enough to cause a typhus epidemic in all EUROPE,' Sharp wrote, given that they were 'all political prisoners (Jews and Communists and anti-Nazi presumably) and as they hear the British are approaching they are sure to attempt to break out'.[47] In order to ensure this did not happen, the camp was to be handed over to the British so that there was no moment when these infected prisoners were out of the military control of guards – whether Axis or Allied – watching the perimeter fence.

This transition in ownership and control was unusual. In most places, liberation was experienced more as a fading away of the old forces of German control, followed by an unsettling hiatus as guards donned civilian clothes and disappeared back into German society and former prisoners were left to fend for themselves. Susan Beer, who was taken from Auschwitz to Ravensbrück in January 1945 and then on to Neustadt-Glewe in February, recalled how on 2 May:

we looked out the window, it was a lovely day, and we saw our guards looked unusual. They were unshaven, they were drunk and they were leaving. So, we sort of knew the end came. And the French prisoners of war cut through some wires . . . And, after we were free, we really didn't feel that free. No one came there, none of the American army who freed this territory didn't know we existed. The town wasn't very far, but they didn't know. And so, no one came then, we didn't know what's our next move. Some people became very unhappy and screamed and cried because they just, it just dawned on them that they are left alone, that all their loved ones were killed off and there was no place for them to come back to.[48]

However, this ultimate fading away of control did not happen at Belsen. Here, the handover of the camp intact meant that control was dramatically reasserted as the British sought to create order out of chaos.

Belsen appeared to the British to be an anarchic place, where prisoners had already breached the internal divisions of a concentration camp broken down into discrete zones. They now threatened to breach the external fence of the camp and break out into the crowded roads of Germany, spreading infection as they went. In response, British troops sought to redraw and harden the boundary around the camp, and implement a tighter degree of segregation and separation. Major Sharp marked out the hinterland as a site of danger with each 'Typhus Danger' notice he posted 'a few miles radius around the whole place'. His superiors limited access into the camp, which could only be entered by those holding an officially issued pass authorizing entry into 'after dusting'.[49] Within the camp there was an attempt to undo the chaos and restore order – in particular an ordering of the world into the world of the living and the world of the dead.

Restoring order involved two things in Sharp's mind: burying the dead and feeding the living and evacuating them to the hospital camps set up in the former SS barracks. Burying the dead was a long process, even making use of mass graves. 'The wretched people are dying at about the same rate as we are burying,' Sharp complained after a few days, 'leaving a balance of about 5000 corpses around all the time.' A little later, he was still worried that 'the burying . . . must be speeded up' given that 'they are dying much faster than we are burying'. The problem posed by the slow progress they were making meant that Belsen continued to be a place inhabited by the dead and the living. On 23 April it seemed to Sharp that 'we are now getting somewhere but it would be a gross exaggeration to say we have things under control'. His confidence that they had finally turned a corner came as he reported that for the first time they had finally managed to bury more corpses (1,700) than the average daily death rate (1,500). Four days later he was able to report the 'lowest death rate since we arrived' (311) on the previous day, and that 'all the accumulated dead have now been buried and all the pit graves filled in and capped off except one'. At a 'conservative estimate', Sharp reckoned they had buried 17,000 corpses in the main camp since they had taken over this place.[50]

Alongside burying the dead another priority was evacuating the living. Prisoners were stripped, wrapped in blankets, and taken from the camp – their emptied barracks burnt to the ground as they were cleared. In the former SS barracks, prisoners were cleansed in what was known as the 'human laundry'. They were washed, shaved, and 'we literally shower the anti-louse powder over them'.[51] One woman remembered 'being sprayed with DDT and loving it, because all the itching stopped, and . . . all the horrible things on my body stopped'.[52] For Lilly Malnik, being washed in the 'human laundry' meant not only a return to cleanliness after the 'filth', 'dirt' and 'decay' that characterized Belsen, but the reassertion of human agency that seemed absent in this place. She was now in the hands of the military and Red Cross who:

> took off all my clothes that I had on and they wrapped me in an army blanket and they took me. And they . . . took and put me in . . . a bathing house and they took the Germans who were the Nazis, they made them put on white uniforms and they took care of . . . the inmates who were very bad off. And they washed me and shampooed me and . . . then they put me in a hospital.[53]

For the British, restoring order ultimately meant erasing the main camp of Belsen from the face of the earth. Major Sharp approved of the decision to burn the camp to the ground once the evacuation of prisoners was complete. On 23 April he wrote that the huts in the main camp were 'now empty' and 'being used as latrines' and recorded his 'wish' that 'we could burn them all down'. A little under a month later his wish came true. Three or four huts were being burnt each day, with the 'final show' scheduled for 21 May. 'It's a fine sight to see those places destroyed by fire,' Sharp wrote. However, when the ceremonial burning of the final hut took place – something reported by the press in a clipping Sharp carefully pasted in to the pages of his diary – he wrote surprisingly little. It seems that this symbolic moment was something of an anti-climax. As he described what he had earlier called the 'final show', Sharp expressed some frustration with new arrivals 'fighting to get in front to . . . take pictures' and with speeches given by prominent men, most of whom had not – like Sharp – 'been here all the time'.[54]

The barracks that had been chosen for the ceremonial burning was especially dressed for the occasion with posters displaying a portrait of Hitler flanked by a swastika and an iron cross. The speech given by Colonel

Bird spoke of the symbolism behind the destruction of the last hut in 'this pestilence-ridden camp'. It was a sign of 'the final destruction for all time of the bestial, inhuman creed of Nazi Germany; the creed by which criminals tried to debase the peoples of Europe to serve their own devilish ends'. Once the hut was aflame, and Belsen was no more, the Union Jack was raised here for the first time. At the entrance gate a sign was erected by the British troops that recorded what had stood here a month earlier:

This is the Site of

THE INFAMOUS BELSEN CONCENTRATION CAMP

Liberated by the British on April 15 1945.

10,000 UNBURIED DEAD WERE FOUND HERE.
ANOTHER 13,000 HAVE SINCE DIED,
ALL OF THEM VICTIMS OF THE
GERMAN NEW ORDER IN EUROPE,
AND AN EXAMPLE OF NAZI KULTUR.[55]

Writing of his sight of the previous huts in Belsen being burnt, one man explained in a letter home: 'Germany is being cleansed of one of its blackest spots; but the crime has yet to be cleansed.'[56]

Epilogue
Returning Home/
Leaving Home

When they liberated Belsen, one thing that struck British soldiers and medics, aside from the overwhelming sight and stench of death and decay in the 'horror camp', was the multilingual nature of this prisoner population. 'There are literally dozens of languages and you'd never believe the international crises that arise,' one British nurse wrote home.[1] 'Russians, French, Italians, Yugoslavs, Poles, Norwegians – all the nationalities on earth seemed to be represented,' noted a British soldier.[2] Others described a place where 'they protested in Polish; they wept in Hungarian; they howled in Roumanian and all spoke together in a sort of German'.[3] A British Red Cross nurse reckoned that twenty-two languages were spoken in the camp.[4] Encountering Belsen was, like the Laks sisters' earlier experience in Auschwitz, a moment of encounter with the continental scale of the concentration camp system that had united in dying those from as far north as Norway, as far south as Yugoslavia, as far east as the Soviet Union, and as far west as France. The multilingual nature of this prison population thrown together in Belsen was, for medic Sister Kath Elvidge, one of the 'chief difficulties' she faced as she worked to repatriate former prisoners who had been moved from the hospital set up in the former

SS barracks into the two transit camps. Writing a letter home at the end of May 1945, she explained how 'the majority of the patients' she was working with 'have some Jewish origin, but are from all the countries under the sun. Russia, Poland, Hungary, Czheckoslovakia [sic], Belgium, Holland, France, and only about four of them have a smattering of English'.[5]

The concentration camp system, as both the Laks sisters and a British nurse like Kath Elvidge came to realize, had brought together Jews and others from across the continent into multilingual fluid prisoner communities that were moved around the expanding and then contracting network of camps. At war's end these prisoners were dispersed across a number of camps, their families separated along gendered lines. Unpicking histories and geographies of familial separation was not a simple task. It often took months or years, and necessitated travelling over considerable distances. For the Laks sisters, the desire to 'put all of the pieces of the puzzle together to see who survived and who . . .' (hard as it still was to say over half a century later) did not survive, drew them eastwards. However, 'that was easier said than done because everybody . . . wanted to get east, further east'.[6]

Boarding a train for the east, the sisters 'started going back home'.[7] Their plan was to head straight for Starachowice 'of course' to find out news of their parents. But they were warned against going to a 'small town' in Poland by a Jewish Russian soldier, who advised them that it would not be 'safe' and so recommended they go to a 'big city' to 'register with the Jewish agents and that's where you can find family, not in a small town'.[8] The sisters followed his advice, making their way to Łódź, a city that became a temporary hub of Polish Jewish life in the immediate post-war years.[9] Here they discovered that one uncle had survived and was also living in Łódź. But it was also here that they 'started finding out what happened, that all these people who were resettled were no longer alive because they were exterminated', and it became clear to them that their parents would not be coming back.[10] After a year in Łódź, the sisters headed west to Germany where they stayed a little under a year before heading further west to the United States in 1947. That movement, first east, then west, was replicated across the continent, as survivors who had ended up being evacuated to the few remaining camps in the shrinking territory of the Reich headed home and then oftentimes quickly left.

This temporary heading home east, before returning west again, was something that the senior Jewish chaplain in the British Army, Isaac Levy, predicted when he wrote to the United Nations Relief and Rehabilitation Administration in mid-May 1945, just after VE Day, recommending the establishment of a Jewish transit camp in the Belsen area. For Levy, it was 'self evident that the majority of these Jews cannot return to the countries of their origin'. Although he noted a 'desire to return' there 'in the hope that they may find some trace of their families', this was very much 'only a temporary measure'.[11] While lists of survivors were being published and circulated in the areas of the former Reich, many travelled home – to the last place where they had been together as a family and the place where they assumed that surviving relatives would therefore return.

In some cases this had been the plan all along. Ruth Krautwirth Meyerowitz explained how she and her mother headed home because 'we had agreed with my father and everyone – you know, my brother and my mother – that whoever would live would try to make his way back to Frankfurt and so we could be united as a family and then see where we would go from there'.[12] For these German Jews, first deported east, and then heading back west in the final years of the war, returning home was a relatively short journey. For most others, it was a much lengthier journey eastwards made in the chaotic days of the immediate post-war years at a time when many were on the road and the trains were crowded.

Bernard Pasternak, deported from Transylvania to Auschwitz before ending up in Buchenwald, headed east in search of family. 'We took trains . . . from one place to another one,' Bernard recalled, with the journey home taking 'weeks and weeks' to make it 'from Germany to Czechoslovakia to Budapest' and finally back to his 'home town' in Romania. With no room inside the train that took him and his travelling companions back to Budapest, Bernard rode on the top, ducking down each time the train came to a bridge. After a series of long and difficult journeys, Bernard finally made it home. However, this was not to be an experience of joyful family reunion. Rather it was a sobering experience of the reality of loss. As Bernard discovered, 'there was nothing left in there in my home town, just a few people came back', which left him bewildered and he 'couldn't work it out'. Like so many others, Bernard and his companions 'packed up whatever we had and we turned back', although as he quickly realized this was easier said than done. The return journey westwards was even more challenging for them, and necessitated being smuggled across a series of border crossings. As Bernard explained, 'the turning back was not so easy because you had to go out of the Russian zone'. Heading into Hungary, they paid a 'Russian guy' with a 'truck' who 'for a fee . . . took you over to Austria'.[13]

This movement first eastwards and then westwards, driven by the overwhelming search for surviving family members, also characterized Miriam Farcus Ingber's post-war journeying. She headed back home to Czechoslovakia at the end of the war, before quickly leaving it in search of 'boys' from other towns who might have news of her brother. Leaving Hungary, she headed first to Romania and then Czechoslovakia. In Prague she heard news that her brother was alive and in Budapest. However, once she got there, she discovered that he had already left to go to Germany, where she eventually caught up with him. Reflecting back on these immediate post-war years spent scouring the continent for her brother who had been 'in a different camp', Miriam explained, 'we were like a gypsy, running around, finding . . . people, finding everybody . . . Did you see this? Did you see that? Did you . . . you saw somebody? You been with somebody?'[14]

The closer to home people got, the more likely they were to find out news of what had happened to family and friends, who had oftentimes been deported together as one local group. What survivors needed to find were other survivors who had also been on those initial transports. They might have some knowledge of the whereabouts of those they had been separated from – either at the initial selections in the case of family members of the opposite sex, or at one of the subsequent selections in the case of those of the same sex. Felicia Berland Hyatt 'wanted to get closer to Chelm' in order to find either her 'mother or others who might know what happened to her'. She eventually did meet someone who had been a fellow prisoner with her mother, and that person told Felicia that her mother had died in Majdanek concentration camp, most likely of hunger.[15]

Heading home after escaping from the evacuations, Hana Pravda sought out anyone with information about her husband Saša. At a hostel in Częstochowa, Hana discovered two friends from Terezín, 'then I slowly discovered some girls from the sister camp of Kreuzbach' and a couple of other survivors who told her what news they had. However, as Hana noted with sadness in her diary:

> in spite of asking everybody about Saša I did not hear anything at all except that he was chosen, as an exceptionally athletic man, for a special group to go to work in a metal factory. His transport was apparently sent to some factory near Leipzig. When he left and where he is now I don't know. Dear God, look after him and bring him back to me! I pray only for this – I don't want anything else![16]

A month later, Hana 'met Dr Krause, a small short man with glasses who had slept next to Saša in Terezín'. However, in her diary, which she was keeping intending to give it to her husband when they finally met again, she wrote 'Dear God, I am meeting all sorts of people – only not the one person I love!'[17]

Less than a week later, she learnt about her uncle who had been in Auschwitz but had left with her cousin for a labour camp. This gave her 'one more little hope that I may meet again somebody from my family!'

However, this got her no nearer to answering her overwhelming question, 'where is my Saša? My dear darling? Please God, watch over him and make him return home to me healthy! My beloved, my dearest!'[18] By the end of March she had almost made it home. In Košice she 'found my Saša's school friend "the small Polak"'.[19] A couple of days later she saw a familiar face – a friend from Terezín. 'It's a nice feeling,' Hana wrote, 'at last a human being I know, but in spite of all this I feel very sad and my longing for Saša is even stronger. I want my husband, not a friend, not a lover, nothing like that, only calm, peace and real love. God, take pity on me, and give him back to me, please!'[20] News continued to trickle in about others, but there was still no news of Saša.[21] It was not until the end of May that she 'got a message from Jirka Wachtl that my Saša died on the 20 May 1945 in the village called Kraslice near Carlsbad. He died on an open wagon surrounded by 21 dead and dying girls brought from Buchenwald. Wachtl, his brother Ota and their father saved themselves from the same wagon so they know what happened there.'[22]

For others, news of the fate of family members took much longer. A survivor from Ravensbrück wrote of her desperate post-war search for her husband. It took her a year to find out that he had died, and over fifteen years to discover the circumstances of his death from male survivors who had been imprisoned with him.[23] It took Abraham Malnik even longer to find out when his mother died. Forty years after the end of the war, Abraham met a woman who had been in the same camp as his mother and seen her die just before liberation. 'At least I know she dies in March,' Abraham reflected. 'At least I know that her soul is not floating empty and . . . every March I say *kaddish* . . . for her soul.'[24] For others, the precise fate of loved ones remained forever unknown.

There were some whose return journeys led to emotional family reunions. In May 1945, Susan Beer and her mother left Neustadt-Glewe to head home in search of her father. 'We didn't know anything about my father,' Susan explained and so they 'wanted to . . . get closer to home' to see whether they could find him or learn of his fate. In her post-war memoir Susan wrote about arriving in the town of Ludwigslust:

> I would have liked to remain in Ludwigslust, but my mother and I were growing tired of wandering and wanted to re-establish ourselves at home. We had to find a way to return to Slovakia and learn about my father. There had been no news of him for several months, and experience had taught me to expect the worst.

They travelled by bus to Celle and then after some time there managed to get seats on a bus heading to Prague, where it seemed they were 'headed closer to home'. In Bratislava they met a man from their home town. He was not only able to tell them news about Susan's father, who had been liberated by the Soviets in Auschwitz in January 1945 and had made his way back to Budapest where he was once again practising medicine, but also to give them 'a scrap of paper that bore my father's name and address in Budapest'. Susan recalled that 'We went on the only train that went from Bratislava to Budapest',where they found her father at the address they had been given, and 'we were together, which was incredible after all that time'.[25]

After a while the whole family returned to their home town, because Susan's father was keen to resume his medical practice there. 'So we went back,' Susan recounted:

> but we couldn't . . . get back our apartment. Our furniture was being used by other people. Most houses in town were occupied by people who didn't belong to them. They just took them. And, someone who offered my father to put his things, put away so good that when my father came to the door, he appeared in my father's suit, shocked that he had returned. And this was an old patient of his. The anti-semitism continued, it was not a very nice place to be, and it was like a ghost town. None of my friends were there, most of the Jews weren't there, it wasn't nice.[26]

Many had this experience of what Susan called 'a sad and painful homecoming'. Home simply did not feel like home anymore. Not only were friends and family no longer there, turning a former home town into a 'ghost town', but it seemed that their previous lives – and homes – had been occupied and were inhabited either by 'strangers' or by known neighbours and acquaintances. Returning to her former home town of Topolcany, Susan found that 'strangers were living in our apartment, and I had to obtain permission from the local police to repossess our furniture', so they 'moved our old furniture into a new, but much smaller apartment'. The mass deportation of Jews from towns and villages across Europe, who had disappeared into the camp network, resulted in absences on the ground that were, as Susan and her family discovered, quickly filled. Jewish homes and apartments did not, as a rule, lie empty during the intervening years. They were quickly occupied by non-Jewish neighbours. It was as if the place of Jews in these towns had been entirely replaced in the months or years between deportation and return. There was literally no home for most to come back to. With pressure it might be possible to get hold of a new apartment and the return of some furniture, as Susan's family did, but it was not the case of slipping back into the familiar place of home. That had gone forever. Not only that, but the town as a familiar social space was also gone.

Although they had been warned to steer clear of the small towns in Poland, the Laks sisters did decide to head back to Starachowice. As Chris explained, 'we just came for the day to find out what's happening'. They quickly decided that it was no longer home. Far from it. After being threatened in the night, they fled the next morning westwards to Łódź, and in a sense kept going ever further west. This sense of running for their lives in the early morning was how Chris painted the picture of 'how I left Starachowice', a place that she 'promised myself never to return' to.[27] But it was not simply that the town of their birth and growing up no longer felt safe or like home. It seemed to Renia that the very soil of the entire continent was tainted. Starachowice itself was seen as dangerous and Europe was a place where 'adjusting to the emptiness' was impossible, and it seemed to Renia that 'the horror . . . was still in the soil . . . European soil'.[28]

It was not only 'horror' that was in the soil. There were also the ashes of men like Hana Pravda's husband Saša. He was buried, as Hana discovered at the end of May 1945, in a mass grave near the railway station in Kraslice. She decided to travel there, to be close to him again. As she wrote in her diary on 30 May 1945:

> I travelled to Kraslice . . . Saša is buried somewhere in a heap of ashes near the railway station. It's a mass grave. Now is the peace we wanted so much. Now is the end of happiness, of love, of hope. The end of my naïve prayers. The end of my youth. The end, instead of a beginning. What remains is a miserable half existence. Saša, I was writing this diary for you. For you I could take the hunger, the cold and reach the end of the road. I didn't want to die. Now it's so difficult to live even from one minute to another. My dear heart, I don't know for how long I'll be able to take it. Perhaps we shall see each other again? I know I'll die and I hope it won't take too long.[29]

Knowing of Saša's fate, the diary entries came to an end through the summer and autumn of 1945. It was only in late November that Hana wrote in the diary again, when she was in Prague and contemplating suicide. Hana was looking to join Saša 'and father, and Jirka Platovský, and Fricek, Aunt Olga, Aunt Rosa, Uncle Ota, Uncle Franci, Jirka Pick, Josefka Neumanová and Maminka!', as she penned a painful list of the dead.[30] Hana's last entry became a suicide note of sorts, with instructions to 'give some of my money to our Theatre. To Anežka give a good ring. Bring my ashes to Kraslice to Saša. I would like to be near him even if so many unknown girls will be around us there. We belong to them.'[31] Ultimately, Hana did not follow through with her plans to commit suicide and be buried at the end of 1945 alongside her beloved Saša. Instead, when she remarried after emigrating to

England, she named her son after the man she had fruitlessly searched for when she headed home.[32]

Hana and Saša's story is a reminder that Holocaust landscapes stretching across Europe included not only the more familiar sites, such as the camp of Buchenwald where Saša was incarcerated, but also the railway tracks at the little-known Kraslice where he died at the very end of the war in the final chaotic phase of the Holocaust. These landscapes included ordinary as well as extraordinary sites and those sites could be, and were, remade across the course of the war. This was very much genocide on the move. Train tracks meant one thing in 1943 and quite another in 1945. The same was true of the concentration camp system. History as well as geography matters. But Hana and Saša's story does not only point to the ways in which the Holocaust was implemented across a vast range of places on the continent. It also highlights that those landscapes were, in many cases, gendered. As Jewish men and women were moved around the continent during the middle years of the Holocaust, they were separated from each other. That gendered separation loosened during the final months of the war, and so Saša lies buried with female prisoners alongside him. However, those prisoners did not include Hana. She and Saša had taken different, if parallel, routes through the landscapes of the Holocaust. As Hana discovered to her great cost – and the Laks sisters and so many others also did – the initial physical and spatial separation of Jewish men and women in the camp system was, in many cases, permanent.

Moving Holocaust Landscapes

A number of threads run through this book that explores a range of Holocaust landscapes. One is a concern with thinking about the Holocaust as a place-making event and the ways that those places were gendered. Another is to consider spatial strategies for survival and the ways that safety was thought of as a place. But there is also another more meta-level thread that runs through this book, which is the broad European continent-wide shift of the events of the Holocaust first eastwards and then westwards (and then in the post-war world back eastwards again). One thing that has always struck me is that the places where the story ended – in the west in the overcrowded camps of Belsen or Dachau in April 1945 – were the very places where post-war engagement with the events of the Holocaust started. In the Cold War world it was the camps liberated by the Western Allies – rather than the camps in the east like Auschwitz, which was liberated by the Soviets – that provided the early visual and imaginative point of reference. The landscapes of these 'horror' camps played a critical role in shaping understandings of the Holocaust as an act of Nazi barbarity.

Gradually, the Holocaust imagination has shifted further eastwards. Starting in the 1960s, but picking up pace in the 1970s and 1980s, Auschwitz began to emerge as the iconic Holocaust landscape, rather than the overcrowded camps liberated by the Western Allies. If Belsen represented Nazi barbarity, then Auschwitz represented something that appeared worse – Nazi clinical efficiency in a factory of death. The dominant mental image was no longer of piles of unburied corpses being bulldozed into pits, but towering smokestacks and the mass gassing and burning of millions in purpose-built assembly-line killing facilities. Belsen seemed to be a landscape from pre-modernity and Nazism a throwback to an earlier, threatening age that had not yet been completely vanquished. But Auschwitz was very much a landscape of modernity, and this raised the spectre that genocide – and genocidal landscapes – lay just underneath the skin of a fragile Western civilization.

Arguably, the last couple of decades have seen us move imaginatively even further east to those places where everything began. It has taken a while to get there, but with the collapse of the Soviet Union in the early 1990s, both new archives and new landscapes have opened up in the east. Here a 'Holocaust by bullets' has – quite literally – been rediscovered. Dispersed across vast swathes of the east, this was a genocide that was both frighteningly local and intimate. It did not involve the infrastructure of genocidal modernity but rather mass shootings into pits dug in sandy soil on the outskirts of town where the victims were marched. There was no need here for the European rail system that played such a central role in transporting bodies to – and out of – places like Auschwitz.

As I have suggested in this book, the complex reality of the Holocaust was that this was an evolving – and constantly moving – genocide that started in the east and then headed westwards within the expanding space of German victory followed by the shrinking space of German defeat. In short, the Holocaust did not happen in one place but many, and was not one single event (with a single landscape) but multiple events that took place in different ways, at different times, in different places. Focusing on these shifting landscapes has the potential to foreground these differences over the course of the war.

But while there were multiple Holocaust landscapes, the starting point for the killings was in the east – in what Timothy Snyder calls the 'bloodlands' and I prefer to call simply the neighbourhood. It has taken us a long time to get back there, but we finally have. We have moved in the post-war world from Belsen to Auschwitz, and in the post-Cold War world to a place like Jedwabne in eastern Poland where, as Jan Gross has shown, around 1,500 Jews were forced into a barn and burnt to death by their neighbours.[1] It seems that in the last few decades, we have finally made it back – imaginatively – to the places where it all started, rather than the places, liberated by the Western Allies, where it all ended.

As we have moved imaginatively further east, the places we have discovered, and what they represent, are arguably more and more threatening to our understanding of self and liberal notions of progress and human perfectability. In the east genocide took place close to home. It was a story of genocide (and hiding) among us. As we have gone further east, and back to the events of 1941 and 1942, my sense is that we have found out that we are still not so great at doing the simplest of things, like living well with those around us. And that, perhaps, is the most depressing of places to end up.

ACKNOWLEDGEMENTS

There are many people who have accompanied me on, and helped me with, this journey through Holocaust landscapes over the past few years. Critical in getting this project underway was the generosity of the British Academy, who awarded me a mid-career fellowship in 2011–12 to begin the process of reading, research and thinking that led to a number of conference papers, journal articles and book chapters as well as ultimately to this book. The British Academy fellowship not only gave me time and space to think, but also the opportunity to visit a number of archives, most importantly the archives of the United States Holocaust Memorial Museum (USHMM) in Washington, DC, and those of the Imperial War Museum (IWM) in London. In Washington, archivist Ron Coleman and his colleagues have been particularly generous with their time and expertise and often suggested things that I should take a look at as I discussed my project with them.

This book relies on a range of diaries, memoirs and oral history interviews with Holocaust survivors. I am very grateful to Alex Pravda for permitting me to use extracts from his mother's moving wartime diary. I am also thankful for the many survivors whose words – whether written or spoken – I draw on. Listening to a lot of oral history interviews over the last few years, I have been particularly struck by the legacy left in a large number of those undertaken by Joan Ringelheim, an interviewer of unusual insight and tenacity. Her lengthy – and quite simply brilliant – interviews with the Laks sisters in particular provide one important strand that runs through this narrative.

But this book – like every book – began long before I embarked on those first forays into writing in 2011. It was a book that in many ways I taught before I wrote, one which emerged out of a third-year lecture response unit that I began teaching at Bristol on 'Holocaust landscapes' a few years earlier. My students who took those classes might recognize some of the ideas first developed alongside them in the classroom. I am lucky to teach exceptionally bright and motivated individuals and they have helped me think about Holocaust landscapes through their questioning and seminar interventions. This book also owes much to the thinking developed alongside a wonderful group of colleagues and friends who make up the 'Holocaust Geographies Collaborative'. Brought together in a window-less basement at USHMM in the summer of 2007 through the receipt of a grant from its Centre for Advanced Holocaust Studies, this group of historians and geographers have been terrific academic sparring partners ever since. Our initial work together culminated in an edited collection – *Geographies of the Holocaust* – in 2014, and more recently our attention has turned to thinking spatially about oral histories, in part through the generous sponsorship of a research workshop hosted at the University of Southern California (USC) by Wolf Gruner and Stephen Smith. I am sure that there are echoes of many conversations with my fellow Holocaust geographers throughout this book.

But in a sense this book also stretches much further back to my time as a PhD student. Starting off as a historian, I shifted to undertake postgraduate research in geography under the supervision of the late Graham Smith. Graham had taken a group of Cambridge geography undergraduates – including a good friend of mine, Matthew Sleeman – on a field trip to Budapest that included a day exploring the former site of the Budapest ghetto. We history undergraduates didn't get to go on field trips, so I was jealous. After the trip, Matthew introduced me to Graham who agreed to become my supervisor – provided I learn Hungarian. I duly did and began working under him in the geography department. There are resonances of that formative intellectual atmosphere in this book where ideas of place and space are central.

One thing that spending time with geographers has convinced me of is the value of field trips in grounding knowledge. Although I ended up teaching in a history department, it is one where place-based research and teaching has been encouraged. In particular I have enjoyed my forays into a diverse range of landscapes with another of my colleagues, Peter Coates, who loves nothing more than getting his boots dirty. Peter is an environmental historian who has encouraged me to think about space and place in more material ways. I don't think I would have thought about something like the mud of Auschwitz without tramping the hills of Wales with Peter discussing environmental histories and reading the articles from him that appeared in my mailbox.

That these ideas have ended up in this format owes much to Robin Baird-Smith, who has long supported my attempts to put my ideas down on paper and has responded with patience to those requests for 'just a little bit more time please'. Robin published my first book, and has never been far from all those that have followed. In the end this book did end up taking a few months longer than I had originally planned. It meant that I finished writing in the summer of 2015 as debates raged in the British press over what the British prime minister, ill-advisedly, called a 'swarm' of migrants. Many of those seeking to enter the UK in the summer of 2015 were refugees fleeing from conflicts across the Middle East and Africa. Their desperate attempts to find a place of safety resonated with some of the stories that I was probing. Of course there are differences between Europe in the 1940s and the world today, but there are commonalities of safety being thought of as a place imagined in terms of national sovereignty, as well as the profound human need to have somewhere safe to call home.

As I have written this book I have been grateful for the kindness extended at home by my long-suffering family – Julie, Alisha and Lauren – and by friends and family who have provided hospitable venues for writing – in particular the Benson family at Pitt Farm and my parents, Roger and Christine Cole. I have also been helped along the way and encouraged by the stimulating and supportive colleagues that I am very lucky to have at the University of Bristol. Robert Bickers has empathized as we have both faced the challenges of balancing a large administrative role with keeping on writing. Josie McLellan and Angela Piccini have read and commented on some of the early articles that emerged from this book project, and suggested things to read that have left their mark in the final manuscript. Jamie Birkett at Bloomsbury offered helpful editorial suggestions and Richard Mason was a very astute editor.

As I completed the book and thought more about some of the threads that run through it, it became clear who I should dedicate it to: my brother Jonathan Cole, and two friends – Jeremy Lindsell and Matthew Sleeman – with whom I first shared a house as a graduate student, and whose ongoing friendship means so much to me. Writing this book has made me think a lot about places but it has also made me think a lot about people. The importance of family and friendship emerges in many of the stories that survivors retell. Given this, it feels entirely appropriate that the book is for Jonathan, Jeremy and Matthew.

Bristol, August 2015

NOTES

Holocaust Landscapes

1 Interview with Joseph Elman (19 May 1998), United States Holocaust Memorial Museum, Washington, DC (hereafter USHMM), RG-50.030*0390.
2 T. Snyder, *Bloodlands* (London: Bodley Head, 2010).
3 P. B. Jaskot and T. Cole, 'Afterword', in A. K. Knowles, T. Cole and A. Giordano (eds), *Geographies of the Holocaust* (Bloomington, IN: Indiana University Press, 2014), pp. 228–9.
4 Interview with Joseph Elman.
5 G. S. Paulsson, *Secret City: The Hidden Jews of Warsaw 1940–1945* (New Haven, CT: Yale University Press, 2004), p. 3.
6 R. Hilberg, *The Politics of Memory: The Journey of a Holocaust Historian* (Chicago: Ivan R. Dee, 1996), pp. 46–8.
7 See for example A. Charlesworth, 'The topography of terror', in D. Stone (ed.), *The Historiography of the Holocaust* (Houndmills: Palgrave Macmillan, 2004), 216–52; T. Cole, *Holocaust City: The Making of a Jewish Ghetto* (New York: Routledge, 2003); T. Cole, *Traces of the Holocaust: Journeying in and out of the Ghettos* (London: Continuum, 2011); Knowles, Cole and Giordano (eds), *Geographies of the Holocaust*; Paolo Giaccaria and Claudio Minca (eds), *Hitler's Geographies: The Spatialities of the Third Reich* (Chicago: University of Chicago Press, 2016).
8 O. Bartov, *Erased: Vanishing Traces of Jewish Galicia in Present-Day Ukraine* (Princeton: Princeton University Press, 2007), p. xiii.
9 The phrase 'choice-less choices' was coined by Lawrence Langer. See e.g. L. L. Langer, 'The dilemma of choice in the deathcamps', in A. Rosenberg and E. Myers (eds), *Echoes from the Holocaust: Philosophical Reflections on a Dark Time* (Philadelphia: Temple University Press, 1988), pp. 118–27.

Prologue: Returning Home/Leaving Home

1 For the similar story of Lore Gang-Saalheimer, see D. Dwork and R. J. van Pelt, *Holocaust: A History* (London: John Murray, 2002), pp. 99–100.
2 Cited in A. Ascher, *A Community under Siege: The Jews of Breslau under Nazism* (Stanford: Stanford University Press, 2007), p. 170.
3 Interview with Gerda Blachman Wilchfort (3 July 1989), USHMM, RG-50.030*0251.
4 Interview with Ernest Heppner (10 May 1989), USHMM, RG-50.030*0095.

5 Ascher, *Community under Siege*, p. 170.

6 M. A. Kaplan, *Between Dignity and Despair: Jewish Life in Nazi Germany* (New York: Oxford University Press, 1998), p. 122.

7 J. Matthäus and M. Roseman (eds), *Jewish Responses to Persecution. Volume 1: 1933–1938* (Lanham, MD: AltaMira Press and USHMM, 2010), p. 350; Kaplan, *Between Dignity and Despair*, p. 120.

8 On the planned spontaneity of *Kristallnacht* see S. Friedlander, *Nazi Germany and the Jews: The Years of Persecution 1933–39* (London: Weidenfeld and Nicolson, 1997), especially pp. 270–1. The extract from Goebbels' diary is cited on p. 272.

9 Interview with Carola Steinhardt (3 June 1996), USHMM, RG-50.030*0368.

10 Dwork and van Pelt, *Holocaust*, pp. 99–100.

11 Interview with Harry Alexander (25 April 1991), USHMM, RG-50.030*0007.

12 Kaplan, *Between Dignity and Despair*, p. 125.

13 Interview with Ernest Heppner.

14 Cited (and translated) in Matthäus and Roseman, *Jewish Responses to Persecution*, pp. 352–3.

15 Matthäus and Roseman, *Jewish Responses to Persecution*, p. 351.

16 Interview with Ernest Heppner.

17 Interview with Gerda Blachman Wilchfort.

18 Kaplan, *Between Dignity and Despair*, pp. 62–73.

19 Ascher, *Community under Siege*, p. 187.

20 Cited in Kaplan, *Between Dignity and Despair*, p. 130.

21 Interview with Gerda Blachman Wilchfort.

22 Interview with Ernest Heppner.

23 Interview with Gerda Schild Haas (12 June 1995), USHMM, RG-50.030*0334.

24 A. Szanto, cited in A. Barkai, *From Boycott to Annihilation: The Economic Struggle of German Jews 1933–1943* (Hanover, NH: University Press of New England, 1989), p. 152.

25 Interview with Gerda Blachman Wilchfort.

26 Kaplan, *Between Dignity and Despair*, p. 143.

27 Interview with Ernest Heppner.

28 Interview with Gerda Schild Haas. On the disproportionate number of German Jewish women left behind see Kaplan, *Between Dignity and Despair*, p. 143.

29 Interview with Carola Steinhardt; interview with Ernest Heppner.

30 Kaplan, *Between Dignity and Despair*, p. 129.

31 Interview with Gerda Schild Haas.

32 Interview with Ernest Heppner.

33 Interview with Gerda Schild Haas.

Ghetto

1 R. Hilberg, S. Staron and J. Kermisz (eds), *The Warsaw Diary of Adam Czerniakow: Prelude to Doom* (New York: Stein and Day, 1979): (18 November 1939), p. 90; (20 November 1939), p. 91.

2   Hilberg, Staron and Kermisz, *The Warsaw Diary* (11 August 1940), p. 183.

3   J. Bauman, *Winter in the Morning: A Young Girl's Life in the Warsaw Ghetto and Beyond* (London: Pan Books, 1987), p. 34.

4   D. Michman, *The Emergence of Jewish Ghettos during the Holocaust* (New York: Cambridge University Press, 2011), pp. 72–3.

5   C. R. Browning, 'Nazi ghettoization policy in Poland: 1939–1941', *Central European History* 19:4 (1986), pp. 343–63; Michman, *The Emergence of Jewish Ghettos*, pp. 84–5.

6   Bauman, *Winter in the Morning*, p. 34.

7   J. Sloan (ed.), *Notes from the Warsaw Ghetto: From the Journal of Emmanuel Ringelblum* (New York: ibooks, 2006): (12–13 October 1940), p. 75.

8   G. Kádár and Z. Vági, *Self-Financing Genocide: The Gold Train, the Becher Case and the Wealth of the Hungarian Jews* (Budapest: Central European University Press, 2004).

9   Y. Gutman, *The Jews of Warsaw, 1939–1943: Ghetto, Underground, Revolt* (Brighton: Harvester Press, 1982), p. 52; Paulsson, *Secret City*, p. 61.

10 On this elsewhere see T. Cole and A. Giordano, 'Bringing the ghetto to the Jew: spatialities of ghettoization in Budapest', in Knowles, Cole and Giordano, *Geographies of the Holocaust*, pp. 123–39.

11 Bauman, *Winter in the Morning*, p. 36.

12 Michman, *The Emergence of Jewish Ghettos*, pp. 74–5.

13 On this in Hungary see T. Cole, *Traces of the Holocaust: Journeying in and out of the Ghettos* (London: Continuum, 2011), pp. 26–32, 56–59.

14 Bauman, *Winter in the Morning*, pp. 38–9.

15 Dwork and van Pelt, *Holocaust*, p. 217.

16 M. Jay, 'Of plots, witnesses, and judgements', in S. Friedlander (ed.), *Probing the Limits of Representation: Nazism and the 'Final Solution'* (Cambridge, MA: Harvard University Press, 1992), p. 103.

17 J. Ringelheim, 'Why women?', in E. Katz and J. Ringelheim (eds), *Proceedings of the Conference on Women Surviving the Holocaust* (New York: Occasional Papers from the Institute for Research in History, 1983), p. 24.

18 Interview with Janina David (14 December 1986), Imperial War Museum Archive (hereafter IWM), 9538.

19 J. David, *A Square of Sky: Memories of a Wartime Childhood* (London: Eland, 1992), p. 121.

20 E. Wiesel, 'Introduction', in R. Braham and B. Vágo (eds), *The Holocaust in Hungary: Forty Years Later* (New York: Columbia University Press, 1985), p. xv.

21 B. Engelking and J. Leociak, *The Warsaw Ghetto: A Guide to the Perished City* (New Haven, CT: Yale University Press, 2009), pp. 47–9.

22 J. Kermisz, 'Introduction', in Hilberg, Staron and Kermisz, *The Warsaw Diary*, p. 53.

23 Bauman, *Winter in the Morning*, p. 63.

24 F. Aldor, *Germany's 'Death Space': The Polish Tragedy* (London: Francis Aldor, 1940), p. 141.

25 Browning, 'Nazi ghettoization policy in Poland', pp. 347–8.

26 Engelking and Leociak, *The Warsaw Ghetto*, pp. 283–84.

27 Engelking and Leociak, *The Warsaw Ghetto*, pp. 416–17.

28 Interview with Janina David; David, *A Square of Sky*, pp. 101–2.
29 Interview with Icek Baum (5 July 1994), USHMM, RG-50.030*0017.
30 Interview with Erwin Baum (6 July 1994), USHMM, RG-50.030*0016.
31 Mary's original name was Miriam Wattenberg. The result of this rewriting is what has been termed a 'diary memoir' or 'hybrid text'. See S. Pentlin, 'Introduction', in S. L. Shneiderman (ed.), *The Diary of Mary Berg: Growing up in the Warsaw Ghetto* (Oxford: Oneworld, 2006), p. xvi; A. Zapruder, *Salvaged Pages: Young Writers' Diaries of the Holocaust* (New Haven, CT: Yale University Press, 2002), p. 444.
32 Shneiderman, *The Diary of Mary Berg* (5 February 1941), pp. 38–9.
33 Shneiderman, *The Diary of Mary Berg* (10 October 1941), p. 101.
34 Shneiderman, *The Diary of Mary Berg* (22 November 1941), pp. 109–10.
35 Shneiderman, *The Diary of Mary Berg* (20 February 1942), p. 124.
36 Interview with David Kochalski (28 July 1994), USHMM, RG-50.030*0001.
37 Interview with Erwin Baum.
38 On the concept of 'third space' see E. W. Soja, *Thirdspace: Journeys to Los Angeles and Other Real-and-Imagined Places* (Oxford: Blackwell, 1996); Bauman, *Winter in the Morning*, p. 52; Engelking and Leociak, *The Warsaw Ghetto*, p. 453.
39 Engelking and Leociak, *The Warsaw Ghetto*, p. 457.
40 Interview with Icek Baum.
41 Interview with Erwin Baum.
42 Interview with Erwin Baum.
43 Cited in A. Polonsky, 'Introduction', in A. Polonksy, *A Cup of Tears: A Diary of the Warsaw Ghetto by Abraham Lewin* (London: Fontana Paperbacks, 1990), p. 2.
44 T. Cole, 'Building and breaching the ghetto boundary: A brief history of the ghetto fence in Körmend, Hungary 1944', *Holocaust and Genocide Studies* 23:1 (2009), pp. 54–75.
45 Interview with Erwin Baum.
46 K. I. Helphand, *Defiant Gardens: Making Gardens in Wartime* (San Antonio, TX: Trinity University Press, 2006), pp. 75–83.
47 Hilberg, Staron and Kermisz, *The Warsaw Diary* (6 December 1941), p. 305.
48 Shneiderman, *The Diary of Mary Berg* (4 April 1941), pp. 45–6.
49 Kermisz, 'Introduction', in Hilberg, Staron and Kermisz, *The Warsaw Diary*, p. 59; Engelking and Leociak, *The Warsaw Ghetto*, pp. 453–8.
50 See e.g. Polonsky, *Cup of Tears* (9 May 1942), p. 66; (18 May 1942), p. 77; (19 May 1942), p. 79; (22 May 1942), p. 89; (4 June 1942), p. 118; (7 June 1942), p. 125.
51 Sloan, *Notes from the Warsaw Ghetto* (mid-September 1941), p. 217; (23 April 1942), p. 256.
52 Polonsky, *Cup of Tears* (18 May 1942), p. 77; (4 June 1942), p. 118; (7 June 1942), p. 124.
53 Hilberg, Staron and Kermisz, *The Warsaw Diary* (18 September 1941), p. 280.
54 Sloan, *Notes from the Warsaw Ghetto* (mid-September 1941), pp. 216–17.
55 Shneiderman, *The Diary of Mary Berg* (15 February 1941), p. 40.
56 Shneiderman, *The Diary of Mary Berg* (20 February 1941), pp. 41–2.
57 Shneiderman, *The Diary of Mary Berg* (12 June 1941), p. 65.

58 Bauman, *Winter in the Morning*, pp. 51–2.

59 Sloan, *Notes from the Warsaw Ghetto* (8 May 1942), pp. 264–5.

60 Interview with Janina David.

61 Bauman, *Winter in the Morning*, p. 39.

62 Bauman, *Winter in the Morning*, p. 39.

63 Sloan, *Notes from the Warsaw Ghetto* (18 May 1941), p. 179.

64 Engelking and Leociak, *The Warsaw Ghetto*, p. 431.

65 Engelking and Leociak, *The Warsaw Ghetto*, pp. 434–5.

66 Sloan, *Notes from the Warsaw Ghetto* (October 1941), p. 222.

67 Shneiderman, *The Diary of Mary Berg* (31 July 1941), pp. 80–1.

68 Shneiderman, *The Diary of Mary Berg* (16 January 1942), p. 122.

69 Shneiderman, *The Diary of Mary Berg* (20 April 1941), p. 48.

70 Engelking and Leociak, *The Warsaw Ghetto*, pp. 594–640.

71 Bauman, *Winter in the Morning*, p. 42.

72 Schneiderman, *The Diary of Mary Berg* (5 February 1941), pp. 38–9.

73 Bauman, *Winter in the Morning*, pp. 52–3.

74 Hilberg, Staron and Kermisz, *The Warsaw Diary* (14 June 1942), p. 366.

75 Interview with Erwin Baum.

76 Interview with Icek Baum.

77 Bauman, *Winter in the Morning*, pp. 39 and 54.

78 Shneiderman, *The Diary of Mary Berg* (20 May 1941), pp. 50–2.

79 Bauman, *Winter in the Morning*, p. 40.

80 Shneiderman, *The Diary of Mary Berg* (17 June 1941), p. 66.

81 Shneiderman, *The Diary of Mary Berg* (29 July 1941), p. 76.

82 Shneiderman, *The Diary of Mary Berg* (31 July 1941), p. 81.

83 Shneiderman, *The Diary of Mary Berg* (10 September 1941), p. 83.

84 Shneiderman, *The Diary of Mary Berg* (3 October 1941), p. 97.

85 Bauman, *Winter in the Morning*, p. 57.

86 Bauman, *Winter in the Morning*, p. 40.

87 Interview with David Kochalski; T. Cole, 'Holocaust tourism: The strange yet familiar/the familiar yet strange', in D. I. Popescu and T. Schult (eds), *Revisiting Holocaust Representation in the Post-Witness Era* (Houndmills: Palgrave Macmillan, 2015), pp. 93–6.

88 Shneiderman, *The Diary of Mary Berg* (25 December 1940), pp. 35–6; (4 January 1941), pp. 36–7.

89 Shneiderman, *The Diary of Mary Berg* (27 February 1942), p. 130; (5 July 1942), pp. 150–1; Bauman, *Winter in the Morning*, p. 58.

90 Shneiderman, *The Diary of Mary Berg* (8 May 1942), p. 145; (5 July 1942), p. 150.

91 Polonsky, *Cup of Tears* (12 June 1942), p. 132.

92 Engelking and Leociak, *The Warsaw Ghetto*, p. 49.

93 Browning, 'Nazi ghettoization policy in Poland', pp. 345–63.

94 Engelking and Leociak, *The Warsaw Ghetto*, p. 730.

95 Bauman, *Winter in the Morning*, pp. 92–7.

96 David, *A Square of Sky*, pp. 214–22.

97   Engelking and Leociak, *The Warsaw Ghetto*, pp. 781–6.
98   Interview with William J. Lowenberg (28 January 1993), USHMM, RG-50.030*0139; Engelking and Leociak, *The Warsaw Ghetto*, pp. 801–2.
99   A. Wójcik, M. Bilewicz and M. Lewicka, 'Living on the ashes: Collective representations of Polish-Jewish history among people living in the former Warsaw Ghetto area', *Cities* 27 (2010), p. 196.

Forest

1   R. Hilberg, *The Destruction of the European Jews*, 3rd edn (New Haven, CT: Yale University Press, 2003), p. 295.
2   E. Greif, *Angels in the Forest* (New York: iUniverse, 2006), pp. 43, 108.
3   Hilberg, *Destruction of the European Jews*, p. 295.
4   Greif, *Angels in the Forest*, pp. 52–3.
5   Greif, *Angels in the Forest*, p. 8; cf. Interview with Earl Greif, USC Shoah Foundation (hereafter USC) 10904; Rachel Minkoff, 'Earl Greif', in California State Assembly, *2008 California Holocaust Memorial Book* http://asmdc.org/members/a42/attachments/HolocaustMemorialBook.pdf. For more on the discrepancies in Greif's account see T. Cole, '(Re)Placing the past: Spatial strategies of retelling difficult stories', *Oral History Review* 42:1 (2015), pp. 30–49.
6   Hilberg, *Destruction of the European Jews*, p. 293.
7   R. Brandon and W. Lower, 'Introduction', in R. Brandon and W. Lower (eds), *The Shoah in Ukraine: History, Testimony, Memorialization* (Bloomington, IN: Indiana University Press, 2010), p. 13; D. Pohl, 'The murder of Ukraine's Jews under German military administration and in the Reich Commissariat Ukraine', in Brandon and Lower, *The Shoah in Ukraine*, p. 28.
8   C. R. Browning and J. Matthäus, *The Origins of the Final Solution: The Evolution of Nazi Jewish Policy, September 1939–March 1942* (Lincoln, NB: University of Nebraska Press, 2004), p. 312.
9   Y. Lozowick, 'Rollbahn Mord: The early activities of Einsatzgruppen C', *Holocaust and Genocide Studies* 2:2 (1987), pp. 221–41.
10   Hilberg, *Destruction of the European Jews*, pp. 304–5.
11   Hilberg, *Destruction of the European Jews*, p. 361.
12   Hilberg, *Destruction of the European Jews*, pp. 382–6.
13   Pohl, 'The murder of Ukraine's Jews', pp. 48–9, 50–1.
14   A. Charlesworth, 'The topography of genocide', in D. Stone (ed.), *The Historiography of the Holocaust* (Houndmills: Palgrave Macmillan, 2004), pp. 221–2.
15   Charlesworth, 'Topography of genocide', p. 222. See also C. R. Browning, *Ordinary Men: Reserve Police Batallion 101 and the Final Solution in Poland* (Harmondsworth: Penguin, 2001), p. 98; P. Desbois, *The Holocaust by Bullets: A Priest's Journey to Uncover the Truth Behind the Murder of 1.5 Million Jews* (Houndmills: Palgrave Macmillan, 2008), pp. 35, 40, 56, 111–16.

16 Charlesworth, 'Topography of genocide', p. 222.
17 Greif, *Angels in the Forest*, p. 7.
18 Hilberg, *Destruction of the European Jews*, p. 406; Pohl, 'The murder of Ukraine's Jews', pp. 53–4.
19 Desbois, *The Holocaust by Bullets*, p. 64.
20 P. Pekerman, 'There was a lot of humiliation', in B. Zabarko (ed.), *Holocaust in the Ukraine* (London: Vallentine Mitchell, 2005), p. 204.
21 T. Snyder, 'The life and death of western Volhynian Jewry, 1921–1945', in Brandon and Lower, *The Shoah in Ukraine*, p. 97.
22 N. Tec, *Defiance: The True Story of the Bielski Partisans* (New York: Oxford University Press, 2008), p. 288.
23 Interview with Josef Perl (15 January 1998), IWM, 17883.
24 Snyder, 'The life and death of western Volhnian Jewry', p. 97.
25 S. E. Paper, *Voices from the Forest: The True Story of Abram and Julia Bobrow* (Bloomington, IN: 1st Books Library, 2003), p. 3.
26 Interview with Samuel Gruber (21 May 1991), USHMM, RG-50.030*0087.
27 Interview with Charlene Perlmutter Schiff (23 March 1993), USHMM, RG-50.030*0203.
28 S. S. Orbuch and F. Rosenbaum, *Here, there are no Sarahs: A Woman's Courageous Fight Against the Nazis and her Bittersweet Fulfillment of the American Dream* (Muskegon, MI: RDR Books, 2009), pp. 71, 74, 77, 81, 91, 92, 102.
29 Paper, *Voices from the Forest*, p. 106.
30 Orbuch and Rosenbaum, *Here, there are no Sarahs*, p. 91.
31 Cited in S. W. Weber, 'The forest as a liminal space: A transformation of culture and norms during the Holocaust', *Holocaust Studies* 14:1 (2008), p. 54.
32 N. Kohn and H. Roiter, *A Voice from the Forest: Memoirs of a Jewish Partisan* (New York: Holocaust Library, 1980), p. 35.
33 C. Lafferty, 'Chaim Melcer's *Voice from the Forest*: Remembering the Holocaust' (PhD Dissertation, Drew University, 2008), p. 75; Paper, *Voices from the Forest*, pp. 202, 206.
34 J. Kagan and D. Cohen, *Surviving the Holocaust with the Russian Jewish Partisans*, 2nd edn (London: Vallentine Mitchell, 2000), p. 91.
35 Kagan and Cohen, *Surviving the Holocaust*, pp. 197–8; Hilberg, *Destruction of the European Jews*, p. 395.
36 Hilberg, *Destruction of the European Jews*, p. 394.
37 Pohl, 'The murder of Ukraine's Jews', p. 52.
38 Interview with Charlene Perlmutter Schiff, USHMM, RG-50.030*0203; First-Person Interview with Charlene Perlmutter Schiff (31 March 2005), USHMM; First Person Interview with Charlene Perlmutter Schiff (19 May 2009), USHMM; H. Altman, *On the Fields of Loneliness* (New York: Yad Vashem and the Holocaust Survivors' Memorial Project, 2006), pp. 117–18; N. Anapolsky, 'We survived thanks to the kind people – Ukrainians and Poles', in Zabarko, *Holocaust in the Ukraine*, p. 9; interview with Sonia Heidocovsky Zissman (25 May 1995), USHMM, RG-50.030*0332.
39 Paper, *Voices from the Forest*, pp. 108–10.

40 Interview with Charlene Schiff.

41 Paper, *Voices from the Forest*, p. 111.

42 Paper, *Voices from the Forest*, p. 129.

43 Interview with Samuel Gruber.

44 Tec, *Defiance*, pp. 87–8.

45 Interview with Rachel Mutterperl Goldfarb (5 September 1991), USHMM, RG-50.030*0082.

46 M. Katz, *Path of Hope* (New York: Yad Vashem and the Holocaust Survivors' Memoirs Project, 2008), pp. 116–17.

47 Katz, *Path of Hope*, pp. 114–15.

48 Interview with Charlene Schiff.

49 Katz, *Path of Hope*, p. 39.

50 Katz, *Path of Hope*, p. 60.

51 Katz, *Path of Hope*, pp. 114–15.

52 Katz, *Path of Hope*, pp. 116, 123, 169–70; L. Reizer, *In the Struggle: Memoirs from Grodno and the Forests* (New York: Yad Vashem and the Holocaust Survivors' Memoirs Project, 2009), p. 173; Greif, *Angels in the Forest*, p. 10.

53 Paper, *Voices from the Forest*, p. 106.

54 Altman, *On the Fields of Loneliness*, p. 119; Paper, *Voices from the Forest*, p. 123.

55 Paper, *Voices from the Forest*, p. 110.

56 Anapolsky, 'We survived thanks to the kind people', pp. 10–11.

57 Greif, *Angels in the Forest*, p. 11; Lafferty, 'Chaim Melcer's *Voice*', p. 76; Kagan and Cohen, *Surviving the Holocaust*, p. 68.

58 Paper, *Voices from the Forest*, p. 110; interview with Sonia Heidocovsky Zissman.

59 Katz, *Path of Hope*, pp. 124–5; Reizer, *In the Struggle*, p. 170; Paper, *Voices from the Forest*, pp. 114–15, 120, 201; interview with Semyon Menyuk (25 October 1990), USHMM, RG-50.030*0159; interview with Sonia Boldo Bielski (11 July 1994), USHMM, RG-50.030*0025; First-Person Interview with Charlene Perlmutter Schiff (19 May 2009).

60 Paper, *Voices from the Forest*, pp. 114–15, 120, 128; interview with Dora Kramen Dimitro (18 July 1996), USHMM, RG-50.030*0372.

61 G. Weinerman, 'The terror of the Jewish population began in the first days of occupation', in Zabarko, *Holocaust in the Ukraine*, p. 42; Katz, *Path of Hope*, pp. 133, 154–70; Greif, *Angels in the Forest*, pp. 54–7. See the gendering of this with Sonia Bielski and her mother both spending the winters outside of the forest: see interview with Sonia Boldo Bielski.

62 Lafferty, 'Chaim Melcer's *Voice*', pp. 30, 75–6.

63 Paper, *Voices from the Forest*, p. 111.

64 Paper, *Voices from the Forest*, p. 125.

65 Kohn and Roiter, *Voice from the Forest*, pp. 35–6.

66 Kohn and Roiter, *Voice from the Forest*, p. 99.

67 Kagan and Cohen, *Surviving the Holocaust*, p. 60.

68 Kagan and Cohen, *Surviving the Holocaust*, pp. 87, 191.

69 Tec, *Defiance*, p. 263.

70   Paper, *Voices from the Forest*, p. 152.

71   Interview with Josef Perl.

72   Kagan and Cohen, *Surviving the Holocaust*, p. 64.

73   Kagan and Cohen, *Surviving the Holocaust*, p. 64.

74   Kagan and Cohen, *Surviving the Holocaust*, p. 88.

75   J. Harmatz, *From the Wings. A Long Journey: 1940–1960* (Lewes: The Book Guild, 1998), p. 85; Paper, *Voices from the Forest*, p. 206.

76   N. Tec, *Resilience and Courage: Women, Men and the Holocaust* (New Haven, CT: Yale University Press, 2003), pp. 270–1; Tec, *Defiance*, pp. 89–93.

77   Tec, *Resilience and Courage*, p. 282.

78   Kagan and Cohen, *Surviving the Holocaust*, p. 83.

79   Paper, *Voices from the Forest*, pp. 180–1.

80   Kagan and Cohen, *Surviving the Holocaust*, pp. 63–4.

81   Tec, *Defiance*, p. 103.

82   Interview with Joseph Elman.

83   Paper, *Voices from the Forest*, p. 153.

84   Harmatz, *From the Wings*, pp. 84–5.

85   Kohn and Roiter, *Voice from the Forest*, pp. 59, 95.

86   Interview with Rachel Mutterperl Goldfarb; interview with Florence Gitelman Eisen (18 August 1994), USHMM, RG-50.030*0260.

87   Paper, *Voices from the Forest*, p. 68.

88   Reizer, *In the Struggle*, p. 157.

89   Reizer, *In the Struggle*, pp. 157–9.

90   Interview with Joseph Harmatz (11 May 1998), IWM, 18221.

91   Kohn and Roiter, *Voice from the Forest*, p. 44; Harmatz, *From the Wings*, pp. 86–8.

92   Interview with Joseph Elman.

93   Interview with Samuel Gruber.

94   Interview with Florence Gitelman Eisen.

95   Tec, *Resilience and Courage*, p. 306.

96   Orbuch and Rosenbaum, *Here, there are no Sarahs*, p. 83.

97   Orbuch and Rosenbaum, *Here, there are no Sarahs*, pp. 94, 85.

98   Interview with Florence Gitelman Eisen.

99   Orbuch and Rosenbaum, *Here, there are no Sarahs*, p. 88.

100   Paper, *Voices from the Forest*, pp. 198–200.

101   Leib, *In the Struggle*, p. 156.

102   Katz, *Path of Hope*, pp. 187–8, 199.

103   Kohn and Roiter, *Voice from the Forest*, pp. 15, 36. 93. On this more generally, see T. Cole, '"Nature was helping us": Forests, trees, and environmental histories of the Holocaust', *Environmental History* 19 (2014), pp. 665–86.

104   Reizer, *In the Struggle*, p. 161.

105   Reizer, *In the Struggle*, p. 171.

106   Katz, *Path of Hope*, pp. 176–7.

107   Katz, *Path of Hope*, p. 179.

108   Hilberg, *Destruction of the European Jews*, p. 276.

Camp

1   On the narratives of this separation see Cole, '(Re)Placing the past', pp. 30–49.
2   For a reinterpretation of this meeting see M. Roseman, *The Villa, the Lake, the Meeting: Wannsee and the Final Solution* (Harmondsworth: Penguin, 2003).
3   Interview with Regina Laks Gelb (20 February 2001), USHMM, RG-50.030*0410. Regina was known as Renia by her sisters, so this is the name I use throughout. See also interview with Bella Simon Pasternak (21 April 1994), USHMM, RG-50.030*0176.
4   'Blockbuch', Auschwitz Birkenau Block 22b (1944), USHMM, RG-65.003M.
5   Interview with Lilly Malnik (10 May 1990), USHMM, RG-50.030*0146.
6   Interview with Nina Kaleska (3 January 1990), USHMM, RG-50.030*0101.
7   J. Bachner, *My Darkest Years: Memoirs of a Survivor of Auschwitz, Warsaw and Dachau* (Jefferson, NC: McFarland and Company, 2007), p. 163.
8   Interview with Ruth Krautwirth Meyerowitz (20 February 1990), USHMM, RG-50.030*0161.
9   Interview with Margaret Jastrow Klug (13 March 1990), USHMM, RG-50.030*0108.
10   D. Dwork and R. J. van Pelt, *Auschwitz: 1270 to the Present* (New York: W. W. Norton, 1996), pp. 336–7.
11   Dwork and van Pelt, *Auschwitz*, pp. 326, 336–7.
12   S. Steinbacher, *Auschwitz: A History* (Harmondsworth: Penguin, 2005), p. 106.
13   T. Cole, 'Crematoria, barracks, gateway: Survivors' return visits to the memory landscapes of Auschwitz', *History and Memory* 25:2 (2013), pp. 102–31; K. Hart, *Return to Auschwitz* (London: Granada, 1983), p. 121.
14   E. Olsson with R. Jacques, *Remembering Forever: A Journey of Darkness and Light* (Bracebridge, ON: Eva Olsson, 2008), p. 94.
15   Interview with Michael Vogel (10 July 1997), USHMM, RG-50.030*0240.
16   H. Morlok, 'Preface', in T. Swiebocka (ed.), *The Architecture of Crime: The Security and Isolation System of the Auschwitz Camp* (Oswiecm: Auschwitz-Birkenau State Museum, 2008), p. 10; cf. P. Setkiewicz, 'The fencing and system for preventing prisoner escapes at Auschwitz concentration camp', in Swiebocka, *Architecture of Crime*, p. 52.
17   Interview with George Havas (26 August 1996), USHMM, RG-50.030*0378.
18   W. Sofsky, *The Order of Terror: The Concentration Camps* (Princeton: Princeton University Press, 1999), p. 51.
19   Interview with Michael Vogel.
20   Interview with Thomas Buergenthal (29 January 1990), USHMM, RG-50.030*0046.
21   Sofsky, *Order of Terror*, p. 55.
22   Olsson, *Remembering Forever*, p. 94.
23   Interview with Lilly Malnik; F. B. Hyatt, *Close Calls: Memoirs of a Survivor* (Washington, DC: United States Holocaust Memorial Museum Holocaust Library, 2000), pp. 94–5.
24   Hyatt, *Close Calls*, pp. 97–8; M. Nitkiewicz, 'Shame, guilt, and anguish in Holocaust survivor testimony', *Oral History Review* 30:1 (2003), p. 9; K. Hart, *Return to Auschwitz* (London: Granada, 1983), p. 83.

25   I. Choko-Sztrauch-Galewska, 'My first life', in D. Silberklang (ed.), *Stolen Youth: Five Women's Survival in the Holocaust* (New York: Yad Vashem and the Holocaust Survivors' Memoirs Project, 2005), p. 42.
26   E. Wiesel, *Night* (New York: Bantam Books, 1960), p. 27.
27   Interview with Leo Schneiderman (23 May 1990), USHMM, RG-50.030*0205.
28   *Nuremberg Trial Proceedings*. Volume 8, Sixty-Ninth Day, Morning Session (27 February 1946).
29   Setkiewicz, 'The fencing and system for preventing prisoner escapes', p. 42.
30   Interview with William J. Lowenberg (28 January 1993), USHMM, RG-50.030*0139.
31   Interview with Thomas Buergenthal.
32   Interview with Regina Laks Gelb; interview with Michael Vogel; interview with William J. Lowenberg; interview with Nina Kaleska.
33   Interview with Regina Laks Gelb.
34   Hart, *Return to Auschwitz*, p. 110.
35   Interview with Magda Blau (11 June 1990), USHMM, RG-50.030*30.
36   Interview with Regina Laks Gelb.
37   Interview with William J. Lowenberg.
38   Hyatt, *Close Calls*, p. 90.
39   Hart, *Return to Auschwitz*, pp. 99, 102–4.
40   Interview with Beno Helmer (25 June 1990), USHMM, RG-50.030*0093.
41   Interview with Rosalie (Chris) Laks Lerman (1 December 1998, 13 January 1999), USHMM RG-50.030*0396. As with Renia, I use the name Chris that the sisters use in their interviews.
42   Hyatt, *Close Calls*, p. 85.
43   Hyatt, *Close Calls*, pp. 89–91.
44   Hart, *Return to Auschwitz*, pp. 89–90, 100.
45   Choko-Sztrauch-Galewska, 'My first life', p. 43.
46   Interview with Magda Blau; Hart, *Return to Auschwitz*, pp. 92–5, cf. pp. 106–7.
47   F. Irwin, '"Remember to be a good human being": A memoir of life and the Holocaust', in Silberklang, *Stolen Youth*, p. 97.
48   Interview with Bela Blau (11 June 1990), USHMM, RG-50.030*0029.
49   Interview with Thomas Buergenthal.
50   Interview with Rosalie Laks Lerman.
51   Interview with Regina Laks Gelb, USHMM, RG-50.030*0410.
52   Interview with Rosalie Laks Lerman.
53   Interview with Anna Laks Wilson (21 February 2001), USHMM, RG-50.030*0411. As with Renia and Chris, I use the name Hania, which is the name the sisters used in their interviews.
54   Interview with Rosalie Laks Lerman.
55   Interview with Regina Laks Gelb.
56   Interview with Rosalie Laks Lerman.
57   Interview with Regina Laks Gelb.
58   Interview with Rosalie Laks Lerman.

59 Interview with Michael Vogel.
60 Interview with Rosalie Laks Lerman; interview with Anna Laks Wilson.
61 Interview with Regina Laks Gelb; interview with Anna Laks Wilson.
62 Interview with Rosalie Laks Lerman.
63 Interview with Ruth Krautwirth Meyerowitz.
64 Zipora B. in I. Rosen, *Hungarian Jewish Women Survivors Remember the Holocaust: An Anthology of Life Histories* (Lanham, MD: University Press of America, 2004), p. 100; Hart, *Return to Auschwitz*, p. 91.
65 Interview with Abraham Malnik (27 February 1992), USHMM, RG-50.030*0145.
66 Hyatt, *Close Calls*, p. 105.
67 Hyatt, *Close Calls*, p. 109.
68 Interview with Lilly Malnik.
69 Interview with William J. Lowenberg.
70 Hyatt, *Close Calls*, p. 95.
71 Interview with Regina Laks Gelb.
72 Interview with Regina Lak Gelb.
73 Interview with William J. Lowenberg.
74 Interview with Rudy Kennedy (16 February 1998), IWM, 17940.
75 Interview with Regina Laks Gelb.
76 Interview with Leo Schneiderman.
77 Hyatt, *Close Calls*, pp. 87–8; Interview with Rose Szywic Warner (12 September 1994), USHMM, RG-50.030*0270; Ariella G. in Rosen, *Hungarian Jewish Women Survivors*, p. 40.
78 Interview with Bella Simon Pasternak.
79 Interview with Bella Simon Pasternak.
80 Interview with Bella Simon Pasternak.
81 M. R. Kalina, 'Surviving a thousand deaths. Memoir: 1939–1945', in Silberklang (ed.), *Stolen Youth*, p. 220.
82 Sofsky, *Order of Terror*, p. 47.
83 Interview with Antoni Golba (29 June 1994), USHMM, RG-50.030*0081.
84 P. B. Jaskot, A. K. Knowles and C. Harvey, with B. P. Blackshear, 'Visualizing the archive: Building at Auschwitz as a geographic problem', in Knowles, Cole and Giordano (eds), *Geographies of the Holocaust*, pp. 179–83.
85 Interview with Michael Vogel; interview with Erich Kulka (8 June 1990), USHMM, RG-50.030*0119.
86 Interview with Rosalie (Chris) Laks Lerman; interview with Nina Kaleska.
87 *Kitty: Return to Auschwitz* (Yorkshire Television, 1979); Hart, *Return to Auschwitz*, pp. 82–3, 128, 220. See also interview with Rudy Kennedy.
88 Interview with Lilly Malnik; Hyatt, *Close Calls*, p. 94.
89 Interview with Magda Blau; Hyatt, *Close Calls*, p. 94.
90 Interview with Hana Bruml (27 February 1990), USHMM, RG-50.030*0043.
91 Ariella G. in Rosen, *Hungarian Jewish Women Survivors*, p. 41.
92 Interview with Carola Steinhardt.
93 Interview with Carola Steinhardt.

94 Irwin, '"Remember to be a good human being"', p. 96.

95 Interview with Ruth Krautwirth Meyerowitz.

96 E. Stroud, 'Does nature always matter? Following dirt through history', *History and Theory* 42 (2004), pp. 75–6, 80.

97 Dwork and van Pelt, *Auschwitz*, p. 343.

98 Interview with David Bergman (18 July 1990), USHMM, RG-50.030*0020.

99 Interview with Michael Vogel.

100 C. Gerlach and G. Aly, *Das letze kapital. Realpolitik, Ideologie und der Mord an den ungarischen Juden 1944/1945* (Stuttgart and Munich: Deutsche Verlags-Anstalt, 2002), pp. 158–71, 375–414.

101 Hyatt, *Close Calls*, pp. 117–18.

102 D. Bloxham, *The Final Solution: A Genocide* (Oxford: Oxford University Press, 2009), p. 251.

103 Interview with George Havas.

104 A. K. Knowles, P. B. Jaskot, with B. P. Blackshear, M. de Groot and A. Yule, 'Mapping the SS concentration camps', in Knowles, Cole and Giordano, *Geographies of the Holocaust*, pp. 18–50.

105 Interview with Gerda Schild Haas.

Train

1 S. Gigliotti, *The Train Journey: Transit, Captivity, and Witnessing in the Holocaust* (New York: Berghahn Books, 2009), pp. 94–5.

2 Ferenczy report (9 July 1944), USHMM, RG-52.009.04/1.

3 Gigliotti, *Train Journey*, p. 4; Alfred C. Mierzejewski, 'A public enterprise in the service of mass murder: The Deutsche Reichsbahn and the Holocaust', *Holocaust and Genocide Studies* 15:1 (2001), pp. 33–46.

4 Raul Hilberg, 'German railroads/Jewish souls', *Society* 35:3 (1998), p. 162.

5 Interview with Rita Kerner Hilton (10 August 1994) USHMM, RG-50.030*0002.

6 Gigliotti, *Train Journey*, p. 54.

7 Hilberg, 'German railroads/Jewish souls', pp. 170–71.

8 Interview with Anna Laks Wilson.

9 Simone Gigliotti, *Train Journey*, pp. 114–16.

10 Interview with Fritzie Weiss Fritzshall (27 June 1990), USHMM, RG-50.030*0075.

11 Interview with George Havas.

12 Interview with Madeline Deutsch (14 May 1990), USHMM, RG-50.030*0060.

13 Interview with Madeline Deutsch. See also the choice of chapter title, '8 Horses – or 96 Men, Women, and Children', in O. Lengyel, *Five Chimneys* (London: Granada, 1972).

14 Interview with Madeline Deutsch. The analogy of being packed like sardines or herrings into a can to explain the degree of overcrowding is widely drawn on; see Gigliotti, *Train Journey*, pp. 100, 170.

15 Interview with George Havas.

16 Franz Stangl cited in Gigliotti, *Train Journey*, p. 50.

17 Wiesel, 'Introduction', p. xv.

18 Interview with Madeline Deutsch.

19 Interview with Madeline Deutsch.

20 Interview with George Havas.

21 On what she terms 'transport shame' see Gigliotti, *Train Journey*, pp. 101–4. Not all survivors remember having a bucket for a toilet. Hania Laks, when asked, told her interviewer that they did not have one and she was not alone in this memory. Interview with Anna Laks Wilson.

22 Interview with George Havas.

23 Interview with Kate Bernath (22 March 1990), USHMM, RG-50.030*0023.

24 Michael Kraus, 'Diary', pp. 26–7, USHMM 2006.51.

25 Interview with Rita Kerner Hilton.

26 Roselia J. in Rosen, *Hungarian Jewish Women Survivors*, p. 62.

27 Interview with Alex Braun (9 July 1990), USHMM, RG-50.030*0036.

28 Gigliotti, *Train Journey*, p. 101.

29 Interview with Rose Szywic Warner (12 September 1994), USHMM, RG-50.030*0270.

30 David Boder interview with Jacob Schwarzfitter (31 August 1946), cited in Gigliotti, *Train Journey*, p. 152.

31 David Boder interview with Nechama Epstein (31 August 1946), cited in Gigliotti, *Train Journey*, p. 153.

32 David Boder interview with Benjamin Piskorz (1 September 1946), cited in Gigliotti, *Train Journey*, p. 155.

33 Interview with Ernest Koenig (12 June 1997), USHMM, RG-50.030*0112.

34 Interview with Leo Bretholz (31 July and 27 September 1989), USHMM, RG-50.030*0038.

35 Interview with Ernest Koenig.

36 Interview with Beno Helmer.

37 T. des Pres, *The Survivor: An Anatomy of Life in the Death Camps* (Oxford: Oxford University Press, 1976), ch. 3; Gigliotti, *Train Journey*, p. 21.

38 Gigliotti, *Train Journey*, p. 27.

39 Interview with Anna Laks Wilson.

40 Interview with Fritzie Weiss Fritzshall.

41 Interview with Madeline Deutsch.

42 Michael Kraus, 'Diary', p. 32.

43 Michael Kraus, 'Diary', p. 31.

44 Interview with George Havas.

45 Interview with Ernest Koenig.

46 Interview with Nina Kaleska.

47 Interview with Meyer Adler (24 April 1991), USHMM, RG-50.030*0005.

48 Gigliotti, *Train Journey*, pp. 159–60, 214.

49 Interview with Leo Bretholz.

50　D. Blatman, *The Death Marches: The Final Phase of Nazi Genocide* (Cambridge, MA: The Belknap Press of Harvard University Press, 2011), p. 41.

51　Interview with David Bergman, USHMM, RG-50.030*0020.

52　Interview with David Bergman, USC, VHA 42574.

53　Interview with David Bergman, USHMM, RG-50.030*0020.

54　Interview with David Bergman, USC, VHA 42574.

55　Interview with David Bergman, USHMM, RG-50.030*0020.

56　Interview with David Bergman, USHMM, RG-50.030*0020; Interview with David Bergman, USC, VHA 42574.

57　Interview with David Bergman, USHMM, RG-50.030*0020.

58　Interview with David Bergman, USHMM, RG-50.030*0020.

59　Interview with David Bergman, USHMM, RG-50.030*0020.

60　Interview with David Bergman, USHMM, RG-50.030*0020.

61　Interview with William J. Lowenberg.

62　Interview with William J. Lowenberg.

63　See also interview with Rita Kerner Hilton.

64　Interview with David Bergman, USHMM, RG-50.030*0020.

65　Interview with David Bergman, USHMM, RG-50.030*0020.

66　Interview with David Bergman, USHMM, RG-50.030*0020.

Attic and Cellar, Mountain and Sea

1　Interview with Gerda Blachman Wilchfort.

2　Interview with Peter Feigl (23 August 1995), USHMM, RG-50.030*0272; A. Giordano and A. Holian, 'Retracing the "hunt for Jews": A spatio-temporal analysis of arrests during the Holocaust in Italy', in Knowles, Cole and Giordano, *Geographies of the Holocaust*, pp. 52–86.

3　On the background to this see G. S. Paulsson, 'The "Bridge over the Oresund": The historiography on the expulsion of the Jews from Nazi-cccupied Denmark', *Journal of Contemporary History* 30:3, pp. 431–64; H. Kirchoff, 'Denmark: A light in the darkness of the Holocaust? A reply to Gunnar S. Paulsson', *Journal of Contemporary History* 30:3, pp. 465–79.

4　Paulsson, *Secret City*, p. 9.

5　Hilberg, *Destruction of the European Jews*, pp. 599–600.

6　Kagan and Cohen, *Surviving the Holocaust*, p. 40.

7　Kagan and Cohen, *Surviving the Holocaust*, p. 41.

8　Interview with Johanne Hirsch Liebmann (19 January 1990), USHMM, RG-50.030*0133.

9　Interview with Max Liebmann (19 January 1990), USHMM, RG-50.030*0134.

10　Interview with Leo Bretholz.

11　Interview with Eva Edmunds (18 October 1990), USHMM, RG-50.030*0064.

12 Interview with Max Liebmann.

13 Interview with Gerda Blachman Wilchfort.

14 Interview with Frieda Belinfante (31 May 1994), USHMM, RG-50.030*0019.

15 Knud in K. Monroe, *The Hand of Compassion* (Princeton: Princeton University Press, 2004), p. 166.

16 P. A. Levine, *From Indifference to Activism: Swedish Diplomacy and the Holocaust, 1938–1944* (Uppsala: Acta Universitatis Upsaliensis Studia Historica Upsaliensia, 1996), pp. 229–45.

17 Interview with Frode Jacobson (30 April 1995), USHMM, RG-50.030*0330.

18 Interview with Niels Bamberger (26 December 1989), USHMM, RG-50.030*0013. See also interview with Frank Meissner (1 December 1989), USHMM, RG-50.030*0158.

19 Interview with Preben Munch-Nielsen (6 November 1989), USHMM, RG-50.030*0167.

20 Interview with Preben Munch-Nielsen.

21 Interview with Niels Bamberger.

22 Interview with Gerda Blachman Wilchfort.

23 Interview with William J. Lowenberg.

24 Hilberg, *Destruction of the European Jews*, p. 627.

25 Interview with Gerda Blachman Wilchfort.

26 D. Barnouw and G. van der Stroom (eds), *The Diary of Anne Frank: The Critical Edition* (London: Viking, 1989): (11 July 1942), p. 216.

27 Barnouw and Van der Stroom, *The Diary of Anne Frank* (27 April 1943), p. 355; (17 February 1944), p. 488; (25 April 1944), p. 617.

28 Barnouw and Van der Stroom, *The Diary of Anne Frank* (11 April 1944), pp. 599–600.

29 B. Moore, *Victims and Survivors: The Nazi Persecution of the Jews in the Netherlands 1940–1945* (London: Arnold, 1997), p. 146.

30 Altman, *On the Fields of Loneliness*, pp. 127, 157, 136–7.

31 Paulsson, *Secret City*, pp. 129–30.

32 Moore, *Victims and Survivors*, p. 155.

33 Interview with Susie Gruenbaum Schwarz (14 February 1990), USHMM, RG-50.030*0209.

34 Hilberg, *Destruction of the European Jews*, p. 627.

35 Interview with Hetty d'Ancona de Leeuwe (13 February 1990), USHMM, RG-50.030*0059.

36 Interview with Helen Waterford (14 November 1989), USHMM, RG-50.030*0246.

37 Interview with Helen Waterford.

38 Interview with Lore Baer (8 June 1990), USHMM, RG-50.030*0011.

39 Interview with Hetty d'Ancona de Leeuwe.

40 Interview with Susie Gruenbaum Schwarz.

41 Diary of Mrs E. J. van Lohuizen (unpublished manuscript), USHMM, RG-680.102, pp. 95ff, 103, 109, 129.

42 J. B. Schor, 'Mamma's ark' (unpublished manuscript), USHMM, 2011.301, pp. 132–5; Moore, *Victims and Survivors*, p. 156.

43   Interview with Susie Gruenbaum Schwarz.
44   Interview with Charlene Perlmutter Schiff, USHMM, RG-50.030*0203.
45   Interview with Lore Baer.
46   Interview with Karel Poons (12 October 1990), USHMM, RG-50.030*0183.
47   Bauman, *Winter in the Morning*, p. 138.
48   Schor, 'Mamma's ark', p. 73.
49   Bauman, *Winter in the Morning*, p. 105.
50   Interview with Susie Gruenbaum Schwarz.
51   Bauman, *Winter in the Morning*, pp. 111–12.
52   Bauman, *Winter in the Morning*, p. 130; Paulsson, *Secret City*.
53   Bauman, *Winter in the Morning*, p. 137.
54   Bauman, *Winter in the Morning*, pp. 101–2.
55   Bauman, *Winter in the Morning*, pp. 140–1.
56   Interview with Carla Heijmans Lessing (29 May 1990), USHMM,
     RG-50.030*0126.
57   Interview with Selma Wijnberg Engel (16 July 1990), USHMM, RG-50.030*0067.
58   Tec, *Resilience and Courage*, pp. 229–31.
59   Interview with Susie Gruenbaum Schwarz; interview with Carla Heijmans Lessing.
60   Katz, *Path of Hope*, pp. 76, 84.
61   Katz, *Path of Hope*, p. 99.
62   Katz, *Path of Hope*, pp. 99–102.
63   Katz, *Path of Hope*, p. 107.
64   Katz, *Path of Hope*, p. 102.
65   Katz, *Path of Hope*, pp. 104–6.
66   Katz, *Path of Hope*, p. 108.
67   Katz, *Path of Hope*, p. 151.
68   Katz, *Path of Hope*, p. 153.
69   Katz, *Path of Hope*, p. 157.

River

1   Cole, *Holocaust City*.
2   Zs. Ozsváth, *When the Danube Ran Red* (Syracuse, NY: Syracuse University Press, 2010), p. 125.
3   Interview with Per Anger (12 March 1990; 14 March 1990; 15 March 1990; 20 March 1990), Uppsala Universitets Arkiv, Raoul Wallenberg Project Archive (hereafter RWPA), F2C 002.
4   Interview with Per Anger.
5   Interview with Eugenia Blau Szamosi (12 September 1990), USHMM RG-50.030*0229.
6   Interview with Per Anger.

7   Interview with István Schalk (18 August 1989; 2 November 1989), RWPA, F2C 303.

8   Interview with Per Anger.

9   Interview with Eugenia Blau Szamosi.

10 Interview with Peter Tarjan (11 April 1989), RWPA, F2C 503; interview with Erszébet Schwartz (1 April 1990), RWPA, F2C 344; interview with István Schalk.

11 A. Cohen, *The Halutz Resistance in Hungary 1942–1944* (New York: Columbia University Press, 1986), pp. 190–3.

12 Interview with Peter Tarjan.

13 Cole, *Holocaust City*, pp. 197–201.

14 K. Lauer to I. Olsen (24 July 1944), cited in P. A. Levine, *Raoul Wallenberg in Budapest: Myth, History and Holocaust* (London: Vallentine Mitchell, 2010), p. 173; H. Johnson to Secretary of State (25 July 1944), cited Levine, *Raoul Wallenberg in Budapest*, p. 235.

15 Levine, *Raoul Wallenberg in Budapest*, p. 206.

16 R. Wallenberg, *Letters and Dispatches 1924–1944* (New York: Arcade Publishing, 1995), p. 245.

17 Wallenberg, *Letters and Dispatches*, pp. 248–9.

18 Levine, *Raoul Wallenberg in Budapest*, p. 263.

19 Wallenberg, *Letters and Dispatches*, p. 251.

20 K. Lauer to I. Olsen (23 August 1944), cited in Levine, *Raoul Wallenberg in Budapest*, p. 257.

21 Wallenberg, *Letters and Dispatches*, p. 253; Levine, *Raoul Wallenberg in Budapest*, p. 268.

22 'PM first report regarding the use of funds, placed at the disposal of the Jewish action' (12 September 1944), cited in Levine, *Raoul Wallenberg in Budapest*, p. 259.

23 Cole, *Holocaust City*, pp. 200–1.

24 Wallenberg, *Letters and Dispatches*, p. 253.

25 Wallenberg, *Letters and Dispatches*, p. 262.

26 Interview with Per Anger. See also Levine, *Raoul Wallenberg in Budapest*, pp. 296–7.

27 Cole, *Holocaust City*, pp. 203–4.

28 Wallenberg, *Letters and Dispatches*, pp. 265–6.

29 Cohen, *The Halutz Resistance in Hungary*, p. 185.

30 Interview with Per Anger.

31 Interview with Per Anger.

32 Interview with Agnes Mandl Adachi (29 November 1990), USHMM RG-50.030*0003.

33 J. Lévai, *Raoul Wallenberg: Regényes Élete, Hősi Küzdelmei, Rejtélyes Eltűnésének Titka*, 3rd edn (Budapest: Magyar Téka, 1948), p. 278.

34 Interview with George Sebök (4 and 5 November 1989), RWPA, F2C 531.

35 'Memorandum concerning the Hungarian Jews' (6 August 1944), cited in Levine, *Raoul Wallenberg in Budapest*, p. 283.

36 Interview with Anna Zafir (6 November 1989), RWPA, F2C 534.

37 J. Brody, 'Unpublished memoir'; interview with JK (17 May 1990), RWPA, F2C 560.

38   Interview with Ahava A. Feldberg, RWPA, F2C 144; J. Lévai, *Black Book on the Martyrdom of Hungarian Jewry* (Zurich: The Central European Times Publishing Company, 1948), p. 316.
39   'Name list of those persons who had Schutzpasses and were under the protection of the Swedish Embassy' (unpublished bound volume, 1944), RWPA, F3A 18.
40   Interview with Naomi Gur (8 December 1990), RWPA, F2C 118.
41   Interview with Ahava A. Feldberg.
42   L. Palosuo, *Yellow Stars and Trouser Inspections: Jewish Testimonies from Hungary, 1920–1945* (Uppsala: Department of History and The Uppsala Programme for Holocaust and Genocide Studies, 2008), pp. 158, 181–2, 235–6; A. Lajos, *Hjälten och offren. Raoul Wallenberg och judarna I Budapest* (Växjö: Svenska Emigrant-institutet, 2004), p. 220.
43   Wallenberg, *Letters and Dispatches*, p. 261.
44   Wallenberg, *Letters and Dispatches*, pp. 257–8.
45   Interview with Peter Tarjan; interview with Naomi Gur; interview with Ivan E. Becker (29 August 1989), RWPA, FC2 508.
46   Interview with Miklósné Váli (1 and 2 April 1990), RWPA, FC2 342.
47   Interview with Anna Zafir.
48   Interview with Mrs Jozsefné Koltai (10 October 1989), RWPA, F2C 310.
49   Interview with István Bélai (1 March 1990), RWPA, F2C 343; interview with Ivan Gabor (17 November 1994), RWPA, F2C 544.
50   Interview with Peter Tarjan.
51   Interview with Alfred Schomberg (7 November 1989), RWPA, F2C 535.
52   I. Z. Gabor and J. Neal, *Echoes of My Footsteps: An Autobiography* (Bloomington, IN: Authors House, 2009), ch. 6.
53   Interview with Agnes Grossman Aranyi (18 July 1990), USHMM, RG-50.030*0008.
54   Interview with Mihály Kádár (18 December 1989), RWPA, F2C 326.
55   Interview with Agnes Grossman Aranyi.
56   Interview with Ödönné Pollai (26 February 1990), RWPA, F2C 325.
57   Interview with Magda Mezei Lapidus (4 September 1990), USHMM, RG-50.030*0122.
58   Interview with Ödönné Pollai.
59   Interview with Francis Körösy (27 October 1989), RWPA, F2C 106.
60   Interview with Valeria Nádas (23 October 1989; 30 October 1989), RWPA, F2C 315.
61   Interview with Lilly Schwarz Gach (9 December 1991), USHMM RG-50.030*0077.
62   Interview with Eva Brust Cooper (9 December 1991), USHMM RG-50.030*0056.
63   Interview with Dr Paul Milch (28 April 1990), RWPA, F2C 518.
64   Interview with István Schalk.
65   Interview with Per Anger.
66   Interview with Per Anger.
67   Interview with Giorgio Perlasca (3 November 1989; 4 November 1989; 5 November 1989), RWPA, F2C 312.

68   Interview with Agnes Grossman Aranyi.

69   Ozsváth, *When the Danube Ran Red*, p. 137.

70   E. Gottlieb, *Becoming My Mother's Daughter: A Story of Survival and Renewal* (Waterloo, ON: Wilfrid Laurier University Press, 2008), p. 98.

71   K. Ungváry, *Battle for Budapest: 100 Days in World War II* (London: I. B. Tauris, 2010), p. 238.

72   Interview with Yehuda Mandel (13 November 1990), USHMM, RG-50.030*0148; interview with Cornelius Loen (11 May 1991), USHMM, RG-50.030*0137.

73   E. Rácz, 'When I was twelve', in K. Pécsi (ed.), *Salty Coffee: Untold Stories by Jewish Women* (Budapest: Novella, 2007), pp. 43–4.

74   A. Biro, *One Must Also Be Hungarian* (Chicago: University of Chicago Press, 2006), pp. 60–3.

75   E. Szép, *The Smell of Humans: A Memoir of the Holocaust in Hungary* (Budapest: Central European University, 1994), pp. 50–173.

76   Mrs M. G. in Rosen, *Hungarian Jewish Women Survivors*, p. 36.

Road

1   J. Bachner, *My Darkest Years: Memoirs of a Survivor of Auschwitz, Warsaw and Dachau* (Jefferson, NC: McFarland and Company, 2007), p. 179.

2   Blatman, *The Death Marches*, p. 9.

3   Interview with Nina Kaleska.

4   Interview with Lily Margules (16 October 1990), USHMM, RG-50.030*0150.

5   J. Katz, *One Who Came Back: The Diary of a Jewish Survivor* (Takoma Park, MD: Dryad Press, 2006), p. 195.

6   Bachner, *My Darkest Years*, pp. 179–80.

7   'Affadavit from a former prisoner – R. Frascht – evacuated from Wattenstedt and Aussenkommando Neunegamme on 6 April 1945', International Tracing Service Archive (Hereafter ITS), 84599785#1.

8   Interview with William Luksenburg (14 April 1991), USHMM, RG-50.030*0140.

9   Interview with Barbara Marton Farkas (27 April 1990), USHMM, RG-50.030*0070.

10   Interview with Fritzie Weiss Fritzshall.

11   Hart, *Return to Auschwitz*, p. 181.

12   Magda G. in Rosen, *Hungarian Jewish Women Survivors*, p. 31.

13   Magda G. in Rosen, *Hungarian Jewish Women Survivors*, p. 32; Hart, *Return to Auschwitz*, p. 183.

14   Interview with Lily Margules.

15   Interview with Miriam Farcus Ingber (30 October 1990), USHMM, RG-50.030*0098.

16   Interview with Barbara Marton Farkas.

17 Irwin, 'Remember to be a good human being', in Silberklang, ed., *Stolen Youth*, p. 99.

18 Interview with Bela Blau.

19 Interview with Guta Blass Weintraub (4 January 1990), USHMM, RG-50.030*250.

20 Interview with Mr Hoffman, IWM, 9091/05/01; interview with Miriam Farcus Ingber.

21 Blatman, *Death Marches*, p. 411.

22 Interview with Regina Laks Gelb.

23 Interview with Edgar Krasa (9 September 2003), USHMM, RG-50.030*0478.

24 Interview with Anna Laks Wilson.

25 Hart, *Return to Auschwitz*, pp. 181–2.

26 Interview with Magda Blau.

27 Interview with Lily Margules.

28 Interview with William Luksenburg.

29 Interview with Rosalie (Chris) Laks Lerman.

30 Interview with Regina Laks Gelb.

31 Interview with Carola Steinhardt.

32 J. Katz, *One Who Came Back: The Diary of a Jewish Survivor* (Takoma Park, MD: Dryad Press, 2006), p. 195.

33 Interview with Miriam Farcus Ingber.

34 Interview with Anna Laks Wilson.

35 Interview with Lily Margules.

36 Bachner, *My Darkest Years*, p. 180.

37 H. Pravda, 'War diary' (26 January 1945) (unpublished manuscript), IWM, 97/3/1.

38 Interview with Edgar Krasa.

39 Interview with Mr Hoffman, IWM, 9091/05/01.

40 Irwin, 'Remember to be a good human being', in Silberklang, ed., *Stolen Youth*, p. 99. See also S. Gigliotti, M. J. Masurovsky and E. B. Steiner, 'From the camp to the road: Representing the evacuations from Auschwitz, January 1945', in Knowles, Cole and Giordano, *Geographies of the Holocaust*, pp. 192–225. See especially figures 7.6, 7.7 and 7.8.

41 Interview with Regina Laks Gelb, USHMM, RG-50.030*0410; interview with Regina Laks Gelb, USHMM, RG-50.030*0078.

42 S. Silas, *Helmbrechts walk 1998–2003* (2003); T. Cole, 'Holocaust roadscapes: Retracing the "Death Marches in Contemporary Europe"', *Cahiers de Géographie du Québec* 57:162 (2013), pp. 449–52.

43 Bachner, *My Darkest Years*, p. 180.

44 T. Ingold, 'Footprints through the weather-world: Walking, breathing, knowing', *Journal of the Royal Anthropological Institute* 16:1 (2010), p. 137.

45 Interview with Susan Eisdorfer Beer (16 May 1995), USHMM, RG-50.030*0326.

46 Blatman, *Death Marches*, pp. 373–4.

47 Blatman, *Death Marches*, pp. 380–2.

48 Blatman, *Death Marches*, p. 418.

49 Pravda, 'War diary' (21 January 1945).

50 Pravda, 'War diary' (26 January 1945).

51 Pravda, 'War diary' (29 January 1945).

52 Magda G. in Rosen, *Hungarian Jewish Women Survivors*, p. 32.

53 Hart, *Return to Auschwitz*, p. 183; interview with Regina Laks Gelb, USHMM, RG-50.030*0410.

54 Interview with Nina Kaleska.

55 Interview with Fritzie Weiss Fritzshall.

56 Interview with Magda Blau.

57 Pravda, 'War diary' (21 January 1945; 26 January 1945).

58 Pravda, 'War diary' (26 January 1945).

59 'Evacuation, refugees and displaced persons in Germany' (10 Feburary 1945), cited in Blatman, *Death Marches*, p. 75.

60 Interview with Magda Blau.

61 Pravda, 'War diary' (29 January 1945).

62 Interview with Regina Laks Gelb, USHMM, RG-50.030*0410.

63 Pravda, 'War diary' (14 February 1945).

64 Interview with Rosalie Laks Lerman.

65 Interview with William Luksenburg.

66 Interview with Nina Kaleska.

67 Interview with Ruth Krautwirth Meyerowitz.

68 Affadavit by Hilde Borodajkewycz, ITS, 84597938#1.

69 'Report of the concentration camp convoy Kochendorf passing Hütten' (1 April 1946), ITS, 84598905#2.

70 Interview with Fritzie Weiss Fritzshall.

Camp

1 Interview with Fela Warschau (9 February 1995), USHMM, RG-50.030*0303.

2 Interview with Solomon Klug (13 March 1990), USHMM, RG-50.030*0109; interview with Chana Mehler (13 December 1993), USHMM, RG-50.030*0275.

3 Interview with Fela Warschau.

4 Interview with Lilly Malnik.

5 Interview with Solomon Klug.

6 'Belsen horror camp' – Photographs taken by Captain Malindine, Lieutenant Wilson, Sergeant Morris and Sergeant Midgley, IWM, BU 3723, 3728, 3732, 3759, 3760.

7 'Belsen horror camp', IWM, BU 3722, 3724, 3725, 3733, 3741, 3742, 3743, 3744, 3754, 3755, 3756, 3757, 3758, 3767, 3769, 3770, 3771, 3772, 3773, 3791, 3793, 3794, 3802, 3803.

8 'Belsen horror camp', IWM, caption accompanying BU 3732 and 3733; caption accompanying BU 3769–3779.

9 Typescript of Richard Dimbleby's despatch (17 April 1945) in B. Flanagan and D. Bloxham (eds), *Remembering Belsen: Eyewitnesses Record the Liberation* (London: Vallentine Mitchell, 2005), p. xi.

10 Brigadier H. L. Glyn Hughes; Private Emmanuel Fisher; Lieutenant-Colonel M. W. Gonin; Sister K. J. Elvidge in Flanagan and Bloxham, *Remembering Belsen*, pp. 10–11, 14, 19.

11 See accounts in Flanagan and Bloxham, *Remembering Belsen*, pp. 7–20.

12 C. P. Sharp, 'Notes. From 1 Jan 45' (unpublished manuscript, 1945), USHMM, 2005.20.1, p. 54.

13 Sharp, 'Notes', pp. 57–8.

14 'Belsen horror camp', IWM, caption accompanying BU 3793–3794 and 3803.

15 Sharp, 'Notes', pp. 53, 57.

16 Lieutenant-Colonel James Alexander Deans Johnston in Flanagan and Bloxham, *Remembering Belsen*, p. 9.

17 Sharp, 'Notes', pp. 53, 58–9, 61.

18 Interview with Bella Jakubowicz Tovey (15 February 1990), USHMM, RG-50.030*0236.

19 Interview with Chana Mehler.

20 Interview with Solomon Klug; interview with Bella Jakubowicz Tovey.

21 Interview with Lilly Malnik.

22 Interview with Bella Jakubowicz Tovey.

23 Interview with Fela Warschau.

24 Interview with Fela Warschau.

25 Interview with Doriane Kurz (10 July 1990), USHMM, RG-50.030*0120.

26 A. J. Herzberg, *Between Two Streams: A Diary from Bergen-Belsen* (London: Tauris Parke, 2008): (17 August 1944), p. 16.

27 Herzberg, *Between Two Streams* (17 August 1944), p. 17.

28 Interview with Doriane Kurz.

29 Interview with Martin Spett (7 November 1989), USHMM RG-50.030*0218.

30 Interview with Doriane Kurz.

31 Herzberg, *Between Two Streams* (15 August 1944), pp. 13–14.

32 Herzberg, *Between Two Streams* (28 August 1944), p. 34.

33 Herzberg, *Between Two Streams* (29 August 1944), p. 36.

34 Herzberg, *Between Two Streams* (19 December 1944), pp. 183–4.

35 Interview with Martin Spett.

36 Herzberg, *Between Two Streams* (31 January 1945), p. 196.

37 Herzberg, *Between Two Streams* (15 February 1945), p. 197.

38 Herzberg, *Between Two Streams* (1 April 1945), p. 206.

39 Herzberg, *Between Two Streams* (1 April 1945), p. 2.

40 Herzberg, *Between Two Streams* (1 April 1945), p. 207.

41 T. Musiol, *Dachau 1933–1945* (Katowice: Instytut Slaski w Opolu, 1968), p. 20.

42 Interview with Nina Kaleska.

43 Interview with Regina Laks Gelb, USHMM, RG-50.030*0410.

44 Interview with Regina Laks Gelb, USHMM, RG-50.030*0410.

45 B. Shephard, *After Daybreak: The Liberation of Belsen, 1945* (London: Pimlico, 2006).

46 Private Emmanuel Fisher, 32 Casualty Clearing Station, cited in Flanagan and Bloxham, *Remembering Belsen*, p. 11.

47 Sharp, 'Notes', pp. 51–2.

48 Interview with Susan Eisdorfer Beer.

49 Sharp, 'Notes', pp. 54–5, and see also 'Certificate of dusting' between pp. 60–1.

50 Sharp, 'Notes', pp. 56, 61, 73–4, 91.

51 Lieutenant-Colonel M. W. Gonin in Flanagan and Bloxham, *Remembering Belsen*, p. 25; Private Emmanuel Fisher in Flanagan and Bloxham, *Remembering Belsen*, p. 34.

52 Interview with Bella Jakubowicz Tovey.

53 Interview with Lilly Malnik.

54 Sharp, 'Notes', pp. 74, 122, 129–33.

55 'Scenes in Belsen concentration camp after its liberation in 1945', IWM, HU 49664–49669; 'Belsen is history. A scene at the burning of the camp. The fires were started with flamethrowers', IWM, BU 6593–6605; 'Burning the last hut at Belsen camp', BU 6670–6676.

56 Cyril Charters (15 May 1945) in Flanagan and Bloxham, *Remembering Belsen*, p. 39.

Epilogue: Returning Home/Leaving Home

1 Miss J. Rudman (letter 14 May 1945) in Flanagan and Bloxham, *Remembering Belsen*, p. 29.

2 Private Emmanuel Fisher in Flanagan and Bloxham, *Remembering Belsen*, p. 11.

3 Robert Collis and Han Hogerzeil in Flanagan and Bloxham, *Remembering Belsen*, p. 81.

4 Anny Pfirter in Flanagan and Bloxham, *Remembering Belsen*, p. 54.

5 Sister K. J. Elvidge (letter 26 May 1945) in Flanagan and Bloxham, *Remembering Belsen*, p. 19.

6 Interview with Regina Laks Gelb, USHMM, RG-50.030*0161.

7 Interview with Anna Laks Wilson.

8 Interview with Regina Laks Gelb, USHMM, RG-50.030*0410.

9 S. Redlich, *Life in Transit: Jews in Postwar Lodz, 1945–1950* (Brighton, MA: Academic Studies Press, 2011).

10 Interview with Regina Laks Gelb, USHMM, RG-50.030*0410.

11 Isaac Levy in Flanagan and Bloxham, *Remembering Belsen*, p. 76.

12 Interview with Ruth Krautwirth Meyerowitz.

13 Interview with Bernard Pasternak.

14 Interview with Miriam Farcus Ingber.

15 Hyatt, *Close Calls*, p. 136.

16 Pravda, 'War diary' (14 February 1945).

17 Pravda, 'War diary' (13 March 1945).

18 Pravda, 'War diary' (19 March 1945).

19 Pravda, 'War diary' (31 March 1945).

20 Pravda, 'War diary' (2 April 1945).

21 Pravda, 'War diary' (1 May 1945).

22 Pravda, 'War diary' (30 May 1945).
23 G. Gluck, *Fiorello's Sister: Gemma La Guardia Gluck's Story* (Syracuse, NY: Syracuse University Press, 2007), p. 109.
24 Interview with Abraham Malnik.
25 Interview with Susan Eisdorfer Beer; S. Beer, 'To Auschwitz and back: An odyssey' (undated, unpublished manuscript), USHMM, RG-02.144.
26 Interview with Susan Eisdorfer Beer.
27 Interview with Rosalie Laks Lerman.
28 Interview with Regina Laks Gelb, USHMM, RG-50.030*0410.
29 Pravda, 'War diary' (30 May 1945).
30 Pravda, 'War diary' (20 November 1945).
31 Pravda, 'War diary' (20 November 1945).
32 Pravda, 'War diary' (Epilogue, 4 January 1996).

Moving Holocaust Landscapes

1 J. T. Gross, *Neighbors: The Destruction of the Jewish Community in Jedwabne, Poland, 1941* (Princeton: Princeton University Press, 2003).

INDEX

Adler, Meyer 111
Anger, Per 154, 155, 156, 160, 168–9
Aranyi, Agnes Grossman 164–5, 169–70
Arrow Cross Party *(Nyilas)* 153, 156, 157, 158–9, 168–70, 172
Aryanization 15
Auschwitz complex 69, 70, 71–2, 74, 77, 79, 91–2, 95, 115, 121, 199
    arrival at 109–11
    deportations to 127
    1945 evacuation 173, 176–8, 179–83, 189
    train journeys to 99–100, 101–2
Auschwitz I: 72, 92, 95, 226
Auschwitz-Birkenau (Auschwitz II) 69, 71, 72–82, 86–7, 92–8, 171
    crematoria 73, 77–8, 79
    deportations from Hungary 151–2
    exchange of information 80–2
    gas chambers 73, 77–8
    mud 92–4
    transfers to/from 69, 92, 95–8
Auschwitz-Monowitz (Auschwitz III) 74

Bachner, James 182–3
Bamberger, Niels 135, 136
Bartov, Omer 6–7
Baum, Erwin 29, 30–1, 32, 37–8
Baum, Icek 28–9, 30–1, 38
Bauman, Janina 21–2, 24–5, 26, 27, 35, 43, 144, 145–6
    education 38
    memoir 39–40, 41
Bauman family 23, 24–5, 149
Beer, Susan 185, 211, 220–2
Belgium 127–8, 136–8
Belsen, *see* Bergen-Belsen

Belzec 4–5, 73
Berg, Mary (Miriam Wattenberg) 36–7
    diary 29–30, 34, 36, 38–9, 40–1
Berg family 35, 36
Bergen-Belsen 196–208, 226
    under British control 196, 197, 200–2, 210–14
    evacuation of prisoners 212–13
    expansion of 207–8
    multilingual nature 215
    sanitary conditions 199, 201, 203, 206, 207
    unburied corpses 199–203
Bergman, David 96, 113, 114–21, 122–5, 152
Bergman family 95–7
Bird, Colonel 213–14
Birkenau, *see* Auschwitz-Birkenau
Biro, Adam 171
Biro family 171–2
Blachman, Gerda 9–10, 129, 133–4
    in Belgium 127–8, 136–8
    emigration 15, 16, 17, 18
black market 31, 33, 38, 42: *see also* smuggling economy
Blatman, Daniel 114, 179
Blau, Bela 83, 177
Blau, Magda 79–80, 83, 180, 189
bloodlands 2, 69, 171–2, 192
Bloxham, Donald 97
Bobrow, Adam 51, 55, 58, 60
Bobrow, Julia 58
Boder, David 106–7
Borodajkewycz, Hilde 192
Braun, Alex 104–5, 106
Bretholz, Leo 112, 133–4
Brody, Judit 161
Bruml, Hana 93

Buchenwald 10
Buergenthal, Thomas 76, 79, 83

camp system 69–98
    breakdown of 198, 203–4, 207–10
    concentration camps 10–11, 69, 72,
        74, 208
    death camps 4–5, 43, 69, 72, 73, 77–8
    food in 195–7, 206
    escapes from 92
    inside jobs 83–6, 93
    labour camps 69, 72, 74
    multilingual nature 215–16
    Operation Reinhard camps 4–5, 43,
        69, 73, 78
    POW camps 72
    separation in 5–6, 77–8, 79–80
    shoes, importance of 93–4
    social networks 87–91
    transfers between camps 89–90, 95
    violence of 19
Central Authority for Jewish Emigration,
    Berlin 18
Charlesworth, Andrew 49
Chelmno 69, 73
Cohen, Dov 59, 60, 131–2
concentration camps 10–11, 69, 72, 74, 208
Cooper, Eva Brust 167
crematoria 73, 77–8, 79
Czech language 85–6
Czechoslovakia 22, 71, 76, 95–6, 100, 101,
    110, 123, 176, 217–18
Czerniakow, Adam 32, 33–4, 37

Dachau 10, 208
d'Ancona de Leeuwe, Hetty 140, 141–2
Danielsson, Carl Ivan 156
David, Janina 26–7, 28, 34–5, 43
death camps 4–5, 43, 69, 72, 73, 77–8
death marches 173–92, 203
    escape from 186–8, 190
    roadside shootings 179, 180, 182,
        183–4, 185–6, 189, 192
    scavenging for food 176, 193

Denmark 128, 134–6
deportation 20, 43, 127–8
    from Belgium 127–8
    from Hungary 151–2
des Pres, Terence 108
Desbois, Patrick 49–50
Deutsch, Madeline 101–2, 103, 110
diaries 11, 13, 14, 42
    Berg 29–30, 34, 36, 38–9, 40–1
    Czerniakow 32, 33–4, 37
    Frank 139
Dimbleby, Richard 200
Dwork, Debórah 25, 73

education
    segregation in 9, 15, 19
    Warsaw ghetto 38
Eichmann, Adolf 18, 151
Einsatzgruppen 47–8
Elman, Benjamin 1–2, 3–4, 130
Elman, Joseph 1–2, 3, 4, 61–2
Elvidge, Sister Kath 215–16
emigration 15–20, 127–9, 130–1
Engelking, Barbara 37
exchange Jews 205, 206

food
    black market 31, 33, 38, 42
    bread 31, 38, 42, 82, 118, 128, 193,
        196, 206
    in camp system 195–7, 206
    from contacts 55
    on death marches 176, 193
    in forest camps 55, 57, 160–2
    as hiding place for valuables 128
    potatoes 31, 33, 55, 176, 195, 196–7
    scavenging for 30, 176, 193
    sharing 196
    stealing 55
    on train journeys 118, 119
forests 45–67
    bunkers in 56–7, 65
    food supplies 55, 57, 60–2
    gender roles in partisan camps 64–5

as hiding places 46–7, 51–66, 143,
   149
as killing sites 46, 47, 49, 123
partisan camps 52–3, 54, 58, 59–64
seasonal adjustments 57–8
vulnerability of women in partisan
   camps 63–4
France 127, 128, 130–1, 132–3, 137
Frank, Anne 139
Frank, Hans 22
Frank family 138–9, 140
Fritzshall, Fritzie Weiss 100, 109, 188,
   192–3

Gach, Lilly Schwarz 166
Gang-Saalheimer, Lore 12
gas chambers 73, 77–78
Gelb, Renia Laks, *see* Laks, Renia
Generalgouvernement, Poland 4–5, 22, 23,
   43, 48, 69, 73, 78
Gelpter, Hans 80, 88–9
Genth, William 185
Germany 22, 173–5
   Buchenwald 10
   Dachau 10, 208
   death marches 174–5
   destruction of synagogues 11
   emigration 15–20, 127–9, 130–1
   Kristallnacht 9–10, 11–14, 15–16
   Ravensbrück 70, 89, 208–9
   Sachsenhausen 10
   see also Bergen-Belsen
ghettos 21–43, 48
   creation of 23–4
   hiding places 43
   Hungary 151–4, 158–9, 161–70
   international ghetto, Hungary 153–4,
      162–9
   liquidation of 43
   Poland 1, 3, 22–3, 46, 48: *see also*
      Warsaw ghetto
Gigliotti, Simone 108, 111
Goebbels, Joseph 11
Greece 71, 72, 99

Greif, Earl 45, 46–7
Greif, Leibel 46–7
Greif, Reizel 45–6
Greif family 45–7
Gross, Jan 227
Gross-Rosen 117
Grossmann, Gertrud 16
Gruber, Samuel 51, 55, 63
Grynszpan, Herschel 11

Hart, Kitty 82, 92–3, 175
Havas, George 75–6, 97–8, 101, 102,
      103–4, 110–11, 113
Heppner, Ernest 10, 13, 14, 20
   emigration 17, 18
Herzberg, Abel 205, 206, 207–8
hiding places 3, 129–30, 136–41, 143–7
   attics 138–9, 143–5, 147–8
   barns 143–5
   cellars 148–9
   claustrophobia of 138–9
   forests 46–7, 51–66, 143, 149
   ghettos 43
Hilberg, Raul 48, 54, 67, 99, 137
Horthy, Miklós 153
Hungary 151–72
   deportations to Auschwitz-Birkenau
      151–2
   division between groups of Jews
      161–3
   ghettos 151–4, 158–9, 161–70
   international ghetto 153–4, 162–9
   Jews as human shield 152–3
   mass shootings into the river 168, 169,
      170–2
   Nyilas (Arrow Cross Party) 153, 156,
      157, 158–9, 168–70, 172
   Spanish protection 154, 157, 165–6
   Swedish protection 154–6, 157,
      159–61, 162–4, 166–7
   Swiss protection 154, 156–7, 159, 168,
      169
Hyatt, Felicia Berland 77, 80, 82, 85–6,
      87, 97, 219

I. G. Farben works 74
Ingber, Miriam Farcus 176–7, 181, 218
Ingold, Tim 184–5
International Settlement, Shanghai 16–17
International Tracing Service 178, 192
Italy 71, 73

Jacobson, Frode 134–5
Jay, Martin 26
Jewish Council, Warsaw 32

Kaleska, Nina 71–2, 111, 173–4, 187–8, 191, 208
Kanada commando 84–5, 93–4
Kaplan, Marion 12, 19
Katz, Menachem 56, 65, 66, 147–9
Katzmann, Fritz 10
killing sites
    forests 46, 47, 49, 123
    villages 50
    see also death camps
Kmiec, Hanka 147, 149
Kmiec, Piotr 147, 148, 149
Kochalski, David 30, 42
Koenig, Ernest 111
Kohn, Nahum 53, 58–9, 62
Krasa, Edgar 179–80, 183–4
Kraus, Michael 110
Kristallnacht 9–10, 11–14, 15–16
Kurz, Doriane 205–6

labour camps 69, 72, 74
Lajos, Attila 163
Lakatos, Géza 153
Laks, Chris 81, 82, 83–4, 85, 181, 222
Laks, Hania 84, 85, 100, 108, 181, 182
Laks, Renia 69, 70–1, 79, 80, 81, 83–4, 85, 87–8, 181, 190, 209, 222–3
Laks sisters 71, 72, 81, 83–4, 85, 86, 87–8, 100, 113, 174, 179, 182, 190, 216–17, 222
Langenbielau I: 117
languages 71–2, 85–7

Law for the Restoration of the Regular Civil Service 15
Leociak, Jacek 37
Levy, Isaac 217
Lewin, Abraham 33, 42
lice 40, 53, 204, 207
Liebmann, Johanne Hirsch 132
Liebmann, Max 132–3
Lowenberg, William 79, 87, 88–9, 121, 137
Luksenburg, William 180, 191

Madagascar plan 23
Majowka labour camp 69
Malnik, Abraham 220
Malnik, Lilly 71, 86, 198–9, 203, 213
Margules, Lily 174, 176, 180, 182
Melcer, Chaim 58
Menaker, Piotr 64
Meyerowitz, Ruth Krautwirth 85, 86, 93–4, 191, 217
Milch, Paul 168
Monowitz, see Auschwitz-Monowitz
mountain crossings 128, 129, 132–3
Munch-Nielsen, Preben 135–6

Netherlands 79, 127, 130–1, 137, 138–40
Nini (Greek teenager) 86
Nisko plan 23
Nuremberg Laws 15
Nyilas (Arrow Cross Party) 153, 156, 157, 158–9, 168–70, 172

Olsson, Eva 74–5, 76
Operation Barbarossa 2
Operation 1005: 49
Operation Reinhard camps 4–5, 43, 69, 73, 78
Orbuch, Sonia 52–3, 58, 62, 63–4
Ostjuden 22

Palosuo, Laura 163
Panchenko, Victor 61
partisans 3, 4
    forest camps 52–3, 54, 58, 59–64

Pasternak, Bella 90
Pasternak, Bernard 217–18
Paulsson, Steve 129, 139, 146
Pekerman, Polina 50
Perl, Josef 50, 60
Perlasca, Giorgio 169
Piskorz, Benjamin 106–7
Plaszów concentration camp 96
pogroms 9–10, 11–14, 15–16
Poland 1–5, 32
    Generalgouvernement 4–5, 22, 23, 43,
        48, 69, 73, 78
    ghettos 1, 3, 22–3, 46, 48: see also
        Warsaw ghetto
    Gross-Rosen 117
    Langenbielau I: 117
    Majowka labour camp 69
    Operation Reinhard camps 4–5, 43,
        69, 73, 78
    pogroms 9–10
    Warthgeau 22
    see also Auschwitz complex; Auschwitz
        I; Auschwitz-Birkenau (Auschwitz
        II); Auschwitz-Monowitz
        (Auschwitz III)
POW camps 72–3
Pravda, Hana 183, 186–7, 189–90,
    219–20, 223–4
Pravda, Saša 219–20, 223–4

rabbit hunts 54–5
Rajzmen, Samuel 78
Ravensbrück 70, 89, 208–9
Reichskommissarat Ostland 48
Reichskommissarat Ukraine 48
Reizer, Leib 62–3, 64, 65
Ringelblum, Emmanuel 33, 34, 35–6
Ringelheim, Joan 26

Sachsenhausen 10
Schalk, István 155–6
Scheneiderman, Leo 77
Schiff, Charlene Perlmutter 51–2, 55, 58,
    63

Schild, Gerda 17–19, 20, 98
Schor, Julia 142, 144
Schwarz, Susie 140, 142–5
Schwarz family 139–40, 142–5
sea crossings 134–6
Sharp, Major Charles Phillip 201–2, 210,
    211–12, 213
Silas, Susan 184
smuggling economy
    Warsaw ghetto 30–1, 32–5, 39, 42
    see also black market
Snyder, Timothy 2, 50, 51
Sobibór 69, 73
Society of Friends 10
Sofsky, Wolfgang 91
Solmitz, Luise 13–14
Sonderkommando 5, 78, 121, 204
Spain 154, 157, 165–6
Spett, Martin 206, 207
Stalingrad, Battle of 53
starvation 173, 197–8
    in Warsaw ghetto 28–9, 30, 35, 42
Steinbacher, Sybille 73
Steinhardt, Carola 93, 181
Stroud, Ellen 94
suicide 3
survivor guilt 183–4
Sweden 134, 154–6, 157–8, 159–61,
    162–4
Switzerland 128, 132–4, 137–8, 149, 154,
    155, 156–7, 159, 168, 169
synagogues, destruction of 9–10, 11, 12
Szamosi, Eugenia 155, 156–7
Sztójay, Döme 151

Tec, Nechama 50, 61
Toporol Society for the Support of
    Agriculture 32
Tovey, Bella Jakubowicz 204
train jouneys 99–126
    arrival at Auschwitz 109–11
    deaths in 105–6, 111, 119–20, 121
    escapes from 112
    food 118, 119

length of journeys 100–1, 103, 109
mass movement of prisoners 112–16
movement of labour resources 116–18
sanitary conditions 103–4, 105, 107
senses heightened in 108–9
travelling conditions 101–9, 111, 115,
    118–22
Treblinka 4–5, 43, 69, 73, 78
typhus 208, 210, 211–12
    Warsaw 28, 39–40, 41

urine for drinking 105–7, 119
USSR 45–9, 61, 66, 69, 72–3, 129, 153,
    205, 226
    German invasion of 20, 43, 45–6, 47
    advances into German territory/
        liberation by 47, 113, 172, 173–4,
        188–9, 221, 225
    partisans 4, 59, 61
    Soviet territory 2, 22, 43, 45–50, 53,
        67, 125, 171

van Pelt, Robert Jan 25, 73
Vogel, Michael 74–5, 76, 84–5
vom Rath, Ernst 11

Wachtl, Jirka 220
Wallenberg, Raoul 154, 155, 156, 157–8,
    159, 161, 162, 163
Warner, Rose 105–6
Warsaw ghetto 21–2, 23–5, 26–7
    artistic life 36–7
    bunkers 43
    death in 27–30, 35, 42
    education in 38
    epidemics in 28, 39–40, 41
    permeability of boundary 30–4
    smuggling economy 30–1, 32–5, 39, 42
    starvation in 28–9, 30, 35, 42
    uprising 43
Warschau, Fela 195–8
Warthgeau, Poland 22
Wiesel, Elie 27, 77